THE WORLD'S WESTWARD MARCH

THE WORLD'S WESTWARD MARCH

Explorers, Warriors and Statesmen

Peter F. Krogh

Hamilton Books
Lanham • Boulder • New York • Toronto • London

Published by Hamilton Books
An imprint of The Rowman & Littlefield Publishing Group, Inc.
4501 Forbes Boulevard, Suite 200, Lanham, Maryland 20706
Hamilton Books Acquisitions Department (301) 459-3366

6 Tinworth Street, London SE11 5AL, United Kingdom

British Library Cataloguing in Publication Information Available

ISBN 978-0-7618-7158-3 (pbk. : alk. paper)
ISBN 978-0-7618-7159-0 (electronic)

∞™ The paper used in this publication meets the minimum requirements of American National Standard for Information Sciences Permanence of Paper for Printed Library Materials, ANSI/NISO Z39.48-1992.

For Christopher and Jennifer

CONTENTS

Foreword ix
Peter Dunkley

Preface xi

Acknowledgments xv

Introduction 1

1 The Vikings 11

2 The Mongols and Genghis Khan 19

3 Before European Hegemony 29

4 The Plague 37

5 The Ottoman Empire 45

6 Mehmet the Conqueror and the Fall of Constantinople 55

7 The Portuguese 65

8 The World of Christopher Columbus 75

9 The Voyages of Christopher Columbus 81

10 Ferdinand Magellan 93

11 Sir Francis Drake 109

12 Captain James Cook 121

13 Thomas Jefferson and the Louisiana Purchase 133

14 Theodore Roosevelt and the Panama Canal 143

15 Winston Churchill 153

16 Dean Acheson 165

17 Deng Xiaoping 175

Conclusion 185

Appendix A: *Guns, Germs and Steel: The Fates of Human Societies* 191
Jared Diamond

Appendix B: *The Wealth and Poverty of Nations: Why Some Are So Rich and Some So Poor* 195
David S. Landes

Appendix C: *The Hungry Spirit: How Fear and Yearning Drove World History* 199
Ying Gao

Appendix D: Further Readings 207

Permissions 213

FOREWORD

Peter Dunkley

Peter Krogh's ambitious book is a welcome addition to the growing literature on epic developmental trajectories—some mutually supportive, others reciprocally antagonistic—that have taken place over a considerable period of time and across intercontinental and transoceanic space. Making sense of these obviously complex aspects of world history, encompassing as they did much of humankind, is a gargantuan task, requiring at the very least a conceptual framework within which to distinguish the forest from the trees. Krogh accomplishes this in a necessarily succinct consideration of how global centers of cultural gravity have shifted ever westward from East Asia, specifically from China, and ultimately to North America over the last half-millennium, until in our own era the process seems poised to leap the Pacific in a return to long-ago Chinese cultural primacy.

This is fascinating and important stuff, made the more so by Krogh's imaginative use of select historical figures as emblems of their age and, more significantly, as historical agents in shaping it. This amounts to more than a resurrection of the well-worn great-man-of-history question and raises some major issues to think about in the unusual context of a planetary narrative. This is especially the case here in that the discussion of these individuals is embedded in his broader interpretive paradigm, of seismic cultural displacements having been driven over the long term according to a kind of geographical teleology, in an apparently inexorable advance of civilizational dynamism from east to west. His figures are well chosen and serve to humanize big historical themes that can often seem in their telling to be overly abstract to most readers when not leavened with the touch of humanity.

The jury is still out on whether that paradigm will hold good in coming generations. It may be that the ebb and flow of earlier shifts in global power have not always conformed to the book's overarching schema, but the general east-to-west tendency is plain enough when viewed from 50,000 feet. Another thing is certain, too, as Krogh makes clear: China's progress has been historically phenomenal since Deng Xiaoping, perhaps his most apt example of the force of human agency in history, turned it into new courses, and did so, we are reminded, a mere handful of decades ago. Anyone interested in the possibility that the last half-millennium of global development elsewhere is prelude to a Chinese-dominated world in the twenty-first century would do well to consult what Krogh has to tell us about how we came to be where we are today.

Peter Dunkley, Georgetown University
March 3, 2020

PREFACE

Some years ago, on summer vacation in my old whaler's cottage on Nantucket Island, surrounded by a small library, I plucked a book from the shelf on Christopher Columbus and dug into it. Its author was the distinguished dean of historians of world exploration, Felipe Fernández-Armesto, and I was swept away by it. In it he observed that Columbus's "discovery" of the "New World" provided critical impetus to the west-

Felipe Fernández-Armesto (left) with the author.

ward shift of the world's "centers of initiative" and "main axis of commerce and communication." This observation struck me as the ideal framework for a little book on tribes and individuals who figured prominently in that relocation of the world's "center of gravity" over the last five hundred years. Those so involved could be labeled as explorers, warriors or statesmen or some combination of the three. Inspired and informed by Felipe (who was to become a close friend and intellectual guru), I set out to identify the leading tribes, individuals and conditions involved in the world's westward march and write a book about them.

My personal choices yielded the following:

- The Vikings: Leif Ericson. The Atlantic became the ocean route that connected the old world with the new. That highway was ultimately heavily traveled as the main axis of commerce and communication shifted westward. The Vikings were the first to travel that route.
- The Mongols: Genghis Khan. The Mongols, under the intrepid leadership of Genghis Khan, established a land-based highway across Eurasia that facilitated east-west contact. That "turnpike" opened the eyes of the West to the riches of the East and made possible what we would now call "a transfer of technology."
- Before European Hegemony: Prior to European hegemony an elaborate, highly successful and nearly global trading system was functioning with Europe at its periphery. The dominant countries or regions, in order of strength, were China, the Middle East and India. When that trading system broke down, the West seized the initiative.
- The Plague: The "Black Death" in the mid-fourteenth century dealt a severe blow to the then existing inter-regional trading system. While it mowed down as much as a third of Europe's population, that region subsequently made the strongest comeback.
- The Ottomans and Mehmet the Conqueror: The Ottomans, led by Mehmet the Conqueror, established a formidable empire headquartered in Constantinople (later renamed Istanbul) that boxed the Europeans in, closing off the land-based route to the Orient and forcing the relatively impoverished Europeans to take to the seas to access the "riches of Cathay."

- The Portuguese: The Portuguese and its mariners, most prominently, Vasco da Gama, Francisco de Almeida, and Alfonso d'Albuquerque, took to the sea in a successful search for an eastern ocean highway to the Orient. Along the way they overpowered and displaced the competition, established trading posts, took over the trading system and grew rich.
- The Spanish: The Spanish, led by Christopher Columbus and Ferdinand Magellan (who were born elsewhere, but entered the service of Spain), pointed in the opposite direction. They opened a western ocean highway and a passage to the Pacific discovering, in the process, a "New World" that was to become a creator of new wealth and a powerful center of gravity.
- The English: Sir Francis Drake and Captain James Cook. The English did not stand idly by. They commissioned voyages that, among other things, solved the problems of fixing accurate longitude at sea and the scourge of scurvy while charting the vast Pacific Ocean, enabling the girdling of the globe and clearing the way for active trans-Pacific commerce and communication.
- The Americans: Thomas Jefferson and Theodore Roosevelt. The North American landmass was initially seen as an inconvenient barrier to getting to the riches of the Orient. But, once settled, its leadership looked westward in order to establish "an empire of liberty" creating, in the process, a "continental behemoth" and then a "path between the seas." Those creations anchored a westward shift in the world's center of influence and economic power.
- The British and the Americans Combined: Winston Churchill and Dean Acheson. World War II had to be won and a secure new order established in the chaos of its aftermath in order to prevent a civilizational retreat. Churchill faced down Hitler's threat and Dean Acheson stepped forward to serve as the principal architect of the post-war American-centered world order.
- The Chinese: Deng Xiaoping. The diminutive Deng Xiaoping engineered a revolution in China that set it in clear forward motion. He awakened a giant and accelerated the westward shift in the world's center of gravity and the emergence of what is now called "The Pacific Century."

This book, focused on world transforming ideas and individuals, follows the world's westward march over the last five hundred years as "centers of initiative" and "the main axis of commerce and communication" moved from East to West.

Sir Vivian Fuchs, the general editor of a series of books on *The Great Explorers*, has offered the following observation that captures the essence of the story and lesson of this book: "Throughout history exploration has advanced through man's curiosity and imagination, brought to fulfillment by the inspiration and drive of an individual." In keeping with that observation, this book focuses on world transforming ideas and individuals who figured prominently in the world's westward march over the last half millennium as "centers of initiative" and "the main axis of commerce and communication" moved from East to West.

As the reader proceeds with the story, flaws in this work doubtless will be discovered. Here I wish to borrow from the distinguished historian of the rise of the West, William McNeill, who, in the preface to his book on *Venice: The Hinge of Europe*, attributed any errors "to my ignorance and to my limited sensibilities and imperfect conceptualization." I now seek the same refuge.

Peter F. Krogh
August 2019

ACKNOWLEDGMENTS

The origin of this book can be traced to the inspiration of Felipe Fernández-Armesto, the dean of historians of world exploration. It was he who introduced me to the concept of "the world's westward march." I first put that concept to work in courses taught at Georgetown University's School of Foreign Service. Those courses often produced insightful student papers, one of which by Ying Gao, entitled *The Hungry Spirit*, appears as an appendix in this book.

For the creation of the book I am indebted to: a long-time collaborator, Charlie Dolgas, who formatted the text in obedience to the famous "Chicago Manual of Style;" my Executive Assistant, Clare Ogden, who zealously tracked down permissions for the use of the epigraphs that introduce each chapter; a former student, Carol Harrison (now an acclaimed photographer) whose photograph of Felipe Fernández-Armesto and me captures the bond between us; and Brooke Bures of Hamilton Books who waited patiently for the manuscript while offering advice on the particulars of its publication.

INTRODUCTION

This book has a guru. His name is Felipe Fernández-Armesto. He established the starting point and source of inspiration for the pages that follow.

Felipe Fernández-Armesto is the dean of historians of world exploration. He is an impressive macro-historian with a gift for unorthodox insight and interpretation. He is the editor of the *Times Atlas of World Discovery* and the author of many notable books including two especially pertinent to the theme of this book; namely: *Millennium: A History of the Last Thousand Years* and *Pathfinders: A Global History of Exploration*.

Fernández-Armesto—whom I consider an intellectual companion and a mentor—was the first to reveal to me a compelling reality and excite me with its educational potential. In the introduction to his small book on Columbus—written on the eve of the 500th anniversary of Columbus's discovery of the New World—Fernández-Armesto observed that a central feature of the last 500 years has been the steady shift of the world's center of gravity—or, as he puts it—its "main axis of commerce and communication"—from East to West—a movement which is bent on coming full circle—as the East rises in power and influence.[1]

This movement was by no means inevitable. In fact, at the dawn of the 15th century it seemed highly improbable. The correlation of forces—an expression much used during the Cold War—was weighted heavily in favor of the East. The East was where people, prosperity and progress resided. The West—that is Europe—was in the main poor and backward.

It was, at the beginning of the fifteenth century, on the periphery and on the defensive.[2]

At the dawn of the 15th century, China was arguably the world's greatest power.[3] It possessed a large population, riches and technology—ironically the very technology that the West would exploit to reach and then dominate the Orient in the 16th and 17th centuries; to wit: printing, the compass and gunpowder. The Chinese invented the compass in the third century and printing in the eighth. They were "the unsurpassed master of astronomy" in the Middle Ages and their sailing ships—the fabled junks of the Chinese "Treasure Fleet"—outclassed anything afloat in the West.

And at the beginning of the 15th century, China was not only powerful and well-equipped, it was on the move in exploration.

> The most famous Chinese explorations of the wider world were accomplished in the early 15th century by the eunuch-admiral Cheng Ho. His fleets, of up to sixty-three ships and with reputedly 30,000 men, visited thirty countries around the rim of the Indian Ocean, in the course of (probably) seven voyages of two years each—sailing as far as Aden. The greatest of these voyages sailed 12,618 miles![4]

The Islamic world also was more powerful and more technologically advanced than the West. It was at that time "the most widely dispersed civilization the world had ever seen."[5] Its "military conquerors, navigators and caravan masters reconnoitered the Middle East itself, north and east Africa, the Mediterranean, the Indian Ocean and even the South China Sea in impressive depth." It was enabled to do so on account of its advanced maritime technology which included the sturdy dhow, the use of both square rigged and lateen sails (for sailing before and against the wind, respectively) and sophisticated stowage containers enabling long-distance voyages.

The Muslim world was not only on the move at sea, it had the West on the defensive on land. In the 15th century the West was mired in intramural strife—most notably the Hundred Years War and the War of the Roses—and by fears of invasion from the East. As we shall see, its internal conflicts—including between the Greek and Roman churches—aided and abetted the Eastern invasions to a near-suicidal degree.

Poised at the dawn of the 15th century to dominate succeeding centuries, China and the Islamic world failed to do so. China precipitously turned inward, as it is wont, periodically, to do.[6] Islam—under the influence of its religious leaders—became nautically timid, preferring to stay on land and predominantly coastal exploration at sea. The initiative in discovery—and the opportunity for world hegemony—passed to the West in the fifteenth century. In the words of William McNeill, the famous historian of the rise of the West: "Within surprisingly few decades, the most active centers of innovative activity shifted from China to the Atlantic face of Europe."[7]

What conditions extant in the West in the 15th century drove and enabled it to seize the initiative and mount an Age of Discovery which transformed the world and placed the West in the driver's seat for the balance of the millennium?

In the introduction to his majestic *Atlas of World Discovery*, Felipe Fernández-Armesto writes as follows:

> Exploring cultures are distinguished by rare combinations of motives and means. They have the technical resources with which to undertake long journeys, to sustain life during them, to find directions in unfamiliar places, and to record and communicate the information gathered. They need sources of motivation such as material exigency, scientific curiosity, missionary zeal, commercial spirit or wanton aggression.[8]

Using this description of motives and means as an outline, let us consider the way in which motives and means converged in Western Europe during the course of the 15th century.

MATERIAL EXIGENCY

The main economic feature of Western Europe at the start of the 15th century was revival following the devastating plague—the Black Death—of the mid-14th century. The plague swept into Europe from Crimea where it was borne by the Tatars. It was carried from the Crimea first into the ports of Italy and then worked its way northwestward. Over a period of roughly three years—from 1348 to 1351—a third of Europe's population was wiped out. As terrible as this was in human terms, it came to the rescue of Europe in economic terms. At the beginning of the 14th century Europe was destitute. By the beginning of the 15th century, with its population substantially reduced, there was more to go around, and per capita wealth surged. That surge, which created "large numbers of new rich," was accompanied by what might be called a "revolution of rising expectations." Europeans had the means to upgrade their standard of living but the commodities that would do so—silks and spices, for example—lay in the East. It is certainly one of history's great ironies that were it not for the plague—that came from the East—the West might not have been in a position to aspire to the riches of the East.[9]

SCIENTIFIC CURIOSITY

At the start of the fifteenth century, the predominant western view of the world was that it was a narrow, neat and orderly place. The representation of this conception was enshrined in the famous O–T maps of the Middle Ages which depicted the world in the shape of a T within a circle. The shaft of the T was the Mediterranean (which stands for "middle of the world"), the cross of the T represented Europe to the north (along the Danube river) and Africa to the south (along the Nile), with Jerusalem situated in between (as the navel of the world) and the Orient, where the forbidden Garden of Eden allegedly resided, resting on top of the T. The O–T maps were theological and political, not geographic and representational.

The stultifying grip of the O–T maps on the worldview of literate Europeans, was broken by the distribution—beginning in the early 1400's—of a new Latin edition of Ptolemy's great, thirteen-hundred-year-old book on *Geography*. Ptolemy's work—although flawed in important particulars—was scientifically based on latitudes and longitudes and it frankly admitted that much of the world was as yet unknown. The reappearance of this scientific (vice theological) work and its wide distribution in the latter 15th century (following the European discovery of printing) excited curiosity about the unknown world and offered a scientific starting point for practically pursuing that curiosity. Western European mariners began probing unknown waters, discovering for example the archipelagoes of the eastern Atlantic. Along the way, the grip of the O–T maps was irrevocably sundered, and gaps filled in, and errors corrected, in Ptolemy's great work.

MISSIONARY ZEAL

At the start of the 15th century, Christendom was in retreat. The Osmanli Turks were on the advance. Muslim's commanded the eastern and southern shores and stretches of the northern shore of the Mediterranean—which sea was considered by Christendom to be the center of the world. Christendom was shrunk in size by the plague and was situated between a rock and a hard place—the rock being Gibraltar and the hard place being the Mediterranean and eastern strongholds of the Muslims. With the failure of successive crusades, the only hope for the extension of Christianity lay in an outflanking movement. The only route to such a movement lay beyond the Pillars of Hercules into uncharted ocean waters.

The temptation to follow this route was heightened by the publication and wide distribution in the middle and late 15th century of two fabled books: the travel account of Marco Polo and the novel of Sir John Mandeville. Marco Polo, among other things, described a Far East that was "accessible to Christian preaching" and Sir John Mandeville described an African kingdom—a paradise on earth—presided over by a Christian emperor, Prester John. Both realms were described as harboring untold wealth, exotica and erotica setting the stage for a coupling of missionary zeal, fueled by Christ's commandment to preach in all corners of the world, and material aggrandizement—a powerful combination.

COMMERCIAL SPIRIT

At the beginning of the 15th century, Europe's commercial opportunities—just like its evangelizing opportunities—were at a dead end. Trade among the European countries was mired in low value-added traffic in textiles, wine and salt. Goods that would bring real profit and simultaneously diversify the daily fare and enhance the quality of life lay abroad. By the time these goods trickled into the West via coastal and overland routes, which were largely in hostile hands, their prices were exorbitant, and the financial beneficiaries were the middlemen, the warlords and the pirates who exacted or extorted payments all along the way. The only way out of this commercial bind lay—as with the missionary effort—in an outflanking movement along highways to and from Africa, India and the Orient. The only such highways available were those located in as yet uncharted stretches of the world's oceans. If Europe wished—as it did—to share in the riches of the world, it was necessary for it to go to sea.

The existence of such riches was given widespread credence by the tales of the real Marco Polo and of the fictional Sir John Mandeville. Excitement about the riches of the East grew exponentially as these two books rolled off the printing presses of the mid to late fifteenth century. They served as both summons and challenge to adventurers seeking the fabled wealth of exotic foreign realms.

WANTON AGGRESSION

The distinguished historian of the rise of the West, William McNeill, has claimed that the "barbarian inheritance—both from the remote Bronze Age invasions and from the more immediate Germanic, Scandinavian and steppe invasions—made European society more thoroughly warlike than any other civilized society on the globe, excepting the Japanese."[10] There is no evidence that Europe at large lacked outlets for those warlike instincts in the 15th century. It was up to its ears in intra-European conflict, in crusades against the Muslims and in rearguard defenses of its citadels along its shrinking eastern front. There was, however, one country relatively insulated from regional conflict at the time and that country was Portugal. It has been said that: "God gave Portugal a small country to live in and the whole world to die in."[11] Until the fifteenth century the Portuguese lived relatively introspectively in their sparse strip of seaboard real estate. But beginning in the 15th century the Portuguese aggressively ventured out into the world and began to lose their lives there. By means of aggression, the Portuguese launched the Age of Discovery and, with the assistance of aggression, charted, opened and dominated selected routes across the eastern ocean highways to the riches of the Orient for a world-transforming century.

TECHNICAL RESOURCES

The Portuguese stole the march on their European neighbors and on their eastern based rivals largely because they were first to acquire the technical resources "with which to undertake long journeys, to sustain life during them, to find directions in unfamiliar places, and to record and communicate the information gathered." Once having done this, the technical means were rapidly acquired by other European countries with which Portugal conducted commercial relations. Commanding and refining these means, communities on Europe's western edge thrust out into the world's oceans and dominated them and the riches to which they led for three hundred years.

The technical resources required were four in number: ships, sails, navigational methods and instruments and shipboard artillery. In combination, these technical means provided Europe with unchallengeable power. The Portuguese led the way in the development of all four and were the first to harness their combined power to national objectives.

Ships were required which could be provisioned for long distance voyages. The solution was found in smaller, lighter ships that required fewer crew and in equipping such ships with watertight casks to preserve provisions (including wine!) for long-hauls. The technology for these casks was borrowed from the Arabs whose dhows had benefitted from them for centuries.

Ships were needed which could make a roundtrip so that the nature of discoveries and the riches that accompanied them could be brought back to the home base. A ship that could sail both before and against the wind was required. The solution resided in fitting out the smaller, lighter ships with both square rigged and lateen sails, the latter capable of holding a ship close to the wind. The design of these sails was also borrowed from the Arab dhows and feluccas.

The smaller, more maneuverable ships fitted out with a new combination of sails came to be called caravels. These were the brand of ship that later would bear Christopher Columbus to the New World.

This new nautical technology was necessary for blue water exploration; but it was not sufficient. Improved navigational methods and devices also were required. The compass was adequate when you were in familiar waters and knew where you were going. But it was inadequate when sailing in unknown waters to unknown destinations. Improved astrolabes were required which allowed mariners trained in their use to determine their latitude in the northern hemisphere with reference to the angle of the pole star and, in the southern hemisphere, with reference to the declination of the sun. Improvements in such means of determining oceanographic location were led by the Portuguese.

Development and deployment of these maritime technologies enabled the Portuguese to begin to reach out into the eastern and southern Atlantic. But, inasmuch as the ships were sparsely manned, it did not give them the means to exert force and to make their presence stick. The answer to this requirement arrived in the form of light shipboard cannon that were mounted on a second generation of Portuguese ships toward the end of the fifteenth century. These cannon, carried on highly maneuverable ships manned by fearless explorers and warriors, placed the balance of world naval power, at the end of the 15th century, temporarily in Portuguese, and subsequently, in European, hands.[12]

The key to it all—and the revolution in technology that was mounted by Europe in the fifteenth century—was the replacement of animate with inanimate power. At the beginning of the 15th century, manned galleys dominated the naval scene. Naval battles were fought by ramming and boarding ships. At the end of the 15th century, power at sea resided with those who had replaced men with sails and boarding parties with cannon.[13] This the coastal Europeans, led by the Portuguese, had done. Their rivals to the East had not. In consequence, the sea-lanes of the world lay open to the power of the West and were, early in the 16th century, placed securely in Western hands.

This book, entitled *The World's Westward March*, chronicles major chapters in what unfolded and focuses on the historic figures who led the way.

NOTES

1. Felipe Fernández-Armesto, *Columbus* (Oxford; Oxford University Press, 1992), x.

2. Felipe Fernández-Armesto, *The Times Atlas of World Discovery* (Italy: Harper Collins, 1991), 373.

3. In the words of the late distinguished historian of world civilization, William McNeill: "An efflorescence of Chinese civilization (between 1000 and 1500 AD) raised China's culture, wealth and power to a new level, far outstripping all the rest of the world for a period of four to five centuries." William H. McNeill, *The Rise of the West* (Chicago: University of Chicago Press, 1991), xvii.

4. For a description of the Chinese "Treasure Fleet" at its height, see: Louise Levathes, *When China Ruled the Seas* (New York: Oxford University Press, 1994), 174.

5. Felipe Fernández-Armesto, *Millennium: A History of the Last Thousand Years* (New York: Scribner, 1995), 35.

6. For a description of China's abrupt abdication of seaborne exploration, see McNeill, op. cit., 526–31.

7. McNeill, op. cit., xxvii.

8. Fernández-Armesto, *Times Atlas*, 16.

9. Fernández-Armesto has put it this way: "The slow shift of the balance of the world's resources and means, in favor of Christendom, may have begun with the Black Death." *Millennium*, 123.

10. McNeill, op. cit., 539.

11. Samuel Eliot Morison, *The European Discovery of America: The Southern Voyages* (New York: Oxford University Press, 1993), 313.

12. For a description of the advantages gained by improvements in ship design, navigational instruments and shipboard fire power, see McNeill, op. cit., 526–31.

13. See Carlo M. Cippola, *Guns and Sails in the Early Phase of European Expansion* (London: Collins, 1965).

BIBLIOGRAPHY

Cippola, Carlo M. *Guns and Sails in the Early Phase of European Expansion.* London: Collins, 1965.
Fernández-Armesto, Felipe. *The Times Atlas of World Discovery.* Italy: Harper Collins, 1991.
———. *Columbus.* Oxford; Oxford University Press, 1992.
———. *Millennium: A History of the Last Thousand Years.* New York: Scribner, 1995.
Levathes, Louise. *When China Ruled the Seas.* New York: Oxford University Press, 1994.
McNeill, William H. *The Rise of the West.* Chicago: University of Chicago Press, 1991.
Morison, Samuel Eliot. *The European Discovery of America: The Southern Voyages.* New York: Oxford University Press, 1993.

I

THE VIKINGS

"The sea was the element in which their superiority was unchallenged. They relied on their mobility and hardiness to see them through."

—Hugh Kennedy, *Mongols, Huns and Vikings*

"Men have fled to the sea and to distant parts to avoid their wives, their creditors and the consequences of their misdeeds."

—G. V. Scammell, *The World Encompassed: The First European Maritime Empires c. 800–1650*

"The crossing of the Atlantic was the work of Norse seamen, who, starting from Scandinavia, reached Iceland and Greenland by stages and touched America."

—Felipe Fernández-Armesto, *Pathfinders: A Global History of Exploration*

In the last quarter of the first millennium AD, the Vikings—those who are now known as the Norwegians, the Danes and the Swedes—burst out from the Scandinavian Peninsula south, east and west. To the south they reached as far as the Mediterranean. To the east, they extended to the Black and Caspian Seas. To the west they stretched as far as Newfoundland. It is this latter thrust that is of special interest in the context of the world's westward march.

The basic questions which organize our inquiry into the Viking reach to the West are: What did they do and why? How did they do it? And with what impact on history?

There is no simple answer as to why the Vikings went "a-viking."[1] Reasons cited by respected historians range from: a shortage of arable land on the vast, but largely inhospitable, Scandinavian peninsula; to the frequency and intensity of Scandinavian internecine struggles which forced those vanquished to flee; to the advanced maritime capability of the Vikings which allowed them physically to reach distant shores, first to raid and then to reside; to "chance, curiosity and the prevailing winds;" and to the consuming Viking compulsion to live as free men on lands of their own.[2] As with most explanations, the truth is likely to be found in an amalgam of factors that might be reduced to a quest for land, riches, fame and freedom coupled to pure "restless energy."[3]

The Vikings were initially domiciled on a vast peninsula spanning sixteen degrees of latitude and covering 800,000 square kilometers. Their numbers in the late 8th century, when they first launched their raiding expeditions, were, in consequence of vigorous breeding, growing rapidly. Scarcity of land was not, however, a problem per se. What they lacked was arable land in temperate climatic zones. Which is to say that, at the beginning of the Viking era, the Scandinavia that we know today as among the most prosperous regions in the world, was largely an infertile wasteland. It is a tribute to the descendants of the Vikings that they have, through their resourcefulness, industriousness, and strategic vision, made a purse of a sow's ear.

Before this purse was made, bands of Vikings, some ad hoc, some with sustained, organized support from the homeland, first plundered the wealth of others and then appropriated their lands and made themselves at home. The first target was the nearest, an island off the northeast coast of England called Lindisfarne. In 793, a raiding party of pagan Vikings landed—as if from Mars—on Lindisfarne and raided an undefended Christian monastery, stripping it of its ecclesiastical treasures. The shock of this first recorded raid was captured by a local chronicler as follows: "On June 8 (793) the ravages of heathen men miserably destroyed God's church on Lindisfarne, with plunder and slaughter. Never before has such terror appeared in Britain as we have now suffered from a pagan race, nor was it thought that such an inroad from the sea could be made."[4] Note this latter phrase carefully: it was not thought that England could be raided from the sea! The Vikings knew just how to do so, for reasons that shall become clear.

From the moment of their first raid on defenseless Christian establishments, the Vikings were seen by Christendom as the Muslims later were; namely, as antichrists and terrorists.

Next, in 795, the Vikings struck Ireland and then settled into a pattern of raiding along the coasts of Scotland and Ireland. The objects of their plunder were ill-defended coastal market towns, and utterly undefended churches, manor houses and well-stocked farms.[5] Prizes were there for the taking and the Vikings took them because they wanted to, and they could. This itinerant, often brutal, and always opportunistic, violence, made successful by the Vikings extraordinary seaborne mobility, soon gave way to the establishment of farming settlements along the plundered coasts.

Successor generations of these settlers, with an inherited westward gravitational pull, began in the 9th century to sail further west. They found, and settled on, seriatim, the Faroe Islands (or Sheep Islands), Iceland, Greenland and Newfoundland. The settlement on Newfoundland was short lived—due to the ravages of weather and of the native inhabitants; but the remains of a farming community in L'Ainse aux Meadow, on the northeast coast of Newfoundland, have earned the Vikings—or the Norsemen—credit for the first known transit of the Atlantic Ocean and the discovery of North America.

Why were the Vikings first? The short answer is that they were extraordinarily self-confident, and they had the means to get the jump on the competition. They were the first to master a seaborne technology that gave them what we today would call "strategic reach." Their maritime methods and skills enabled them first to terrorize and plunder exposed coastlines and then to transport themselves as settlers to distant shores.

The Viking methods and skills had, apparently, been acquired and developed in the course of fighting one another. Before raiding the coastlines of offshore folks, the Vikings raided their own coasts and folks. In the process of their "close and unrelenting" internal struggles, they mastered a maritime technology, and accompanying tactics, which enabled them to invade from the sea along their own coastlines that rimmed the North and Baltic Seas.[6] The technology so utilized featured long (circa seventy-five feet), narrow (circa seventeen feet), flexible, shallow drafted (circa three feet) ships powered by both sail and oars. It was "the genius of the Vikings to combine the two methods" of locomotion in a ship possessed of both "strength and elasticity."[7] These ships could transport, and deploy on a shore, up to a hundred Viking warriors. It was, in effect, a new a technology—perfected in internecine practice—that facilitated a lightening fast strike before defenses could be alerted and an equally lightening fast retreat before a counterattack could be mounted. It was the best seaborne raiding technology of its day, enabling the Vikings to be "quick in and quick out."[8] One prominent historian has described it this way: "Viking bands moved with speed and secrecy striking unheralded and enjoying all the tactical advantages of mobility, flexibility and surprise that ship power could then confer."[9]

The ancient Scandinavian word "vik" means "a creek."[10] To go viking (or to go a-viking) apparently meant to go up someone's creek. In the event, creeks were inlets or estuaries and they carried Vikings—in their ships—to their rendezvous with assorted destinies. When the creeks at home ran out of possibilities, the Vikings sought creeks abroad and, by virtue of their technology and daring, bent them to their will. The river systems of outlying lands became the routes of access and egress for marauding Vikings. In the marauding, they found fame, riches, adventure, land, women, danger, destruction and comradeship—elements which proved to be an intoxicating, almost irresistible, combination.[11]

The Vikings were not only skilled in the technology of seaborne warfare. They were skilled in the construction and navigation of vessels dedicated to seaborne commerce.[12] Before, during and after their eruption in all directions, the Vikings were active traders, shipping throughout the Baltic and along the east Atlantic coast what they were able to hew from their homelands—or capture elsewhere! This consisted chiefly of furs, hides, walrus ivory, wax, ships cables and slaves that were traded for precious metals, jewels, fabrics and wine. The ships required for this seaborne commerce led the Vikings to develop sturdy, broad-beamed sailing vessels roughly fifty feet long capable of transporting a cargo of about forty tons. It was these ships that enabled the Vikings to "dominate the trade routes of the North Atlantic and to graduate from their opportunistic North Sea raids to their history making trans-Atlantic voyages—to make the transition from piracy to colonization."[13]

The first extended Atlantic voyages to Iceland, which commenced in the mid-9th century, were made without compass or chart. (The magnetic mariner's compass was not introduced in Europe until the 13th century.)

The Vikings, sometimes described as "among the greatest sailors the world has known," relied solely on "latitude sailing" tracking their course across the Ocean Sea with reference to the altitude of the sun by day and the Pole Star by night.[14] Their initial crossings to Iceland—some of which were "storm driven west across the ocean"—would have taken Viking mariners between a week and a month.[15] In a good twenty-four hour day, the Vikings could make "make 120 miles or more."[16] By 860, Vikings were reaching Iceland in large numbers, many apparently seeking freedom from subjugation by tyrannical Scandinavian kings, others arriving as criminal and political outcasts. Among this latter group was Eric the Red.

Expelled from Norway for manslaughter, Eric the Red sailed to Iceland where he soon also resorted to violence. In 982, having been banished from Iceland for three years, he sailed a course to Greenland that had been charted by a wayward Norwegian sailor some fifty years before. Eric explored and charted Greenland and established a small colony there. Upon his return to Iceland, he arranged the reinforcement of the Greenland colony. Under his eldest son, Leif Ericsson, it became the staging ground for the discovery of the New World.

In the year 1000, Leif set a course from Greenland that had been charted by a Norwegian sailor, Bjarne Herjolfsson, who had sighted land to the west when he had overshot Greenland in a storm. Leif bought Bjarne's ship, recruited some of his crew and sailed Bjarne's course in reverse. He first made landfall in Labrador and then on "the northern extremity of Newfoundland" where a modest settlement was established in a land he called Vinland. Returning to Greenland a year later, Leif found that his father had died. Assuming his late father's responsibilities, Leif dispatched his younger brother, Thorvald, to reoccupy the Newfoundland settlement. Thorvald was killed there by the natives and the remaining settlers were soon driven off by the depredations of the natives and the weather.

Within twenty years at most, Viking settlements in the New World—unreinforced and at the end of impossibly long lines of communication and commerce—essentially died on the vine (excuse the pun). They provided the initial evidence that a colony cut off from organized homeland support and beyond the outer rim of an organized sphere of commerce and communication could not survive. England, in particular, painfully relearned that lesson in Virginia a half a millennium later.

The Vikings essentially peaked as explorers in the 11th century. The weather turned against them as glaciers advanced across northern Europe. Their maritime superiority declined and, in the middle of the 14th century, the Black Death eliminated a third of them at home. Even in their prime, the Vikings were few in number and divided among themselves as fiercely independent Danes, Norwegians and Swedes. Their modest numbers and their own rivalries ultimately worked against them. Gradually, the Vikings became 'stay at homers' as the old seaborne Viking aristocracy, that prized adventure and combat, was replaced by chieftains who "were landed men, concerned with stability and peaceful development."[17] The end of the Viking Age was marked by the conversion of the Vikings to Christianity and the "assertion of royal power over unruly subjects."[18] The Viking became "an anachronism at home and abroad."[19] By the mid-eleventh century the Vikings had either been rousted out of their destinations or absorbed (as in the case of England) within them.[20]

The Viking legacy, however, endured. Their migrations scattered "across Europe and momentarily into the New World, a number of remarkably energetic, enterprising and adaptable peoples."[21] Their comingling produced new tribes known for their fierce independence (in Normandy, Brittany and Ireland, for example). Greenland is a part of Denmark. And Iceland evinces a strong Nordic orientation. The Viking vocabulary "penetrated every domain of language" as the following "English" words of Viking origin indicate: law, by-law, outlaw, riding, husband, fellow, awkward, take, want, birth and to die.[22] And the Viking reach to a new world—enabled by their self-confidence, their inexhaustible energy, their advanced maritime technology and their fierce quest for independence—established both the means and the ends of the subsequent, European led, world-transforming voyages of exploration.[23]

How best to sum up the Vikings? They were resourceful and vengeful, exploitative and collaborative, strong and weak. Their strengths resided in skill, daring, mobility and an unquenchable thirst for new horizons. Their weaknesses resided in overreach, internal conflicts and a shortage of manpower. The Vikings were deficient in numbers and organization; in consequence, their presence in the western Atlantic faded, ultimately to be overshadowed by countries with physically sustainable imperial ambitions; to wit: the Spanish, English, French and Dutch. But credit must be given to the audacious Vikings for first transiting the Atlantic and making the first recognized discovery of the New World. It took another five hundred years for Columbus to follow-up and for permanent sea lanes to be established between an old world and a new, providing the ocean highways transited in the course of the world's westward march.

NOTES

1. See Barry Cunliffe, *Europe Between the Oceans* (New Haven: Yale University Press, 2008), 459. In his words: "Why the raids began and generated such momentum is a complex issue. There was no single cause but rather a series of factors that interacted and fed each other."

2. James Graham-Campbell, et al. (eds.), *Cultural Atlas of the Viking World* (Oxford: Andromeda, 1994), 164.

3. William H. McNeill, *The Rise of the West* (Chicago: University of Chicago Press, 1991), 547.

4. Graham-Campbell, op. cit., 124.

5. Gwyn Jones, *A History of the Vikings* (Oxford: Oxford University Press, 1984), 22.

6. Jones, op. cit., 183.

7. Graham-Campbell, op. cit., 75 and Jones, op. cit., 187.

8. Hugh Kennedy, *Mongols, Huns and Vikings* (London: Cassell & Co., 2002), 10.

9. G. V. Scammell, *The World Encompassed: The First European Maritime Empires c. 800–1650* (Berkeley: University of California Press, 1981), 12.

10. Jonathan Clements, *The Vikings* (London: Constable and Robinson, Ltd., 2005), 7.

11. Jones, op. cit., 202.

12. See Kennedy: "While the Vikings lacked arable land at home, they had plenty of wood—especially oak—available for shipbuilding!" Kennedy, op. cit., 186.

13. Graham-Campbell, op. cit., 38.

14. Scammell, op. cit., 14.

15. Ibid., 14.

16. Jones, op. cit., 192.

17. Ibid., 391.

18. Kennedy, op. cit., 201.

19. Jones, op. cit., 392.

20. Scammell, op. cit., 25.

21. Ibid., 27.

22. Graham-Campbell, op. cit., 422.

23. See Scammell, op. cit., 31.

BIBLIOGRAPHY

Clements, Jonathan. *The Vikings*. London: Constable & Robinson Ltd., 2005.
Cunliffe, Barry. *Europe Between the Oceans*. New Haven: Yale University Press, 2008.
Graham-Campbell, James, et al. (eds). *Cultural Atlas of the Viking World*. Oxford: Andromeda, 1994.
Jones, Gwyn. *A History of the Vikings*. Oxford: Oxford University Press, 1984.
Kennedy, Hugh. *Mongols, Huns and Vikings*. London: Cassell & Co., 2002.
McNeill, William H. *The Rise of the West*. Chicago: University of Chicago Press, 1991.
Scammell, G. V. *The World Encompassed: The First European Maritime Empires c800–1650*. Berkeley: University of California Press, 1981.

2

THE MONGOLS AND GENGHIS KHAN

> "In twenty-five years, the Mongol army subjugated more lands and people than the Romans had conquered in four hundred years . . . the scale and scope of Genghis Khan's accomplishments challenge the limits of imagination."
>
> —Jack Weatherford, *Genghis Khan and the Making of the Modern World*

> "The real importance of the denser communications across Asia which the Mongol conquests opened up . . . lay . . . in the penetration into Moslem and Christian lands of certain key elements of Chinese technology, notably gunpowder, the compass, and printing. The importance of these devices for western European history can scarcely be overestimated."
>
> —William McNeill, *The Rise of the West*

In his writings, Felipe Fernández-Armesto identifies an early turning point in world history that led to the emergence of western hegemony. He cites the establishment of the Mongol Empire in the 13th century. The establishment of that empire in the early 13th century by Genghis Khan, and its enlightened utilization in the late 13th century by Kublai Khan, put East and West in direct operational touch with each other for the first time.[1] A route from Europe to Cathay—that previously was occupied by warring tribes—was cleared and then heavily traveled by merchants, missionaries and "tourists" (which is what Marco Polo might be labeled).[2]

This contact shattered Europe's conception of itself as the center of the world and opened it to the knowledge, inventions and treasures of Asia. It effectively joined two worlds that had historically been sundered. Ultimately the balance of the benefit of that joining favored the West, motivating and enabling it to extend its reach.

The story of the creation of the Mongol Empire is spellbinding. It features the towering ability and accomplishments of a single man—Temuchin—better known as Genghis Khan. The historic magnitude of his life's work can be best understood by comprehending the scope of Mongol conquests, the means by which they were achieved and sustained and, most importantly, their legacy.

The scope and pace of Mongol conquests are breathtaking. In roughly 20 years between 1206 and 1227 (when Genghis Khan died at the age of 60), the heartland of Eurasia, from Peking in the east to the Black Sea in the west, was conquered under the leadership—and on account of the genius—of a single man. At the time of Genghis Khan's death (symbolically in the "Year of the Horse"), the Mongol Empire was "four times the size of Alexander's and more than twice the size of the Roman Empire."[3] It has been termed the mightiest realm that ever existed in the world. "From the Sea of Japan to the Caspian, from Korea to the Caucuses, Genghis Khan's rule was law."[4] Never before or since has so much territory—roughly a third of the earth's surface—been conquered so quickly and by so few. Genghis Khan compacted "the nomadic races" and forged them into a "mighty weapon" which was used relentlessly to trample adjacent realms "under the feet of his horses."[5] Ultimately, the trampling covered four-fifths of Eurasia.

When in 1206 Genghis Khan launched his campaigns of conquest from the eastern wastelands of Mongolia, he stood at the head of an army of no more than 100,000 nomadic horsemen. This force erupted with ferocity to subdue vastly more populous and better-equipped civilizations. By the time of his death, successor Khans were able to lead into combat a veritable avalanche of a "perfectly equipped army."[6] Why and how was this done?

The establishment of the Mongol Empire began as an act of intertribal vengeance. As a young man, Temuchin and his tribe were betrayed by an allied tribe and became fugitives in their own land. Temuchin vowed to take revenge and set about dividing and conquering, one by one, the diverse Mongolian tribes and integrating them into his army.[7]

His daring, courage and tactical brilliance won him battles, followers and, uncharacteristically for the Mongolians, loyalty.

The successful pursuit of revenge, which ultimately led to a unification of a Mongol nation under Genghis Khan's absolute control, was then coupled to the pursuit of opportunity. Opportunity appeared in the form of grazing lands to the west, to which nomads were instinctively attracted, and riches to the east, with China as the plum.

In the pursuit of opportunity, vengeance was never far beneath the surface. One of the most spectacular examples of applied vengeance in the history of the world, may have been Genghis Khan's response to the mistreatment of his envoys by the Shah of Khwarizm.[8] Khwarizm was a large empire that stretched from India to the Volga River. It was a world center of splendor and culture located in Bukhara in what is now Uzbekistan. Genghis Khan destroyed it. The invasion involved "an audacious ride into the unknown beside which Napoleon's and Hannibal's crossing of the Alps pale."[9] Khwarizm's population was ravaged, its edifices reduced to rubble and its civilization practically extinguished.

The "why" of Mongolian conquest was intimately related to the "how." The Mongolians conquered Eurasia because they had the means to do so and because they were nomads with an instinctive lust for new lands. Every Mongolian from childhood grew up on the back of a horse and trained in archery. This formation produced a natural warrior class and, among the nomad peoples of Asia, "the most successful in the practice of mounted archery."[10] Genghis Khan capitalized brilliantly on this inherent Mongolian capability. His career "is the most dramatic example in all history of the potentialities of nomad warfare."[11]

The means of conquest were centered on the Mongolian horse. It was quick, agile and tough. And its riders were skilled at steering their horses with stirrups (probably invented in China) leaving their hands free from the reins to launch fusillades of arrows at their adversaries (or even lasso them!). The Mongol cavalrymen were lightly armored and thus highly mobile.[12] They were utterly fearless, placing a higher premium on battle and slaughter than on "clinging to life and prosperity."[13] In their time, they were the best horse-borne combatants in the world. Just as in their time, the Vikings were the best seaborne warriors in the world.

For the Mongols the horse was much more than a fighting platform. It was a complete survival kit. It was a source of meat, milk, cheese, yogurt and alcohol (distilled mares' milk called "koumis"). The horse transported the Mongolian encampments to new grazing grounds. And it enabled the Mongol's favorite pastime, the hunt. Genghis Khan brilliantly capitalized on this pastime for military purposes by transforming the hunt into a simulation of combat, honing his warrior's skills in ambushing and encircling their prey. "The pursuit of quarry became the pursuit of the enemy."[14]

The horse also served as the postal system of an expanding empire. As territory was acquired it was linked by a transportation and communication route—called "The Yam"—which featured a pony express. A route transiting the empire was constructed with way stations where provisions and fresh mounts were available every twenty-five miles. The express riders slept on their mounts and changed horses at full gallop. They were capable of covering up 300 kilometers in a day.

For the Mongols, the horse was practically everything. But, in the event, while necessary, it was not sufficient. Genghis Khan augmented the cavalry with sophisticated catapults, grenades, and firebombs utilized to reduce fortresses and citadels to rubble. His combination of laying siege to a theater, and finishing it off with his cavalry, was studied by legendary contemporary field commanders, including Field Marshall Rommel and General George Patton.[15]

As the Mongols campaigned across the heartland of Eurasia they were normally at a numerical disadvantage. Once having conquered, they remained at a decided numerical disadvantage. The gap in both respects was closed by sheer terror. The Mongols would teach a whole people, a whole civilization a lesson by virtual obliteration. The demonstration effect struck fear and trembling in the hearts of those contemplating resistance or subversion.

A heavy price was paid for the scorched earth tactics of the Mongols. Virtual genocide was a commonplace. Centers of culture, especially in Persia and Mesopotamia, were practically extinguished. In sharp contrast to the Romans, the Mongols were not the spear-carriers of an advanced civilization. The harshness of their native environment precluded the development of language, culture and the arts.[16] But they were custodians of admirable practices and developments for which they deserve historic credit:

- The Mongols were advocates and practitioners of religious tolerance. As they worshiped their own idols, they believed others should be left alone to worship theirs. Genghis Khan proclaimed, "Under my rule everyone may pray to any god he please."[17] This enlightened outlook was captured in an observation offered by Mongke Khan, Genghis Khan's grandson, recorded circa 1253: "We Mongols believe there is one God, by whom we live and by whom we die and towards him we have an upright heart. But just as God gave different fingers to the hand, so has he given different ways to men."[18]

- Genghis Khan established a system of laws for the governance of his empire. Required behavior was codified and enforced, removed from arbitrary and capricious local hands. "Peace and order ruled in the empire and trade flourished."[19]
- The Mongols established a turnpike across the heartland of Eurasia. They created a "transcontinental union" which was their most "brilliant creation."[20] Safe passage along that turnpike was guaranteed by the "Pax Mongolica" setting in train an historic encounter between East and West. The West became the principal beneficiary of that encounter as it was exposed to the wisdom, technology and treasures of the East. The absorption of the elements of that exposure ironically equipped the West to later eclipse the East. It was a dramatic demonstration of the dictum that "the principal factor promoting historically significant social change is contact with strangers possessing new and unfamiliar skills."[21]

This book focuses on individuals as shapers of history. Some question such a focus, placing higher priority on other determinants—environmental (as in David Key's *Catastrophe*), economic (as in David Landes's *The Wealth and Poverty of Nations*), epidemiological (as in Jared Diamond's *Guns, Germs and Steel*). Genghis Khan, however, provides powerful raw material for the determining role of the individual. Starting literally from scratch, in a desolate region, and down and out until he was in his mid- to late thirties (which qualified him as a senior citizen in his time), he led—in 20 years—the conquering, pacification and unification of the world's—and history's—largest, contiguous land-based empire.[22] What vision, qualities, abilities and character enabled him to do so?

Genghis Khan had a vision of "a realm of warriors ruled by one Emperor."[23] The achievement of that vision required enabling Mongolians to add up to more than the sum of their parts. This involved pacification and unification of a heretofore intensely tribal structure and the establishment of command and control emanating from a single source. An absolute autocracy was imposed.

That autocracy was based on an army, cohered and inspired by Genghis Khan's own audacity and fearlessness. Genghis Khan was undoubtedly one of the greatest generals of all time. That greatness rested on his constant preparedness to take greater risks than his adversaries. Strategic and tactical risk taking won him victories on the battlefield and the loyalty of his army. The army quickly replaced the tribe as the focus of the nomad's loyalty and the army, in turn, owed its loyalty to Genghis Khan.

The autocracy of Genghis Khan was promulgated in laws and administered with wise counsel. The laws governing the empire were set forth in 1206 at the commencement of Genghis Khan's conquests in a document called the Yasa. They were administered throughout his reign with the wise counsel of a captured Chinese sage by the name of Yeh-lu, who must go down as one of the wisest, most versatile imperial counselors in the annals of history.[24]

Genghis Khan's most notable qualities included: (1) undaunted courage; (2) unbending will and determination; (3) spontaneous generosity (Genghis Khan was known to "take off his own cloak and give it away, or dismount his own horse and bestow it as a gift.");[25] (4) scrupulous attention to the needs of his warriors; and (5) a preparedness to seek and accept wise council.

The Mongols penetrated Europe as far as the Danube; but, in the main, Europe was spared Mongolian conquest. It was spared both by chance and by choice. In 1242, with the Mongols "poised to overwhelm Eastern Europe," Genghis Khan's son and successor, Ogodei, died and the Mongolian forces withdrew to reassemble in the east to resolve the issue of succession.[26] Thereafter, by choice, the Mongols did not believe that Europe—a backwater—was worth the effort it would take to conquer it. The Mongols concentrated their fire power instead on "the two great civilizations of the era," the Chinese and the Islamic.

The core of the Mongolian Empire was built upon by Genghis Khan's successors, especially by the Golden Horde which extended the Mongol reach into Russia and by the famous Kublai Khan, who succeeded in unifying northern and southern China. It was under Kublai Khan—who ruled for thirty-four years (1260–94)—that the Mongolian Empire reached its apogee. Under his rule, traditional Chinese insularity "was swept aside" as Kublai Khan reached out in all directions from the Middle Kingdom. He encouraged and facilitated active trade "under the custody of Mongol world dominance" and, in consequence, Europe enjoyed direct contact with Cathay for the first time through the medium of merchants. "Gunpowder, printing and the compass, three critical factors in Europe's ascension to world leadership after 1500 . . . reached the Far West during the time when the political unification of northern Eurasia by the Mongols made movement back and forth across the whole continent unusually safe, frequent and easy."[27]

The Pax Mongolica as it came to be called was a relatively short-lived affair. The heirs of Genghis Khan warred among themselves and the Mongols, as hereditary nomads, were genetically ill-suited to govern large, sedentary populations. The first of their conquests to "revert to native control" were the two most prized, namely China and Persia.[28] An early 14th century outbreak of the plague contributed to the breakup of the trans-Eurasian world sponsored by Kublai Khan.

But while that world lasted, Europe benefitted enormously. Its eyes were opened to the world, the lure of the Orient was implanted and the means to get there—including the compass—imparted. It could be argued that the creation, and utilization for intercontinental commerce, of the Pax Mongolica sparked "the Age of Discovery."[29] Recall that when Christopher Columbus embarked in 1492, he did so in search of a western sea route to Cathay—a route that would replace the former land route to the realm of "the Great Khan."[30]

NOTES

1. Jack Weatherford, *Genghis Khan and the Making of the Modern World* (New York: Random House, 2005), xix.

2. For a succinct description of Marco Polo's travels and what he discovered en route that so excited the Europeans see: Felipe Fernández-Armesto, *Times Atlas of World Discovery* (Italy: Harper Collins, 1991), 156–57.

3. Robert Marshall, *Storm from the East* (Berkeley, University of California Press, 1993), 64.

4. Michael Prawdin, *The Mongol Empire: Its Rise and Legacy* (New York, The Free Press, 1961), 198.

5. Ibid., 233.

6. Ibid., 301.

7. Weatherford, op. cit., 52.

8. Ibid., 4.

9. Prawdin, op. cit., 159.

10. Hugh Kennedy, *Mongols, Huns and Vikings* (London: Cassell & Co., 2002), 117.

11. William H. McNeill, *The Rise of the West* (Chicago: Chicago University Press, 1991), 491.

12. For a description of the organization and provisioning of the Mongolian army see Prawdin, op. cit., 157–58.

13. Ibid., 142.

14. Marshall, op. cit., 42.

15. See Kennedy, op. cit., 14. "It was the field of military that Genghis Khan's genius really became apparent."

16. See Amy Chua, *Day of Empire: How Hyperpowers Rise to Global Dominance—and Why They Fall* (New York: Doubleday, 2007), 88. "The nomadic Mongols had no science, engineering or written language of their own."

17. Prawdin, op. cit., 182.

18. Marshall, op. cit., 168.

19. Paul Ratchenevsky, *Ghengis Khan: His Life and Legacy* (Oxford, UK: Blackwall Publishers Ltd., 1991), 199.

20. For a description of the turnpike, see Prawdin, op. cit., 329–30.

21. McNeill, op. cit., xvi.

22. See Ibid., 491.

23. Prawdin, op. cit., 27.

24. See Chua, op. cit., 101.

25. Prawdin, op. cit., 42.

26. See Chua, op. cit., 109.

27. McNeill, op. cit., xix–xx.

28. Marshall, op. cit., 233.

29. For a succinct account of the birth of *The Age of Discovery*, see Prawdin, op. cit., 508–12.

30. Marshall, op. cit., 18.

BIBLIOGRAPHY

Chua, Amy. *Day of Empire: How Hyperpowers Rise to Global Dominance—And Why They Fall.* New York: Doubleday, 2007.

Fernández-Armesto, Felipe. *The Times Atlas of World Exploration.* Italy: HarperCollins, 1991.

Kennedy, Hugh. *Mongols, Huns and Vikings.* London: Cassell & Co., 2002.

Marshall, Robert. *Storm from the East.* Berkeley: University of California Press, 1993.

McNeill, William H. *The Rise of the West.* Chicago: University of Chicago Press, 1991.

Prawdin, Michael. *The Mongol Empire: Its Rise and Legacy.* New York: The Free Press, 1961.

Ratchenevsky, Paul. *Ghengis Khan: His Life and Legacy*. Oxford, UK: Blackwall Publishers Ltd., 1991.

Weatherford, Jack. *Genghis Khan and the Making of the Modern World.* New York: Random House, 2005.

3

BEFORE EUROPEAN HEGEMONY

"Of crucial importance is the fact that the 'Fall of the East' preceded the 'Rise of the West,' and it was this devolution of the preexisting system that facilitated Europe's easy conquest."

—Janet L. Abu-Lughod, *Before European Hegemony: The World System AD 1250–1350*

"The East enabled the rise of the modern West."

—John M. Hobson, *The Eastern Origins of Western Civilisation*

"In the race across early modern oceans, it helped to come from behind."

—Felipe Fernández-Armesto, *Pathfinders: A Global History of Exploration*

"For all we know, the displacement of the Far East by the Far West that took place in the sixteenth century may be reversed."

—William H. McNeill, *The Rise of the West*

There is a single point upon which all historians seem to agree about the world before European—or Western—or Christian—hegemony. That point is that Europe was the least likely region in the then known world to achieve hegemony. It was least likely because it lacked the capabilities to do so. It was decidedly inferior to other regions: culturally, technologically, economically and militarily.[1] Worse, it was a backwater, not only peripheral to the main action in the world that was located in the East, but even irrelevant to that action. By most accounts, to be a European in the 13th and 14th centuries was to be a barbarian, a beggar and an outlier. It was embarrassing to be from the West.

Prior to European hegemony, the dominant countries or regions in order of strength and reach were: (1) China; (2) the Middle East; and (3) India.

Before moving on to inventory the assets of these three regions, let us pause for a moment to record such strengths as "poor" Europe possessed as the mendicant, the weak sister, in the world system in the 13th and 14th centuries.

Europe's strengths within the extant system of world commerce resided in the city-states of Italy. Venice and Genoa were the richest and most powerful European entities in the 13th and 14th centuries. They were rich because they were integrated into the world trading system. They were the vanguard of the West in the world, the middlemen between the riches of the East and the consumers of the West. They were powerful because they could afford to be and because they had to be in order to maintain their access to the world trading system and protect their monopolies as middlemen. This having been said, it would be a mistake to exaggerate the relative power of the Italian city-states in the world system at the time. As John Hobson reminds us: "While Italy indeed led the inferior or backward European subcontinent it was none the less a mere bit player in the larger global arena, at all times playing second fiddle to the more advanced Islamic polities and merchants of the Middle East and especially North Africa."[2]

The international trading system before European hegemony consisted of three overlapping and interlocking circles of commercial exchange and three very separate routes traversing—and linking—the circles.

The first circle extended from the eastern Mediterranean to the western coast of India, the second stretched from the Persian Gulf to the Strait of Malacca, and the third circle reached from the eastern coast of India to the South China Sea. The first circle "belonged" to the Muslims, the second to the Indians, the third to the Chinese. But the overlapping of the circles led to a comingling of the respective cultures and regions to a degree that, in practice, obviated a monopoly and the hegemony of a single power. Save for piratical interdictions and "tolls," goods moved relatively unhindered across regions and among distinct powers and cultures. There was no "clash of civilizations." There was, instead, a trading system that has gone by the name of "oriental globalization."[3]

The three separate routes connecting the circles consisted of a northern route, a middle route and a southern route. What follows is a description of these routes west to east.

The northern route travelled via the Black Sea, and then overland through the vast Central Asian landmass to Cathay (or China). This route had the advantage of terra firma and of being independent of the direction of the wind. It had the disadvantage of being extraordinarily arduous and of depending upon the goodwill of tribes in control en route.[4] It was not uncommon for a journey across the northern route to take the better part of a year. This was the route of Marco Polo in the late 13th century.

The middle route ran from the Levant in the eastern Mediterranean to Baghdad and thence to Basra, the Persian Gulf and on to the west and east coasts of India and across to the Strait of Malacca, the "gullet" entrance to the South China Sea. (Baghdad was the mother city of this route and when the route was in its heyday in the 11th century, Baghdad was among a handful of the most magnificent cities in the world.) This route had the advantage of the easily navigable waters of the Persian Gulf and the coastal sailing of India. It not only was the easiest route, it was generally the cheapest.

The southern route departed from Alexandria on the Mediterranean, overland to the Red Sea, and thence across the Indian Ocean to the Malabar Coast of India and on to the South China Sea. This route had the advantage of clear passage from the mouth of the Red Sea to the Malabar Coast of India but the disadvantage of navigational challenges in negotiating the rocky shoals of the Red Sea and the blue water passage across the Indian Ocean.

In the thirteenth century all routes were fully functioning. There was, thus, an active and mutually profitable exchange of goods taking place across the interlocking spheres dominated by the non-Western regional powers: the Muslims, the Indians and the Chinese. The central participants (which did not include Europe) were prosperous. One by one each of the trading routes closed down. And in the final closing, the West figured centrally. Europe then proceeded to reconfigure and control the routes of international commerce and to become, en route, the most powerful region in the world.

How did the old routes collapse, providing an opportunity for the Europeans?

The northern route was sundered by internal rivalries within the Mongolian Empire, which, at its apogee in the 13th century, reached across Eurasia. Genghis Khan established that empire and it was maintained by his successor, several times removed, Kublai Khan. Upon his demise, the empire fell into disarray. By the early 14th century, a combination of internecine conflict among the Mongols and the decimation of their ranks by the plague left the northern route essentially impassable. In Daniel Boorstin's words, a land wall descended upon Europe's overland route to the East. "The last date for which there is any evidence of Genoese merchants using the land route to Cathay is in 1344."[5]

The middle route was disrupted almost simultaneously when the Muslim Mamluk slave regime of Egypt drove the West out of its remaining Crusader-gained footholds in the Levant, and Baghdad, for its part, was conquered by the Mongols. The Egyptians effectively barred Western traders from the points of departure in the eastern Mediterranean and diverted trade from the middle route into their own channel, which was the southern route.

The Egyptians, commanding the entrance to the southern route (today's Suez Canal) then teamed up with the rich Italian city states of Genoa and Venice to dominate trade with the East, via the southern route, for the duration of the 14th and 15th centuries. "Egypt gained virtually exclusive control over the sea gateway to India and China."[6] The Genoese provided the Egyptians slaves for their unrelenting military requirements and the Venetians provided them with a market in the West and a supplementary naval capacity to protect the sea lanes of their trade. In the 14th and 15th centuries, there was a symbiotic relationship between the two strongest entities in Christendom and the then strongest entity in the expanding Islamic world. Cairo was the "mother city" of the southern route that was by the early fourteenth century "the single thread connecting the two bodies of water that comprised the central axis of the then known world."[7]

In the middle of the fourteenth century, this de facto triple trading entente of Egypt, Genoa and Venice suffered a serious setback, a casualty, ironically, of its formidable outreach. Deployed to the east at the frontiers of international trade, Egyptians, Genoese and Venetians were the first to suffer the ravages of the plague, which was imported from the East. The bacillus carrying the Black Death, was transported by a Genoese ship from the Crimea to Europe, where it spread inland from seaports. The populations of Genoa and Venice were, by the mid-fourteenth century, reduced by at least a third, and the population of Egypt, their link to the southern route east, may have been reduced by close to half.

The international trading system anchored in its western extremities by the Genoese, Venetian, Egyptian triumvirate, though weakened by the depredations of the plague, managed to struggle on. The international trading system, at a reduced level, remained intact until the end of the first third of the fifteenth century when it was dealt an even more catastrophic blow.

Throughout the centuries-long existence of commercial contact and exchange between the West and the East, the region with the most coveted wares was China. China, in the fifteenth century, "was by far the most powerful and civilized state in the world."[8] Its indigenous products, and the exogenous products accessible to it within its sphere of trading dominance, featured precious silks, exquisite porcelains and exotic spices and herbs. The lowly Europeans, in contrast, were offering in trade, rough textiles, salt, copper and silver. Not only were China's exports superior, so too was its technology across-the-board. Its paper, its iron and steel, its weaponry, its ships were all in a class by themselves. In consequence, China was the engine of the international trading system. And it had the capacity—but not the will—to become the world's hegemonic power.[9]

By the end of the first third of the fourteenth century, China decided to pull its engine off the tracks of the world economy. It turned inward. In doing so it derailed the system, created "an enormous power vacuum" and left the international trading system vulnerable to a predator.[10]

After an interregnum of 75 years, Portugal made its appearance as the predator and began the process of reconfiguring the international trading system along lines that enriched the West. It did so—as Mao Tsetung would appreciate—through the barrel of a gun—or through what has been aptly called "armed long-distance trade."[11] Its ship-mounted guns made their first appearance in the Indian Ocean on the fleet of Vasco da Gama, whose rounding of the African cape in 1498 led quickly to the Portuguese usurpation of the southern route to the Orient. There was no equivalent firepower deployed to resist them.

But there could have been. Had the Chinese, who "certainly possessed the technical resources to have anticipated the Portuguese in the Indian Ocean" not have turned inward, the Portuguese, instead of sailing into a vacuum, would have faced " a powerful Chinese empire in possession of the principal ports and strategic gateways of the Indian Ocean in 1498."[12]

Janet Abu-Lughod asks the provocative question, "Did the West rise or did the East fall?" She argues that the East had already substantially fallen (due to the destruction or interdiction of trading routes by conquest, the plague and the withdrawal of China from the system) before the Portuguese men-of-war appeared in the Indian Ocean. That weakened world was a plum ripe for the taking. "No special 'virtue' inhered in the conquerors; they took control of the remnants of a preexisting world system, one they then ruthlessly honed to serve their own needs."[13]

NOTES

1. See: John M. Hobson, *The Eastern Origins of Western Civilisation* (Cambridge: Cambridge University Press, 2004), 20.
2. Ibid., 117.
3. Ibid., 82.
4. For a description of the passage and the time it took to traverse it see: Janet L. Abu-Lughod, *Before European Hegemony: The World System 1250–1350* (Oxford: Oxford University Press, 1991), 154–55.
5. Ibid., 69.
6. Ibid., 213.
7. Ibid., 148.
8. J. H. Perry, *The Establishment of the European Hegemony: 1415–1715* (New York: Harper and Row, 1966), 5.
9. Ibid., 322.
10. Ibid., 259.
11. Kenneth Pomeranz, *The Great Divergence: China, Europe, and the Making of the Modern World Economy* (Princeton: Princeton University Press, 2000), 20.
12. William H. McNeill, *The Rise of the West* (Chicago: Chicago University Press, 1991), 526.
13. Abu-Lughod, op. cit., 260.

BIBLIOGRAPHY

Abu-Lughod, Janet L. *Before European Hegemony: The World System AD1250–1350*. Oxford: Oxford University Press, 1991.

Hobson, John M. *The Eastern Origins of Western Civilisation*. Cambridge: Cambridge University Press, 2004.

McNeill, William H. *The Rise of the West*. Chicago: University of Chicago Press, 1991.

Parry, J. H. *The Establishment of European Hegemony*. New York: Harper and Row Publishers, 1966.

Pomeranz, Kenneth. *The Great Divergence: China, Europe and the Making of the Modern World Economy*. Princeton: Princeton University Press, 2000.

4

THE PLAGUE

"Because diseases have been the biggest killers of people, they have also been decisive shapers of history."

—Jared Diamond, Guns, *Germs and Steel*

"The slow shift of the balance of the world's resources and means, in favour of Christendom, may have begun with the Black Death."

—Felipe Fernández-Armesto, *Millennium: A History of the Last Thousand Years*

The story told within these pages moves from east to west. And so too did the plague. It arrived in Europe from Asia in the 1340s as a death reaping import. It wreaked human devastation on a vast scale. But in the process it may have helped lay the basis for the initiatives that led to Western hegemony.

There has been—and probably always will be—a fascination (however morbid) with epidemics which have taken horrible human tolls. A contemporary example is the AIDS epidemic. Historically the epidemic that has dominated Western historical literature is the bubonic plague, the Black Death, of the mid-14th century. It is viewed in the West as "the king of all epidemics."[1] Its stature is such that it defines, in common parlance, the very meaning of the word "plague."

"The plague" has generated a substantial literature. But that literature does not—even to this day—definitively establish the origins, the means of transmission, or the consequences of "the plague." In fact, it does not establish beyond a shadow of a doubt that there was, in fact, a plague. For example, David Herlihy's little book challenges the widely accepted assumption that the bubonic plague was actually the culprit in the 14th century. Perhaps, he suggests, it was tuberculosis or anthrax (today's biological warfare fear) or both.

With all respect to this distinguished medievalist, let us proceed on the basis that the plague was the plague; to wit, a disease born by the bacillus Pastuerella pestis, and carried by infected fleas from infected rats to human beings that mowed down as much as a third of Western Europe's population in a span of little more than a decade.[2]

Where did this plague originate, how was it transmitted and diffused, what and where was the human toll, and what longer–range effects did it have?

The best available answers to these questions are found in a book by the famous historian of world civilization, William McNeill. McNeill has dealt with these questions in detail in a groundbreaking book entitled, *Plagues and Peoples*. The following central points emerge from that learned treatise.

In the fourteenth century, the plague was transmitted to the West by Mongolian horse-borne warriors. They had been exposed to the disease in the mid-13th century in their raids upon China that had penetrated as far south as the Burmese/Indian border. It was in this region that the bubonic disease pool resided. The infected fleas of this region were then horse borne back to the Mongolian steppe where they took up residence among the burrowing rodent populations of that steppe. From those residences infected fleas periodically invaded human hosts who became victims (and carriers!) of the plague.

In 1345, Mongolian forces laying siege to the Black Sea Genoese trading port of Kaffa fell victims to an outbreak of bubonic plague. They withdrew their siege, but not before hurling some of their own victims into the beleaguered city (an earlier day equivalent of biological warfare). Those Genoese traders in residence who quickly returned from the Crimea to Italy carried the plague with them.[3] It first "closed a deadly noose" on the great port cities of Venice and Genoa and then fanned out into hinterlands and on to seaports in neighboring countries essentially following routes of trade. It struck Western Europe in successive waves, moving south to north, taking the heaviest toll in the Italian city-states most exposed to "world" commerce and in England, a seafaring and trading nation.

The human loss in the Italian city-states ranged from a third to half of the population. Having grown rich in trade with the East, those centers of trade paid the price in the ravages of a bacillus that invaded them from the East on their very own ships. For reasons not entirely clear—but perhaps related to the sparseness of population—Portugal and Spain—later to seize the vanguard of world exploration—escaped the first round of the plague relatively unscathed.

It was, of course, not only the West that reeled from the plague. We know that Egypt, which was linked to Genoa and Venice in the trading system of the 14th century, was devastated by the plague. Egyptians basically lived in densely populated Cairo or Alexandria. They had difficulty fleeing the plague, unlike Europeans who had hospitable alternative environs to which to flee. In consequence the death toll in Egypt approached fifty percent. In central Asia, and in China itself, the death toll was—as Janet Abu-Lughod has made clear—disastrous. There is evidence that China's population in the latter half of the 14th century was cut in half by the plague, from 120 to 60 million.

The plague changed the demographic vital statistics of the world's Eurasian heartland. In doing so, it ultimately worked in favor of the West in the following respects:

- The erosion it caused in the ranks of the Mongolians contributed to the breakup of the formidable Mongolian empire and its attendant formerly secure trade route across the Eurasian heartland.[4] A threat to the West from the East was thus attenuated and an economic artery that had nourished the Chinese economy was severed. China, in partial consequence, turned inward. With its own demographic ranks substantially diminished, China withdrew from the high seas, creating a blue water vacuum in the East—a vacuum that the West ultimately filled.
- The southern trade route, anchored in Egypt, continued to function. But it was substantially weakened and thus vulnerable to competitors or predators, and especially to a combination of the two! A century and a half later, the Portuguese and their men-of-war provided that combination.

- The West, for its part, after absorbing the initial blow, began to gain strength. With its ranks thinned out, labor commanded a higher price.[5] Wages rose two to three times above pre-plague levels. At the same time, there was more to go around as fewer people (by at least a third) laid claim to the existing pie. The standard of living of common people rose, and with it, their desire for more—more goods, more luxury, more riches. There ensued, in effect, a revolution of rising expectations as even the lower social classes "manifested an extravagant taste for food and attire."[6] Those expectations could only partially be satisfied within their own region, because most of the "more" lay elsewhere, primarily in the East.
- The reduction in the labor pool in the West catalyzed a search for labor saving devices, providing an impetus for what later became the industrial revolution. The invention in the West of moveable type followed on the heels of the plague. So too did the design of new ships which were larger but required smaller crews and were thus able to "remain long at sea and sail directly from port to port."[7]
- Before the outbreak of the plague, Western Europe was over-populated, underfed, overtaxed and poor. It was caught in what Herlihy describes as a "Malthusian deadlock" which obviated a transition to a higher level of development. The plague broke that deadlock and "gave to Europeans the chance to rebuild their society along different lines."[8] The nature of those different lines was defined by new ideas that can also be seen as a byproduct of the plague. The pestilence precipitated an attack on multiple conventional wisdoms and spawned, in its aftermath, greater inquiry and greater diversity. In the words of David Herlihy: "Europe proved to be a strong patient and emerged from its long bout with pestilence healthier, more energetic and creative than before."[9]

In these respects, it is possible to view the plague—however terrible, even grotesque, its human toll—as providing a breakthrough for the West.

At this point in the story, it is appropriate to segue from the specific case of the plague to the general role that disease played in the "rise of the West." What follows anticipates the story of the Western thrust into "the New World," but it fits with the consideration of the role played by disease in the development of Western world hegemony. That role is so substantial that it has led William McNeill to conclude that "bacteriology was at least as important as technology" in accounting for the establishment of Western primacy.

At the beginning of the fifteenth century, the known world consisted of the Eurasian landmass, the Middle East and Africa. For centuries, the peoples of the regions of this world—through travel and trade—had been directly or indirectly in contact with each other. In the process, diseases initially specific to one region had been disseminated to other regions. By the fifteenth century most of the diseases extant in the then known world had been effectively shared with the entire population of that world. Along the way, a certain tolerance for these diseases—smallpox and measles for example—had evolved after an initial severe die-off rate. The body's immune system gradually adjusted itself to new bacteriological threats. Thus by the middle of the millennium, the Old World had established, more or less, a common disease pool and some degree of resistance to the diseases within the pool.

The same was not true of the New World. It was isolated from the Old World disease pool. Moreover, it apparently harbored very few diseases of its own, most probably because there were very few domesticated animals in the New World from which humans contract many of their diseases. In this respect it is possible to view the New World as a true state of nature in which healthy human beings resided in harmony with their habitat. That harmony was abruptly and brutally disrupted when the Old World arrived and imparted its disease pool to a virgin population. "Once contact had been established, the Amerindian population of Mexico and Peru became the victims, on a mass scale, of the common childhood diseases of Europe and Africa."[10]

That disease pool was ship-borne on Columbus's ships, the *Santa Maria*, the *Pinta* and the *Nina*. It was reinforced as an export as successive waves of conquistadores transited the sea-lanes opened by Columbus. As soon as the diseases endemic to the Old World were imparted to vulnerable residents of the New, the results were catastrophic. Measles and smallpox were the principal reapers of death among the biologically unprotected Amerindian population. Upon the arrival of Columbus, it is estimated that the population of the Caribbean and what we now call Latin America, stood at around 65 million. Several decades later, it had been reduced, chiefly by Old World diseases, to around 10 million. In less than fifty years, the population of Mexico that had stood, pre-Cortez, at

25 million was reduced to 3 million.[11] On some islands and in some regions of the New World, entire populations were wiped out.[12]

The near eradication of indigenous peoples provides evidence of the role played by disease in the establishment of Western hegemony. First, disease was a decisive weapon responsible for the defeat of native Amerindians. It is, for example, quite clear that the small body of conquistadores led by Cortez could not have prevailed over the Aztecs had the Aztec ranks not been decimated by the sudden ravages of smallpox. Second, the immunity of the conquerors to diseases that were felling their victims, imparted to the conquerors the image of divine protection. This image greatly assisted the Spaniards in their work of converting Amerindians—or what was left of them—to Christianity. Thus, as William McNeill points out, "the lopsided impact of disease upon Amerindian populations (offers) a key to understanding the Spanish conquest of America—not only militarily but culturally as well."[13] Ironically retribution later befell the Spaniards as an outbreak of plague on the Iberian peninsula in the late 16th century and again in the mid 17th century substantially reduced the Spanish population. "Pasteurella pestis must thus be considered as one of the significant factors in Spain's decline as an economic and political power."[14]

The only significant disease that the Old World blames on the New is syphilis. But even this is disputable. There is evidence that the first cases of syphilis in Europe predated Columbus's voyage. There also is evidence that syphilis is a relative of an old European disease known as yaws. In any event, syphilis has never been a demographically significant disease. The number of its victims pales in comparison to the number of those in the New World stricken by diseases from the Old.

NOTES

1. David Herlihy, *The Black Death and the Transformation of the West* (Cambridge: Harvard University Press, 1997), 18.
2. William H. McNeill, *The Rise of the West* (Chicago: University of Chicago Press, 1991), 179.
3. For a succinct account of this episode see Philip Ziegler, *The Black Death* (Folio Society: St. Edmundsbury Press, 1999), 3.
4. 4McNeill refers to the "disembowelment of steppe society" by the plague. McNeill, op. cit., 205.

5. Ibid., 193.
6. Herlihy, op. cit., 49.
7. Ibid., 30.
8. Ibid., 39.
9. Ibid., 81.
10. McNeill, op. cit., 211.
11. William H. McNeill, *Plagues and Peoples* (New York: Doubleday, 1977), 180.
12. "For instance, the Indian population of Hispaniola declined from around 8 million, when Columbus arrived in 1492, to zero by 1535." Jared Diamond, *Guns, Germs and Steel: The Fates of Human Societies* (New York: W. W. Norton & Company, 1999), 213.
13. McNeill, *Plagues and People*, 2.
14. Ibid., 152.

BIBLIOGRAPHY

Diamond, Jared. *Guns, Germs, and Steel: The Fates of Human Societies*. New York: W. W. Norton & Company, 1999.

Fernández-Armesto, Felipe. *Millennium: A History of the Last Thousand Years*. New York: Touchstone, 1995.

Herlihy, David. *The Black Death and the Transformation of the West*. Cambridge: Harvard University Press, 1997.

McNeill, William H. *Plagues and Peoples*. New York: Doubleday, 1977.

———. *The Rise of the West*. Chicago: University of Chicago Press, 1991.

Ziegler, Philip. *The Black Death*. Folio Society: St. Edmunsbury Press, 1999.

5

THE OTTOMAN EMPIRE

> "The Ottoman state was above all else a universal empire. The wide span of its rule was so all-embracing as to cover, in its contrasting cities and plains, river valleys, mountains, and deserts, countless disparate racial, social, and especially religious communities."
>
> —Lord Kinross, *The Ottoman Centuries: The Rise and Fall of the Turkish Empire*

The Ottoman Empire commands attention in the context of the world's westward march for multiple reasons: (1) The Ottomans were the most dynamic event in the world on the eve of the Age of Discovery; (2) Ottoman dynamism and reach in the Near East and Southeast Europe drove the Western Europeans to sea from which location they trumped the Ottomans and established world hegemony; (3) The Ottoman Empire at its apogee in the mid-16th century raised the Islamic world to its greatest heights of respect and effect, accommodating diverse peoples, cultures and practices in a unified, though decentralized, empire. As the East rises and the Islamic world reasserts itself in today's world, and the Christian world scrambles to respond, a path toward peaceful and fruitful coexistence and collaboration might be found in Ottoman formulas for balancing unity and diversity, community and identity.

The Ottoman Empire dates from 1280 and spanned over six centuries through to its final dismemberment in the aftermath of World War I. The years that are of particular interest leading up to the Western "Age of Discovery" are those between 1413 and 1481. These years witnessed the secure establishment of the Empire, its conquest of Constantinople and its initial and extensive conquests in southeastern Europe which, combined, placed Western Europe on the defensive, with its back to the sea.

The Ottomans were a nomadic tribe of Turkomans, initially from Outer Mongolia. They were a "hardy, tenacious and disciplined race."[1] They had, in the 9th century, converted to Islam. By the 13th century they were living as "ghazis"—or fighters for the Muslim faith against the infidel—in western Anatolia, the heart of modern-day Turkey. "Apart from such moral virtues as endurance, self-discipline and foresight, the nomadic way of life had bred in them a combative spirit, the habit of mobility, equestrian skill, and unusual dexterity as archers in combat."[2] The lives of the Ottoman ghazis involved opportunistic raiding of the decadent Byzantine Empire, expanding their holdings of real estate, slaves and treasure in the process. They were, if you will, the Eastern, mid-millennium equivalent of the Vikings, save that they had strong religious motivations and were horse-borne rather than ship-borne. Like the Vikings, who were the best in their time and neighborhood at what they did (namely, raiding and plundering vulnerable Christian coast lines in shallow drafted, oar and sail propelled ships), the Ottomans were the best at what they did in their time and neighborhood (namely, routing armored Christians with bow and arrow aimed from their galloping horses and then sacking their cities).[3]

The Ottoman's awesome prowess on horseback—pitting mobile Muslim archers against heavily armored, axe and pike wielding Christians—carried the day in western Anatolia and parts of the Balkans.[4] Ottoman holdings and power grew rapidly there. Their power did not, however, carry the day in the East, in Asia Minor. In 1402 when the fourth Ottoman emperor, Beyazit I, gratuitously challenged Tamurlane's Mongol empire in the East, Tamurlane prevailed. He routed Beyazit's forces at Ankara, captured him and proceeded to dismember the nascent Ottoman Empire.[5]

In 1413, the Ottomans began to rise from their ashes, under first the leadership of Mehmet I and then of Murat II, the father of the famous Mehmet the Conqueror.

The resurrection of the Ottoman Empire in the first half of the fifteenth century is too complicated a process to detail here. Suffice it to identify the principal elements. First, factional disputes within the Ottoman regime, chiefly between a traditional, conservative Turkish noble class and an aggressive "New Force," the Janissaries (about whom more later), was progressively settled in favor of the restless and warlike "New Force."[6] Second, a priority was attached to western conquests of the infidel, expanding the empire chiefly at Byzantine expense, deferring eastern extension until strength permitted. Third, administrative practices were instituted which featured: religious tolerance within an overarching Ottoman administration; abolition of feudalism; lighter taxation; and provision of law and order. These practices helped to win the loyalty of conquered peoples and consolidate an expanding multicultural empire.

With these elements in place, the Ottomans in the 15th century literally surged to the world's fore, "filling the void left by the decline and fall of the Byzantine empire."[7]

The story of the rapid rise of the reach of Ottoman power is one of the most fascinating in the annals of history. It bears all the hallmarks of a convergence of skill and luck; ability and opportunity; force and diplomacy; tolerance and zealotry; accommodation and ruthlessness. Perhaps all of these qualities in juxtaposition compose the alchemy of momentous, historic change.

With respect to skill, the Ottoman Turks, springing from nomadic roots, were masters of mounted archery. En route to their extensive conquests they developed mobile, agile military tactics that incorporated elements of attrition, ambush and encirclement. They were lightly armored and quick. They possessed a first-class intelligence service and were rarely caught by surprise.

The Ottomans also quickly perceived the need for a standing, professional army, for the most modern artillery and for a navy. The professional army was provided by the Janissary corps (Yeni Ceri—or "New Force"). It was composed of captured Christian boys who were converted to Islam. They became the Sultan's shock troops, loyal to, and rewarded directly by, him.[8] And they effectively placed the Ottomans on a constant war footing with an armed force that would fight until victory had been won. In contrast, European kings often employed mercenaries who "fought well and often but they fought only as long as they were paid."[9]

The Ottoman's modern artillery was first "borrowed" from the Christians and then improved upon and substantially augmented by inventors hired away from less generous European patrons. It is one of history's great ironies that the ordinance responsible for the successful siege of Constantinople was designed by a Christian from Hungary. The Janissaries in particular were equipped with the most modern weaponry.

The Ottoman navy was built from scratch and, in the mid-fifteenth century, at a pace that rivaled the rapid construction of the famous Chinese "treasure fleet." It became an indispensable element in the successful siege of Constantinople.

With respect to luck, the Ottomans were assisted at every turn by the disunity of the West and by acts of God. In this latter respect, most notable was the loss to the plague of two of Christendom's greatest warriors, John Hunyadi of Hungary and St. John Capistrano of Italy. They had demonstrated a capacity to defeat Ottoman forces in the field; but they were lost to a disease that had its origins in the East.

Christian disunity repeatedly played into Ottoman hands. Latin Christians, supposedly on a Crusade in the early 13th century, stormed Constantinople instead, seized it from the Byzantines and ran it down over a period of 60 years. Constantinople was weakened by a Latin Christian conquest and never fully recovered. When the Byzantines recaptured Constantinople, some factions used expedient alliances with the Ottomans to strengthen their hand against opponents. These alliances acquainted the Ottomans with Byzantine weaknesses and left the receding Byzantine Empire increasingly vulnerable. Further West, the Venetians and Genoese alternately and opportunistically allied with the Ottomans in their own selfish fight for commercial advantages in the East. The Ottomans literally had a field day exploiting divisions within Christendom and within Byzantium itself.

With respect to ability, the Ottoman Turks were gifted in the art and science of government (and in "the wiles of manipulation and intrigue").[10] By attending to essential details without micro-managing, they incorporated diverse tribes in an expanding realm which featured both unity and diversity, both centrality and autonomy. At a time in the Middle Ages when much of the rest of the world was chaotic, the Ottoman Turks developed an extraordinary degree of political, economic and military coherence among geographically, religiously and ethnically disparate communities. They seemed to have an instinctive feel for a brand of leadership that saw the forest from the trees. In Kinross's words, "they had a constructive sense of statecraft."[11] "They had the patience and the will and the tolerance; they acquired the practical, constructive experience to adapt themselves to the social and economic conditions of the lands in which they ruled."[12]

With respect to force, the Ottoman's applied it brutally when opposed. So too did the Christians. If adversaries accepted Ottoman authority, however, and paid a required head tax, their lives, property and religion were protected. Force was frequently coupled with diplomacy, which was used expediently to achieve both tactical and strategic gains. Force and diplomacy were seen as interchangeable and mutually reinforcing. For the Ottomans, they were opposite sides of the same coin. Whichever implement worked better for longer was employed.

Tolerance does not immediately spring to mind as a hallmark of the Ottomans. Indeed, as ghazi—as religious warriors bearing the standard of Mohammed—their image is the opposite. But the Ottomans followed "the traditional Islamic policy toward zimmis or 'people of the book'—Christians, Jews and others who accepted the same God."[13] That policy permitted—even encouraged—the maintenance of traditional religious practices so long as the suzerainty of the Sultan was acknowledged. In the event, the Ottomans more often than not co-opted their captives by permitting them to live and worship as they had before, albeit as relatively autonomous minorities within an overarching Islamic and Ottoman regime. One historian put it nicely: "The Ottomans waged war hard, but they goverened their conquests with a light hand."[14]

The Ottoman Empire, for example, was "a paradise" for Jews who were persecuted in the West and who immigrated to Ottoman lands in large numbers. As for Orthodox Christians, many preferred the fez to the miter, that is to say the relative tolerance of the Ottomans to the perceived bigotry of the Roman Catholics. This tolerance bought the loyalty of subjects enabling the Ottoman Empire to stage one of the largest and longest imperial runs in the annals of history.

The Ottoman "golden age" featured the reign of Suleyman the Magnificent (1494–1566) who was a "giant figure on the stage of Reformation Europe." The following description of him provides a glimpse of the power and splendor of the Ottomans at their height.

> Suleyman was a statesman, warrior, administrator, law giver, poet and patron of the arts. . . . His armies were the terror and admiration of the West, while his fleets dominated the Eastern Mediterranean and North Africa and ravaged the coasts of Italy and Spain. The arts flourished with the vast flow of booty and tribute which was augmented by trade in spices, coffee and raw silk, as well as precious gems, rock-crystal and porcelain. Suleyman's architects transformed the face of the great

> cities of his empire, while Istanbul, the seat of his court, exercised a powerful attraction to craftsmen from Europe, Iran and the Ottoman Empire. They produced works of art—textiles, carpets, illuminated manuscripts, goldsmiths' work, arms and armour—which were the envy of Europe."[15]

Across the years ahead, the power and splendor displayed by Suleyman the Magnificent eroded owing to a combination of factors inventoried by Jason Goodwin in his splendid book entitled *Lords of the Horizon*. The factors included the following:

- Gradually the Ottomans lost their fighting spirit. In the early centuries—the 14th, 15th and 16th—they had literally lived to fight. Led into battle by the sultan himself, they were organized as a fighting machine. But over time they lost their taste for battle. The sultan stayed at home, preferring wine to war. So too did the Janissaries, who, beginning in 1523, were allowed to marry. The Ottomans, like the Vikings before them, metamorphosed from invaders to stay-at-homers. They got soft and indulgent.
- They also abandoned the practice of fratricide which Mehmet the Conqueror had instituted in 1451. This practice insured that the empire would not be weakened and divided by dynastic quarrels. It was ended by Sultan Mehmet III in 1595 and replaced by locking younger brothers up in a "cage" in Topkapi where they wiled away their time in "suspended animation," isolated from real life and amusing themselves with the occupants of the harem. When their elder brother, the Sultan, died, they were—if they were still alive—hauled out of the cage in turn and—bewildered and often deranged—enthroned. Generally, and not surprisingly, the former occupants of the cage proved to be incompetent occupants of the sultanate.
- The transition from strong, aggressive sultans to debilitated ones is evident in the names accorded them. The early ones were known as Mehmet the Conqueror, Suleyman the Magnificent and Selim the Grim. Their successors were known as Selim the Sot, Ibrahim the Mad and Abdullah the Damned.
- As the sultans grew weaker, the institutions of the sultanate grew stronger and more influential, each vying for power. These included the harem itself and the increasingly unruly Janissary corps. Power

"slid from the sultans to their slaves."[16] Historians write of years labeled "The Sultanate of the Harem" or "of the Women" and "The Sultanate of the Janissaries." Special interests, intrigue and instability replaced overarching interests and steadfast authority.

- The Ottomans facilitated wealth creation by maintaining a largely privatized economy and by administering it with a light hand. But they were not, it seems, wealth creators themselves. They were in the business first of plunder and then of taxation. Gradually their expenses mounted and the taxes followed suit, progressively draining the sources of income. No new conquests appeared on the horizon to fill the gap. The empire slipped into bankruptcy.
- This bankruptcy was accelerated by the European discovery of the ocean highways to the riches of the East, formerly transshipped through the eastern Mediterranean. European discoveries turned the eastern Mediterranean into a "backwater" and the "lines of trade and wealth" which had intersected at Constantinople were rerouted. At the same time, cheap European silver from the New World undermined the Ottoman currency "forcing de facto devaluation of it and concomitant inflation."[17]
- The progressive economic deterioration of the Ottoman Empire is best captured by a quote from William McNeill in which he describes the decline of the preceding Byzantine Empire:

> Government becomes a great siphon concentrating wealth in the hands of a small group of insiders, whose cultured luxury may disguise the rapacity of the regime which sustains them. Taxation easily becomes confiscation and the tax gatherers soon come to resemble marauding robbers. Economic devolution and radical retrogression become the unintended result.[18]

- Meanwhile, the Ottomans got full of themselves. In possession of Constantinople, they saw themselves—as others did—as being at the center of the world. A first they swaggered. Then, as their expenses outstripped their income, they faked. The empire became a sham as officials lived off earlier conquests and unearned income. The imperial center slipped behind "a veil of fantasy" as all major actors pretended to be what they were not.[19] The Sultan pretended to be omnipotent. The officials pretended that they were actually governing a thriving empire. The Janissaries pretended that they were still warriors.

- All the while, the Ottomans were locked in the intellectual mausoleum of Islam. Gradually they went into a "shell" constructed of belief in their inherent superiority.[20] Innovation was actively discouraged. The printing press was not allowed in Istanbul until 1729. Clocks were not permitted until the 19th century. And thus the world around the Ottomans overtook them technologically. This became increasingly evident in the maritime sciences, as western warships gained ascendancy and in the military sciences as new weaponry (the highly mobile field cannon, for example) and new tactics were developed in the West. The cavalry and the siege cannon had been Ottoman comparative advantages. By the late 16th century, these assets were trumped in the West by well-armored infantry units. The Ottoman's rode to power with archers on horseback and siege cannon drawn by oxen. They lost power to well-armed foot soldiers and field artillery drawn by strong horses.
- En route to gaining technological advantages, the West also gradually came to its senses and formed alliances against the Ottomans—essentially adopting forms of collective security. Thus, a combined European fleet (that included Cervantes!) defeated the Ottoman fleet in the Battle of Lepanto in 1571. It was the largest naval battle of recorded history involving a total of 487 ships, 245 of which were Ottoman. Two hundred of those ships were sunk by the European armada. It was the first major Ottoman defeat in 200 years. A century later, in 1683, Polish and German troops came to the rescue of Vienna, putting the Ottomans to rout and delivering a historic blow to Ottoman expansion, pretension and reputation.
- Finally, the decentralized administrative practices of the Ottomans, which were well suited to the medieval period, proved deficient for the modern period that increasingly featured nation states. It is one of the great ironies of history that the Ottomans facilitated the creation of nation states by leveling the feudal citadels of eastern and central Europe with their massive cannon. The larger entities thus created outgrew the Ottoman's administrative structure and practices.

The Ottoman sultanate was pathetic at the time of its ultimate collapse in the immediate aftermath of World War I. By then the glories of the Ottoman Empire were distant memories. But some of those glories were resurrected by Kemal Ataturk, the founder of modern Turkey, who stands as one of the giants of the 20th century.

NOTES

1. Lord Kinross, *The Ottoman Centuries* (New York: Morrow, 1977), 34.
2. Ibid., 16.
3. Jason Goodwin, *Lords of the Horizon: A History of the Ottoman Empire* (New York: Henry Holt and Company, 1999), 4.
4. See Stanford J. Shaw, *History of the Ottoman Empire and Modern Turkey* (Cambridge: Cambridge University Press, 1976), 6.
5. Ibid., 35.
6. Ibid., 55.
7. Kinross, op. cit., 19.
8. See Goodwin, op. cit., 66.
9. J. M. Rogers and R. M. Ward, *Suleyman the Magnificent* (Seacaucus, N.J.: The Wellfleet Press, 1998), 8.
10. Kinross, op. cit., 43.
11. Ibid., 16.
12. Ibid., 25.
13. See Goodwin, op. cit., 90.
14. Ibid., 91.
15. Rogers and Ward, op. cit., Book jacket.
16. Goodwin, op. cit., 192.
17. Ibid., 174–75.
18. William H. McNeill, *The Rise of the West* (Chicago, University of Chicago Press, 1963), 17.
19. Goodwin, op. cit., 257–58.
20. Ibid., 265.

BIBLIOGRAPHY

Goodwin, Jason. *Lords of the Horizon: A History of the Ottoman Empire*. New York: Henry Holt and Company, 1999.

Kinross, Lord. *The Ottoman Centuries*. New York: Morrow, 1977.

McNeill, William H. *The Rise of the West*. Chicago, University of Chicago Press, 1963.

Rogers, J. M. and R. M. Ward. *Suleyman the Magnificent*. Seacaucus, N.J.: The Wellfleet Press, 1999.

Shaw, Stanford J. *History of the Ottoman Empire and Modern Turkey*. Cambridge: Cambridge University Press, 1976.

6

MEHMET THE CONQUEROR AND THE FALL OF CONSTANTINOPLE

"The capture [of Constantinople] established a stranglehold on European trade with the hinterlands to the north and east . . ."

—Stanford Shaw, *History of the Ottoman Empire and Modern Turkey: Volume One*

"The immediate backdrop to the voyages [of discovery] lay with the Ottoman seizure of Constantinople in 1453 which triggered a major crisis in Christendom."

—John M. Hobson, *The Eastern Origins of Western Civilisation*

The fall of Constantinople in 1453 was a turning point in history. It is viewed by some as a "dividing line between the Middle Ages and the modern era."[1] It crystallized the concerted advance of Muslim forces from the East and the fragmented retreat of Christian forces in the West. This advance and that retreat had been going on for seven centuries prior to the fall of Constantinople. In this connection it has been observed that it is less remarkable that Constantinople fell in 1453 "than it did not fall before." But the capture of this geostrategic citadel by "infidels"—commanding as it does access to two of the world's great continents—Europe and Asia—drove home a historic and ominous reality. For Christendom a citadel that had been considered inviolate and invulnerable ("under Heaven's protection") had fallen and Christendom at large had not effectively raised a hand to defend it.

The capture of the historic capital of the Byzantine Empire by a jumped-up band of Ottoman Turks only four generations old, signaled to the Christian world that its central sea, the Mediterranean, would be implacably controlled, on its eastern and southern shores, by Muslims. The Turks for their part—by capturing Constantinople—made known their designs on Europe while positioning themselves to control the rich Asiatic trade with that continent. Possession of Constantinople gave the Ottoman Turks a seat of power from which to leverage a fundamental shift in the world's correlation of religious, political and economic forces. It gave them a base from which to establish an empire that, along the way, revived and reunited the Islamic world.

The Ottoman Sultan who, at the age of 20, planned and staged the successful siege of Constantinople was the living embodiment of the juxtaposed qualities that drove the imperial reach of the Ottomans. His name was Mehmet II, better known to history as Mehmet the Conqueror.

Mehmet was born in 1432, the son of a Christian slave in the harem and the second youngest of four sons born to Murad, the fourth Ottoman Sultan. Conveniently for Mehmet, his two older brothers died in their youth, leaving Mehmet the heir apparent at an early age. His father, a courageous and contemplative man, died in 1451. Mehmet, at the age of 19, immediately succeeded him.

Murad, who had defeated the last major Christian crusade at Varna in 1444, was an able warrior but essentially a man of peace. He was known for his "justice and mildness" and for fighting "in self-defense."[2] Mehmet was the exact opposite in every respect. He was a warrior and a conqueror.

Upon assuming the mantle of Sultan, his nature was immediately displayed when he ordered his younger brother—his only potential rival—killed. He subsequently legalized fratricide and established it as a practice underpinning the stability of Ottoman royal succession.[3]

Mehmet was an unruly and heretical youth. He had rebelled against education and flirted with fringe religious doctrines. But his father had imposed instruction on him by force and interdicted his confessional waywardness, so that Mehmet emerged as a liberally educated and doctrinally reliable young man. He was well read in literature and philosophy and eventually conversant in six languages: Turkish, Greek, Arabic, Latin, Hebrew and Slavic.

Physically Mehmet was short but broad shouldered, muscular and handsome as defined by the prevailing aquiline facial features fashionable in his time and place. He was at his core a fighter of whom Gibbon said that while "peace was on his lips; war was in his heart." His "intelligence, his energy and his determination commanded respect."[4]

Upon assuming the mantle of Sultan his single purpose—indeed his obsession—became the capture of Constantinople, which had twice before—beginning in 1422—successfully survived concerted Ottoman assaults. He proceeded swiftly and systematically to mount a siege of the Byzantine capital that by then existed as an Orthodox Christian enclave surrounded by real estate controlled by the Ottomans.[5]

First, he built a fortification on the European side of the Bosporus directly opposite a fortification constructed by his late father on the Asian side. He completed this enormous project within three and a half months, gaining thereby strategic control of a point at which seaborne traffic to and from Constantinople (and the Black Sea) could be choked off. It was aptly referred to by the Turks as the "cutter of the strait" or the "cutter of the throat."[6]

The fortification constructed for this purpose was 800 feet long, rose at its highest point 200 feet above the sea and was equipped with huge brass cannon capable of firing 450-pound projectiles.

Mehmet then hastened to build the mother of all field artillery pieces. Employing a Hungarian cannon founder, Urban by name, Mehmet commissioned the construction of several cannon capable of hurling 1,000-pound projectiles.[7] This invention, practically overnight, placed the walled citadels of Christendom, beginning with its most formidable, Constantinople, at grave risk.

Not content with establishing superiority on land, he ordered the construction of a fleet of ships that, on the eve of the assault, numbered 235.

Thus equipped, on Friday, April 6, 1453, he hurled 80,000 thousand Ottoman troops (reinforced by 1,500 Christian Serbian mercenaries!) against the fourteen mile wall of the imperial capital populated by just thirty thousand citizens and defended by seven thousand combatants.[8] He besieged the citadel by land, by sea (after transporting seventy-two ships overland to the Golden Horn, outflanking a barrier which had been placed at its entrance) and by air (with his massive projectiles). After a truly heroic seven week long defense (and only after Mehmet, in a last ditch effort, reinforced the martial spirit of his troops by offering them three days of unlimited plunder within the citadel), the walls were breached and Ottoman warriors surged through the city slaughtering and looting.[9] Mehmet entered on their heels, to pray at the Orthodox Cathedral of Hajia Sophia that he immediately converted to a mosque.

Having raised Ottoman military prowess to its highest demonstrable effect, Mehmet proceeded to rebuild and repopulate Constantinople by employing those qualities for which his predecessors—and many of his successors—were especially noted. Extending a hand of accommodation, he incorporated Byzantine personages of influence in the city's governance structure while killing those who engaged in intrigue. Practicing tolerance, he protected the Greek Orthodox community within a precinct of the city, while converting their cathedral into his mosque and cannibalizing other places of worship for materials with which to build his imperial palace or seraglio. Welcoming foreign merchants and craftsmen into a re-born city, he slotted them into neighborhoods structured along traditional Muslim lines consisting of a central mosque surrounded by a hospital, school, artisan studios and a central market. As a center of urban commercial gravity he had built the great covered market of Istanbul which today still stands as one of the greatest bazaars in the world.

Having captured Constantinople and renamed it Istanbul (after the ancient Greek "is tin pol" or into the city), Mehmet turned himself systematically to his larger ambition; to wit: the establishment of a single world empire with Istanbul as its center. In this pursuit, Alexander the Great was his heroic model.[10] But the direction of the military movement was just the reverse. While Alexander's armies moved east to conquer the Orient, Mehmet's armies moved relentlessly west to conquer the Occident. Over the thirty-year period which spanned Mehmet's reign, a single unified empire was established which reached from Mesopotamia to the Adriatic.

Central to this remarkable accomplishment were critical factors that placed the balance of military power in the field in Ottoman hands. Chief among these factors was the utter, selfish and shameless, disunity of Christendom. This disunity was multidimensional running along religious, political and commercial lines. And it was so deep as to be, in effect, suicidal.

Religious disunity began at the top with the doctrinal cleavage between the Latin and Greek churches.[11] This cleavage was accompanied by such hostility that in 1205 Latin Christendom itself had invaded Constantinople during the Fourth Crusade and deposed its emperor, setting up a Latin empire which collapsed within fifty years.[12] Some Greek Orthodox leaders in the besieged Byzantine Empire preferred to succumb to Muslim rule than forge a defensive alliance with Roman Catholics. Roman Catholic leaders, for their part, operated within a spectrum that ranged from ignoring to welcoming the plight of Eastern Orthodox Christians. The eventual price those leaders paid for their malignant, or benign, neglect, was to witness Ottoman forces plundering Italy and threatening the seat of the Papacy itself.

Political rivalry within Christendom mainly featured dynastic struggles and territorial disputes and ambitions. Europe was literally littered with rival princes seeking opportunities to prevail and engaging in such intrigue as to sap Christendom of any reliable, durable strength. These rivalries were well known to, and adroitly exploited by, Mehmet through the creation and effective operation of a far-reaching espionage service.

Commercial rivalries were best illustrated by the competition among the Italian city-states of Venice, Genoa, Milan and Florence. In the year Constantinople fell, Italy was at war within itself with Milan, Florence and Genoa engaged in an alliance against Venice and Naples. After the fall of Constantinople, each sold out the other to gain commercial advantage with the Ottomans. The Venetians stood first and foremost in this game by seeking to protect their trade with the Orient, immediately entering into a treaty with the Ottomans that —at the expense primarily of the Genoese—gave them an effective Western monopoly on overland trade with the Orient. The Ottomans, however, coveted Venetian possessions and when Venice, increasingly boxed-in, declared war on the Ottomans, the surrounding Italian city states, instead of being frightened into an alliance, were delighted to pick up what pieces they could. Thus, the Venetians faced the Ottomans alone and were ultimately forced to make a humiliating peace involving strategic territorial concessions that placed all of Italy at risk.

Periodic attempts were made in the West to overcome its suicidal disunity, most notably by Pope Pius II between 1458 and 1464. But his appeals for a united crusade, while arousing fervor and rhetorical commitments, foundered on the rock of selfish, mindlessly petty rivalries. In addition to Pope Pius II, two extraordinarily talented Christian military leaders comprehended the dimensions of the threat from the East and came close to mounting the strength required to stop the Ottoman hordes. These were John Hunyadi of Hungary and Skanderbeg of Albania. They took courageously and brilliantly to the field and achieved some remarkable victories; but at the end of the day the needed reinforcements from neighboring Christian provinces or cities failed to materialize and the redoubtable Hunyadi, at a critical juncture, was felled by the plague.

Mehmet stood against the divided western world as an implacable monolith. He carried the banner of a single, unified and fanatical faith. He eliminated internal dynastic rivalries by legalizing royal fratricide that guaranteed that there would be a single successor. He minimized internal political dissent by accommodating local political cultures within the iron-fisted rule of his omnipresent regime. He minimized internal commercial rivalry by strictly and efficiently centralizing the administration of the commercial and financial affairs of his rapidly growing empire. Secure in the unity and loyalty of the ground he occupied, Mehmet pursued with breathtaking success a policy of divide and conquer in Europe.

This success was driven by the military superiority of the Ottomans. This superiority can best be illustrated in three of its dimensions: the mobility of its cavalry, the power of its cannonry and the fanatical loyalty of the Janissary.

With respect to cavalry, battlefield imagery tells the story. Western knights entered the field of battle heavily armored in an effort to come out alive. The mounted Ottoman *ghazis* entered the field with no defenses save their weaponry and their agility, throwing all caution or thoughts of self-preservation to the wind. Mobility, dexterity and utter fearlessness more often than not prevailed over the ponderous, shielded Christian forces.[13]

Lightness worked for the Ottomans in the field; but it was not an asset when the business at hand involved the siege of a citadel. Here heavy artillery was required, and the Ottomans were the first to employ massive cannons on a large scale to breach the walls of strategic, well-fortified citadels. For this purpose, cannon were cast on the spot at the very gates of the citadel to be taken. Unbelievably, some citadels withstood the relentless barrage; but most could not. Once breached, the Ottomans poured through the walls and unmercifully slaughtered, ravaged, or carried off as slaves, the inhabitants.

At the core of the sultan's military machine, stood the Janissary corp. It has been viewed as the world's first professional standing army.[14] While in the West, armies needed to be mustered, the Ottomans were in a constant state of readiness in the form of the Janissaries who during Mehmet's reign grew in numbers to around 10,000. The Janissaries were in effect a fraternal order of cavalrymen composed of Christians who had been captured as youths, converted and forged into a fighting force driven by religious fanaticism, intense loyalty to the sultan and a lust for spoils. Their ranks were constantly refreshed by the so-called "levy of boys" imposed upon Christian villages throughout the Ottoman Empire. And their loyalty—that included a vow of celibacy—was purchased with perks, generous wages and the fruits of war. The Janissaries were, in effect, the institutionalized expression of Mehmet's obsession with war and, hence, with war-readiness.[15]

In later centuries, the Ottoman advantages in the 15th century would become liabilities. Subsequently, armor found its place on the battlefield. Light rather than heavy artillery carried the day. And the Janissary corps grew increasingly mutinous and subversive.[16] But in the fifteenth century, the combination of Ottoman mobility, heavy artillery and disciplined readiness carried the day.

It has been said of Mehmet that he is one of the most notable figures in world history. His conquests fundamentally changed the world's political, cultural and economic order. One of the world's most enduring empires was, under his insatiable thirst for war, securely established. Christian and Muslim peoples were intermingled creating in effect a new culture. Meanwhile, Christendom was reduced in size and its trade routes to the East via the eastern Mediterranean and the Black Sea interdicted. Western Europe was thus forced out to sea, where its intrepid mariners proceeded to open routes, make discoveries and establish empires that, in turn, fundamentally changed the world order.[17] Mehmet's conquests contributed—if they did not directly precipitate—the world transforming age of discovery. He is thus viewed as a transitional figure between the Middle Ages and the modern period.

But what are we to think of this transitional figure as a human being? This is a difficult assessment to make because of a lack of primary sources on the man, because of the nature of the age in which he lived and because he was a "collection of contrasts"—both "cruel and gentle, ruthless and tolerant."[18]

Most contemporary sources are unreliable in the appraisal of Mehmet the man because they are either sycophantic or blindly critical. But one contemporary appraisal seems to stand the test of time and of the scholarship dedicated to Mehmet in the 500 years since his death. This description is owed to Giacomo de' Languischi, who visited Istanbul as part of a Venetian delegation several years after the fall of Constantinople. He wrote:

> The sovereign, the Grand Turk Mehmet Bey, is a youth of twenty-six, well-built, of large rather than medium stature, expert at arms, of aspect more frightening than venerable, laughing seldom, full of circumspection, endowed with great generosity, obstinate in pursuing his plans, bold in all undertakings, as eager for fame as Alexander of Macedonia. . . . He speaks three languages, Turkish, Greek and Slavic. He is at great pains to learn the geography of Italy . . . and how many kingdoms there are in Europe. He possesses a map of Europe with the countries and provinces. He learns of nothing with greater interest and enthusiasm than the geography of the world and military affairs; he burns with desire to dominate; he is a shrewd investigator of conditions. . . . He says the times have changed, and declares that he will advance from East to West as in former times the Westerners advanced into the Orient. There must, he says, be only one empire, one faith, and one sovereignty in the world. . . . It is with such a man that we Christians have to deal.[19]

And how did this man deal with the Christians? He killed large numbers of them. It is estimated that Mehmet the Conqueror was responsible over a thirty-year period for 850,000 deaths, most of whom were Christians. That is an average of 29,000 per year. And many of these were killed in horrible ways. Thus Mehmet must be viewed as one of history's cruelest and most bloodthirsty tyrants. And so he was. But so too were others of his era who happened to be "Christians." Such notorious despots as Ferrante of Aragon and Sigismondo Pandolfo Malatasta of Rimini "show an astonishing resemblance to the Conqueror."[20] The field for the indulgence of their vengeful, violent and arbitrary rule was simply not as extensive as Mehmet's.

While Christians died directly at Mehmet's hands, they also died indirectly at his hands through their own internecine rivalries. Worshipping narrow interests, the West failed to mount a united front to face the threat from the East. This was a mistake that Winston Churchill was determined not to repeat when he and the Western democracies faced a modern-day threat from the East.

The fall of Constantinople and the subsequent extension of the Ottoman Empire from Mesopotamia to the Adriatic, provided a direct impetus to the Age of Discovery mounted by the West toward the end of the 15th century. Commercially, historic land routes for East-West trade were paralyzed or destroyed. Historic water ways for East-West commerce—from the coastal cities of the Black Sea, through the Dardanelles and from the eastern Mediterranean—were similarly interrupted or closed.[21] Religiously, the spread of Islam under the shadow of the Turkish crescent challenged the divided Western world to look elsewhere for converts to redress the confessional balance of forces. New routes of commerce and new sources of converts—given the failure of the West to mount a unified campaign against Turkish power—lay in an outflanking movement over unknown ocean highways. That movement quite rapidly placed the balance of world power in western hands and condemned the Ottoman Empire to eventual decline.

NOTES

1. Franz Babinger, *Mehmet the Conqueror and His Time* (Princeton: Princeton University Press, 1978), 98.

2. See Ibid., 3. "Murad found no satisfaction in war."

3. See Ibid., 65–66.

4. Steven Runciman, *The Fall of Constantinople* (Cambridge: Cambridge University Press, 1965), 59.

5. See Philip Mansel, *Constantinople: City of the World's Desire* (New York: St, Martin's Press, 1996), 4. "Constantinople was a Greek island in an Ottoman sea."

6. Runciman, op. cit., 66.

7. For a description of Urban and his cannon, see Babinger, op. cit., 98.

8. Runciman, op. cit., 85.

9. For a blow-by-blow description of the heroic Christian defense of Constantinople, see Runciman, op. cit.

10. See Mansel, op. cit., 6. "Mehmet wished to exceed the glory of Alexander the Great."

11. For a description of the divide between the churches, see Runciman, op. cit., 7–8.

12. See Jason Goodwin, *Lords of the Horizon: A History of the Ottoman Empire* (New York: Henry Holt, 1998), 12.

13. Stanford J. Shaw, *History of the Ottoman Empire and Modern Turkey* (Cambridge: Cambridge University Press, 1976), 6.

14. See Goodwin, op. cit., 66.

15. For a description of the Janissaries see Babinger, op. cit., 438–49.

16. For Mehmet's treatment of Janissaries who failed him in battle, see Babinger, op. cit., 351. "He had them all tied and thrown into the river with stones attached to their necks."

17. See Babinger, op. cit., 346. "It is no exaggeration to say that even the discovery of the new Atlantic trade routes, with its crucial consequences for the economic life of the West, resulted in part from Ottoman expansion in the Black Sea area. The voyages of discovery to the New World were undertaken in hope of creating a new, substitute route to India and Central Asia."

18. Mansel, op. cit., 21.

19. Ibid., 112.

20. Ibid., 421–22.

21. See Shaw, op. cit., 57.

BIBLIOGRAPHY

Babinger, Franz. *Mehmed the Conqueror and His Time.* Princeton: Princeton University Press, 1978.

Goodwin, Jason. *Lords of the Horizon: A History of the Ottoman Empire.* New York: Henry Holt, 1998.

Mansel, Philip. *Constantinople: City of the World's Desire.* New York: St. Martin's Press, 1996.

Runciman, Steven. *The Fall of Constantinople.* Cambridge: Cambridge University Press, 1965.

Shaw, Stanford J. *History of the Ottoman Empire and Modern Turkey.* Cambridge: Cambridge University Press, 1976.

7

THE PORTUGUESE

"No other people in history made such extensive geographical explorations as the Portuguese."

—Bailey W. Diffie and George D. Winius,
Foundations of the Portuguese Empire: 1415–1550

"The Portuguese were the pioneers in the great movement of European exploration and expansion."

—George Winius (ed.), *Portugal, the Pathfinder*

"Portuguese nautical science in the later fifteenth century and much of the sixteenth was more advanced than that of any other European country."

—Eric Axelson (ed.), *Dias and his Successors*

The westward shift in the world's center of commercial and cultural gravity was set inexorably in motion by the intrepid mariners who, operating from bases on the Iberian Peninsula, discovered, charted and opened the great ocean highways of the world. Once these highways were opened, they were jammed with merchants and missionaries, colonists and conquerors, immigrants and imperialists, scientists and idealists whose travels, exploits and enterprises, in just half a millennium, totally transformed the world. It is a process of transformation that is carrying us briskly into a new era that now is being called *The Pacific Century*.

When, where and why did this transformation begin? Who led it and how?

It began in the course of the 15th century and was driven by a series of events which, when combined, produced the motivations and the means that led to an awesome age of exploration and discovery. Preceding chapters have covered some of the main events and several bear revisiting briefly.

The "Black Death" of the 14th century, invading Europe from the Caucuses and ravaging it from south to north, figures prominently. Along the way, one-quarter to one-third of Europe's population was exterminated and the overland route to trade with Asia collapsed. As dreadful as this was, it left those who survived better off than they were before—the existing pie could be shared with fewer people. Thus the fewer people became, comparatively, wealthier per capita. In these circumstances in the 15th century, there was essentially a revolution of rising expectations. People with more means at their disposal wanted "access to rare and valuable goods that could not be found at home."[1] Those goods, for example gold, porcelains, silk and spices, lay abroad—in Africa, in the first instance, and ultimately in "the Indies."

Europe entered the 15th century wanting more. At mid-point in that century, in 1450 (just a year before Columbus was born) moveable type was introduced and books began to be published. These books transmitted knowledge of worlds elsewhere—or at least speculations about worlds elsewhere. Geographic texts, cosmological treatises and, most influential, the account of the alleged travels of Marco Polo became more or less available. These books excited the imaginations of the learned, raised the expectations of the wealthy and informed the planning of adventurers. In this latter connection, it has been observed that: "the makers of Iberia's Atlantic destiny came from a world steeped in the idealization of adventure."[2]

Then, in 1453, the Osmanli Turks—led by Mehmet the Conqueror—successfully laid siege to the capital of the Byzantine Empire, Constantinople. Constantinople had been a trans-shipment center between Europe and Asia, providing Europeans with secure though expensive access to products from the Orient. The Ottoman Islamic conquest of this citadel placed this vital trans-shipment center in hostile hands. Meanwhile, North Africa was also in hostile Islamic hands, standing between Europe and the riches south of the Sahara.

So in the 15th century—with the desire for and knowledge of riches elsewhere—Europe, lying on the periphery of the world trading system, was effectively trapped, confined to its own marginalized premises. The only escape lay in the uncharted ocean seas.

This escape was led by Portugal, a small, sparsely populated sea-locked country clinging to the western extremity of the Iberian Peninsula. At the time, it had a population of "barely more than one million, a few thousand able-bodied sailors, and a few hundred blue water ships."[3]

It has been said of Portugal that God gave the Portuguese a small country to live in and the whole world to die in.[4] In the late fifteenth and early sixteenth centuries, the Portuguese died in droves in the wreckage of their armadas.[5] But in the process, they opened up an ocean highway to the East, connected the Orient to the Occident, established a formidable and highly profitable seaborne trading empire and effectively launched a European led era which lasted for centuries.[6] How did such a small place do all that?

The driving force was Portugal's geographic position—sea-locked on the southwestern extremity of the European continent with "access to favorable winds and currents." Once those winds and currents were "de-coded" the mariners of the Iberian Peninsula "had privileged access to much of the rest of the world."[7] Deprived of a hinterland and of access to continental Europe by Spain, the Portuguese had no place to go but to sea. But this geographic position by itself would not have led Portugal to launch the age of exploration absent strategic decisions and enlightened and determined leadership.

First among the strategic decisions was to wrest the Moroccan Mediterranean entrepot of Ceuta away from the Moors and to establish a Portuguese trading center in its place on the south coast of the Mediterranean. This was accomplished in 1425 under Queen Phillipa of Portugal. It placed in Portuguese hands a storehouse of gold from Guinea that was warehoused in Ceuta—a treasure chest that was then applied to financing the Portuguese exploration of the south Atlantic. And it "established a foothold in Africa from which they could continue to explore and trade further to the south."[8]

Five years after capturing Ceuta and its riches, a member of the Portuguese royal family, Infante Dom Henrique—later known to history as Prince Henry the Navigator—established himself in the southwestern coastal corner of Portugal and utilized his royal resources to enrich himself while becoming a patron of maritime science and Portuguese exploration.[9] Under his aegis, information on winds and currents acquired from passing ships was compiled, seafaring charts were elaborated, a new generation of ships designed and Portuguese exploration of the south Atlantic encouraged and rewarded. Most critical were the newly designed ships—the caravel and the carrack—which featured lateen sails (borrowed from the Arab dhows) that enabled a ship to sail close to the wind and thus beat a course against a prevailing wind.[10]

At this time—around 1430—the Portuguese objective was to sail down the western coast of Africa in search of slaves, gold and spices. The problem was that mariners refused to sail beyond the western bulge of Africa because of two fears: (1) they would be unable to sail home against the wind and (2) they would be scalded to death by the alleged boiling waters of the equatorial zone. The first fear was allayed by the invention of the caravel. The second was allayed by courage. Thus in 1434 a Portuguese mariner, Diogo Cao, under the patronage of Prince Henry, rounded the African bulge and returned to report that the waters were navigable and there was no cauldron in sight. The Portuguese then began in earnest to thrust their way south along the west coast of Africa, establishing forts and trading posts at strategic intervals. Along the way, as they were sometimes blown out to sea, the Portuguese stumbled upon and settled the Madeira and Cape Verde Islands.

While the Portuguese were well rewarded by their seaborne African trade and its attendant coastal fortifications, factories and trading posts, the big prize lay in the Indies. The challenge lay in discovering, charting and securing an ocean highway to those riches. The breakthrough came in 1488 when the captain of a small Portuguese fleet—Bartholomew Diaz—was accidentally blown around the Cape of Good Hope in one of its famous violent tempests.[11] He discovered that he was in the Indian Ocean when he saw the sun rising over the ocean rather than over land.[12] After some exploration of the southeastern coast of Africa he doubled back around the Cape and reported his findings to the Portuguese King, John II. While the King reflected on how to capitalize on Diaz's discovery, Columbus sailed across the Atlantic under the Spanish flag, and returned claiming to have found a short western route to the riches of the Indies. This bogus, but blockbusting, news, galvanized Portuguese efforts to secure an eastern route to Asia and the race was on.

The ground rules for the race were laid down by the Pope in a treaty—the Treaty of Tordesillas—in 1493. In this treaty the Portuguese were allotted ownership of all discoveries that lay east of a globe girdling longitudinal line set at 1,200 miles west of the Cape Verde Islands; the Spanish were allocated all discoveries that lay west of that line. With this Papal division and guarantee of ownership of lands yet discovered in hand, the Portuguese set about deploying, in the Indian Ocean, armadas of ships designed and fortified not only to carry the Portuguese to distant shores but to enable them to win coastal battles along the way and to secure their position once they arrived. This new generation of ship—the carrack—was substantially stronger and larger and featured—below a full deck—a half deck on which artillery was mounted.[13] Such were the formidable ships that Vasco da Gama led around the Cape of Good Hope in 1498 and that he utilized in the Indian Ocean to put to rout the Egyptian and Venetian fleets which, until then, had a stranglehold on trade with the Indies.

Adam Smith ranked the voyage of Vasco da Gama right up there with that of Christopher Columbus with respect to its impact on history. It was a long and difficult voyage spanning two years and covering 28,000 miles, of which 6,000 unbroken miles were spent out of sight of land. In this respect alone, it can be considered "one of the most remarkable achievements of its time."[14] En route the Portuguese acquired knowledge of the wind systems of the South Atlantic that could carry them around the Cape of Good Hope and of the seasonal monsoon winds that facilitated seaborne commerce throughout the Indian Ocean. Once these wind systems had been mastered by the Portuguese, "world commerce would never be the same."[15] An "important stage in the globalization of trade" unfolded from which the West disproportionately benefitted.[16]

While giving da Gama credit for a major western breakthrough, it is difficult to give him credit for much else. Columbus can be credited with superb seamanship. Not so da Gama who, on his return trip from the Malabar Coast of India, caught the wrong wind, lost one of his ships and half his crew while making "almost every mistake imaginable."[17] Coupled to faulty seamanship was a faulty personality that featured paranoia and brutality.[18] Perhaps some cover for da Gama is provided by the fact that he was not alone among Portuguese admirals in displaying and deploying these qualities while commanding armadas throughout the Indian Ocean.

Successive armadas—led most notably by Francisco de Almeida and Alfonso de Albuquerque—reinforced and extended the reach of Portuguese seaborne power across the Indian Ocean to Malacca and on to the Spice Islands of the Java Sea. Thus by the early 1500s, while Columbus, then on his third voyage, continued to claim that he had reached the Indies, the Portuguese were really, actually, operationally there.

They also had—quite by accident—established a foothold in the new world as a Portuguese armada bound for the Indian Ocean, captained by Pedro Cabral, tacked too far west before bending a course for the Cape of Good Hope and was blown onto the coast of Brazil. Not only did the Portuguese discover and claim what is now Brazil, they were responsible for naming the entire continent as a passenger on a subsequent Portuguese voyage to the coast of South America, a Florentine, Amerigo Vespucci, artfully attached his name to what Columbus had, in the very first instance, discovered.[19]

Thus by the turn of the 16th century, tiny Portugal reached from the mouth of the Amazon through the Strait of Malacca. It utilized this reach to establish an effective monopoly on the spice trade between the Indies and continental Europe. That spice trade included: gums and resins which were integral to European manufactures of the day; pepper, cloves and nutmeg to preserve and flavor an otherwise bland European diet; and aphrodisiacs and embalming fluids coveted by a more specialized clientele. Such was the European demand for spices writ large that the Portuguese trading monopoly in the 16th century placed the King of Portugal at the top of that century's Fortune 500 list.[20]

What enabled Portugal to establish this monopoly and maintain it for a century? And why and how did that monopoly abruptly collapse in the early 17th century?

First of all, the Portuguese were tough. They overpowered those who stood in their way—and with good reason as they brought their firepower ruthlessly and relentlessly to bear on those with the temerity to oppose them.[21] But as violent as the Portuguese could be, aggression was not the key to their success. The key lay in capturing existing entrepots and slotting into extant trading patterns.

The Portuguese empire was a seaborne and seaboard empire, hugging the coasts where commerce mounted the ocean highway.[22] It was an empire without a hinterland—just as Portugal is a country without a hinterland. It was not an empire—as was the Spanish—based on colonization. It was based on facilitating the trade of the region at hand, capturing the profit to be made by the middleman. Thus the indigenous rulers of the realms marginally occupied by the Portuguese found their presence not only palatable, but profitable as the Portuguese served as purveyors of indigenous products to the markets beyond. In Oman on the Persian Gulf Strait of Hormuz, in Goa on the western coast of the Indian subcontinent, in Malacca on the entrance to the Java Sea, in Macao in the sea-lanes of the South China Sea, symbiotic relationships were established between the native held hinterlands and the Portuguese held entrepots. It was the network of such relationships constructed within a universe of traditional trading patterns that enabled a scrawny country like Portugal to establish and sustain the first European seaborne empire in the East.

Ironically, Portugal's grip on that empire was broken when a symbiotic relationship was ruptured in Europe. While Portugal held a monopoly on the importation of spices from the Indies to Europe, they contracted out the European distribution of the spices from Lisbon to the Dutch merchant marine. In 1580 a new King of Portugal—who was simultaneously King of Spain, Philip II—got greedy and broke the contract with the Dutch. Not to be denied, the Dutch mariners—sailing on taut and efficient ships—headed for the Indies and rousted the Portuguese out of their stronghold in Malacca. By early in the 17th century, the Dutch overtook the Portuguese in the spice trade and Portuguese fortunes in the Indies declined. Thereafter Portuguese imperial activities were concentrated in Brazil and later in Africa, most notably in Angola and Mozambique. Still, the remnants of its original seaborne empire remained until the contemporary period with Goa reverting to India in the early 1960's, East Timor taken over by the Indonesians in the late 1970's and the last redoubt, Macao reverting to China at the turn of the century.

The establishment of the Portuguese empire in the East marked the opening of a European era that spanned the 16th, 17th, 18th and 19th centuries. It led to an age of globalized trade and "made possible the long, slow process by which European economies, enriched by the pickings of the Orient, began to catch up with those of the Indian Ocean rim."[23]

NOTES

1. William H. McNeill, *The Rise of the West* (Chicago, Chicago University Press, 1991), xxvii.

2. Felipe Fernández-Armesto, *Pathfinders: A Global History of Exploration* (New York: W. W. Norton & Company, 2006), 195.

3. William J. Bernstein, *A Splendid Exchange: How Trade Shaped the World* (New York: Grove Press, 2008), 169.

4. There is a Portuguese expression that captures the perils of taking to the ocean highways: "If you want to learn how to pray, go to sea!" Bailey W. Diffie and George D. Winius, *Foundations of the Portuguese Empires: 1415–1580* (Minneapolis: University of Minnesota Press, 1977), 201.

5. It is estimated that between 1550 and 1650, on the homeward voyage from Goa to Lisbon, between 112 and 120 ships were lost. See Eric Axelson, ed., *Diaz and his Successors* (Cape Town: Saayman & Weber Ltd., 1988), 49.

6. It has been observed that: "Probably no nation so tiny has ever established its influence more widely or against greater odds—nor done so more deliberately." Diffie and Winius, op. cit., 195.

7. Fernández-Armesto, op. cit., 149–50.

8. . William D. Phillips, Jr. and Carla Rahn Phillips, *The Worlds of Christopher Columbus* (New York; Cambridge University Press, 1992), 54.

9. It has been argued that Prince Henry was essentially an "entrepreneur." Diffie and Winius, op. cit., 122. For a colorful reflection on Prince Henry, see: Fernández-Armesto, op. cit., 129–35.

10. For advances in ship design, see Diffie and Winius, op. cit., 124.

11. For a brief description of the voyage of Diaz, see Axelson op. cit., 2–4.

12. See Diffie and Winius, op. cit., 160.

13. For a detailed description of the kinds of ships built and deployed by the Portuguese as they secured an ocean route to the Indies, see: Axelson, op. cit., 39–41.

14. Bernstein, op. cit., 169–70.

15. Ibid., 174.

16. Fernández-Armesto, op. cit., 182.

17. Ibid., 182.

18. Bernstein, op. cit, 177.

19. See Felipe Fernández-Armesto, *Amerigo: The Man Who Gave His Name to America* (New York: Random House, 2007).

20. For a brief reflection on the gravitational pull of spices, see: Charles Corn, *The Scents of Eden: A Narrative of the Spice Trade* (New York: Kodansha America, 1998), xvii–xv.

21. Felipe Fernández-Armesto, *Millennium: A History of the Last Thousand Years* (New York: Simon and Schuster, 1996), 248.

22. Ibid., 245.

23. Fernández-Armesto, *Pathfinders*, 182.

BIBLIOGRAPHY

Axelson, Eric, ed. *Dias and his Successors.* Cape Town: Saayman & Weber Ltd., 1988.

Bernstein, William J. *A Splendid Exchange: How Trade Shaped the World.* New York: Grove Press, 2008.

Boorstin, Daniel. *The Discoverers: A History of Mans' Search to Know His World and Himself.* New York: Random House, Inc., 1983.

Corn, Charles. *The Scents of Eden: A Narrative of the Spice Trade.* New York: Kodansha America, Inc., 1998.

Diffie, Bailey W. and George D. Winius. *Foundations of the Portuguese Empire: 1415–1550.* Minneapolis: University of Minnesota Press, 1977.

Fernández-Armesto, Felipe. *Millennium: A History of the Last Thousand Years.* New York: Simon and Schuster, 1996.

———. *Pathfinders: A Global History of Exploration.* New York: W. W. Norton & Co., 2006.

———. *Amerigo: The Man Who Gave His Name to America.* New York: Random House, 2007.

Phillips, William D. Jr. and Carla Rahn, *The Worlds of Christopher Columbus.* New York: Cambridge University Press, 1992.

8

THE WORLD OF CHRISTOPHER COLUMBUS

"The Genoese contexts between which Columbus moved are vital to an understanding of his career."

—Felipe Fernández-Armesto, *Columbus*

"Columbus was a true son of Genoa."

—G. V. Scammell, *The World Encompassed: The First European Maritime Empires c. 800–1650*

"Columbus's exploits marked the convergence of two long-term trends in Europe: the search for direct contact with Asia and the gradual mapping of the Atlantic Ocean."

—William D. Phillips Jr. & Carla Rahn Phillips, *The Worlds of Christopher Columbus*

Felipe Fernández-Armesto in his classic book on Columbus, calls him "a crank."[1] And that he clearly was. But he was just as clearly a world-class sailor—maybe the best ever. The combination of his eccentricity and virtuosity ultimately took Columbus to the New World. But perhaps most important, Columbus was a beneficiary of the westward march which preceded his voyage. Columbus was, to be sure, the right man. But he was the right man, in the right place, at the right time.

The man (Columbus) and his mission (to find a westward route to the Orient) can be placed securely in the context of the world's westward march that was unfolding practically across-the-board in the second half of the 15th century. The story begins with Genoa, the trading city-state of Columbus's birth.

For several centuries prior to the voyages of discovery, Genoa had been a maritime power.

> Until almost the end of the 16th century, Genoa was of prime importance in the maritime life of Europe, opening in the late 1200s a sea route from the Mediterranean to the north dominating with the Norse the earliest stages of the continent's oceanic expansion and energizing directly and indirectly an influence out of all proportion to her resources.[2]

Genoa had been a primary European beneficiary of the work of Genghis Khan, capitalizing on the Eurasian highway created and protected by the Mongols, by establishing trading entrepots in the Black Sea (the most famous of which was Kaffa). These entrepots served as points of exchange for east–west trade. The wealth thereby gained underpinned Genoa's robust and aggressive maritime outreach which included, in the mid-1200's, a failed attempt by the Vivaldi brothers to sail down the west coast of Africa and round the cape (a feat that awaited another 250 years to be accomplished by the Portuguese who benefitted from Genoese resources).

Following the fall of Constantinople, the Genoese were driven out of the Black Sea as it rapidly became an Ottoman lake. Genoa's arch maritime rival, Venice, maneuvered to fill the middleman gap left by the expulsion of the Genoese. Genoa, for its part, looked for new opportunities and found them on the Iberian Peninsula. Thus, in consequence of the fall of Constantinople, very substantial Genoese capabilities were placed in the service of the world's westward march.[3] It is surely one of history's great ironies that an act of conquest designed to throttle the West actually provided it with the resources needed to first escape the Ottoman grasp and then establish the world dominance that the Ottoman conquerors themselves had sought.

The capabilities the Genoese offered the Age of Discovery were diverse:

- Advanced maritime technology, including improved ship design and enhanced geographical knowledge and navigational capabilities.[4] The improved ship design was a smaller version of what later became the famous caravel. The enhanced navigational capabilities included advances in the design and mounting of compasses.
- Powerful commercial and maritime families, familiar with exploration, investment and the development of business.[5] These families—one of whom, the Centuriones, employed Columbus—were involved, for example, in the discovery and commercial exploitation of the eastern mid-Atlantic islands—Madeira, the Canaries and the Cape Verde Islands. It was the success of this commercial exploitation of newly discovered lands—especially the production of sugar—that drove more exploration.
- Financial capacity and expertise that qualified the Genoese as the initial and most substantial lenders to Iberian royalty.
- The Genoese also took to the west personal qualities which were their hallmarks, and which were prominently featured in the age of discovery; to wit: ruthless energy, unbridled individualism, greed and accompanying brutality.[6]
- Finally, the Genoese took their native son, Christopher Columbus to the West.

Columbus was born into a Genoese family of modest means. He apparently had a burning ambition to rise above his socio-economic origins and to establish himself and his heirs among the ranks of the nobility. This he sought to do by, in his own words, "going to sea at a very small age."[7] For twenty years he sailed as a Genoese, reportedly travelling all of the known western seas, as far north as Iceland and as far south as the Guinea coast. Along the way, he acquired sailing skills that rose to a level of virtuosity.

His maritime training and experience in the Genoese service deposited him on the coast of Portugal in 1485.[8] At that time Portugal was a veritable maritime laboratory, reaping the benefits of the earlier work of Prince Henry the Navigator. Columbus was introduced in Portugal to the maritime advances in train and to the serious study of recently acquired geographic and navigational knowledge.

- This knowledge itself reflected the westward movement of significant capabilities. Inventions or re-inventions were appearing in the West in the 13th, 14th, and 15th centuries.
- Eyeglasses were invented—probably in Pisa, Italy—in the early 14th century, doubling the working life of skilled craftsman.
- The mechanical clock—invented by the English or Dutch in the late 13th century—led the way to inquiry based on accuracy and precision.
- And the printing press—reinvented by Guttenberg in 1456—enabled the mass publication in the West of world transforming books, most notably, for exploration, the fictional "Tales of John Mandeville," the less fictional "Travels of Marco Polo" and the geographic opus by the ancient Greek scholar Ptolemy.[9] The former excited and titillated the European imagination of the exotica and erotica of the Orient and the latter broke the grip of the theocratic O–T maps on the European world view.
- The travel books off the press reinforced motivations to explore while advances in geographic knowledge and maritime technology provided the means. These latter advances featured the combining of Mediterranean and North Atlantic ship and sail design—pioneered by the Genoese and incorporated in the construction and fitting out of the famous caravel sporting, as it did, both square rigged and lateen sails and carrying improved fresh water casks (a technology, like the lateen sail, borrowed from Arab mariners).
- The westward movement of capabilities—of which Columbus became a beneficiary—was itself a reflection of the westward movement of the center of initiative in the world.

The very concept of a center of initiative is a powerful one. Felipe Fernández-Armesto first introduced me to it. It connotes a concentrated center of constructive activity producing world-wide reverberations.[10] For centuries the center of initiative in the world resided in China. Following the mothballing of the famous Treasure Fleet at the end of the first quarter of the 15th century, the center of initiative shifted to the Islamic world, incorporated in the dynamism of the Ottomans. But while the Ottomans flexed their muscles and showcased their firepower and a high order of statecraft, they exhibited no curiosity about the unknown. Their high priests—their *ulema*—assured them that all that was worth knowing was already known by the keepers of Mohammed's legacy. The Muslim world began to live off its past. An intellectual complacency, comparable to the Chinese cultural complacency, set in just as the West set forth.

The West was not afflicted by either cultural or intellectual complacency. The conditions did not exist for it. Its expanding knowledge of the East, including the acquisition of technologies therefrom, stimulated ambition and innovation. And the Renaissance served to liberate inquiry which acted as an archenemy of intellectual complacency. In Columbus's day, Europe, politically, economically and culturally was a restless center of activity. The center of initiative was shifting to where he was physically located. His voyages then symbolized and dramatized that historic shift.

NOTES

1. Felipe Fernández-Armesto, *Columbus* (New York: Oxford University Press, 1991), vii.
2. G. V. Scammell, *The World Encompassed: The First European Maritime Empires c800–1650* (Berkeley: University of California Press, 1981), 201.
3. Ibid., 170.
4. Ibid., 193–94.
5. Ibid., 180.
6. Ibid., 156.
7. Fernández-Armesto, op. cit., 6.
8. "This lucky landing in Portugal was the turning point in Christopher's career, for chance had washed him ashore in the world center of oceanic voyaging and discovery." Samuel Eliot Morrison, *Admiral of the Ocean Sea: A Life of Christopher Columbus* (Boston: Little Brown & Co., 1992), 27.
9. Scammell writes: "Polo's glowing description of the east was to fire the imagination of Christopher Columbus," 217.
10. Fernández-Armesto, *Millennium: A History of the Last Thousand Years* (New York: Touchstone, 1995), 17.

BIBLIOGRAPHY

Fernández-Armesto, Felipe. *Columbus,* New York: Oxford University Press, 1991.

———. *Millennium: A History of the Last Thousand Years.* New York: Touchstone, 1995.

Morison, Samuel Eliot. *Admiral of the Ocean Sea: A Life of Christopher Columbus.* Boston, Little Brown & Co., 1942.

Scammell, G. V. *The World Encompassed: The First European Maritime Empires c800–1650.* Berkeley: University of California Press, 1981.

9

THE VOYAGES OF CHRISTOPHER COLUMBUS

"Only a heroic individual could be credited with changing the dimensions of the world that Europeans knew in 1492."

—William D. Phillips, Jr. & Carla Rahn Phillips,
The Worlds of Christopher Columbus

"It probably helped to be a visionary, with a flair for the fantastic, to achieve what he achieved."

—Felipe Fernández-Armesto, *Columbus*

This is a book on explorers, warriors and statesmen who share the distinction of having helped to drive—wittingly and unwittingly—the world's westward march. The chapters focus on individuals—their qualities and character, their contexts and their accomplishments.

While each individual is, by definition, unique, the subjects have in common decisiveness in their contributions to world history. Each individual not only dramatically affected his own time, but also left what might be called a paradigm changing legacy; that is, the world was altered by them. The impact of their accomplishments saw to that.

In studying individuals who changed the world, it is possible to take some measure of the qualities required to lead breakthroughs. It also is possible to cultivate a deeper appreciation of the alchemy of leadership;

that is, the admixture of events, preparedness and action that produce great, virtuoso, history-making individual performances.

This same study of historic figures whose achievements are justly famous also reveals what are normally considered to be character weaknesses and personality flaws. Their imperfections are among their hallmarks. Correctness, solicitude and modesty emerge as the hobgoblins of the pedestrian and the enemies of the heroic.

A study of those who shaped history is inevitably idiosyncratic, reflecting the student's historical preferences and heroic role models. In my case, I have chosen to be interested in those figures who made seminal contributions to what Felipe Fernández-Armesto calls "the westward displacement of civilization's center of gravity."[1]

This westward displacement of civilization's center of gravity was given historic impetus by Christopher Columbus.

Columbus entered the world stage in the middle of the fifteenth century at a time when the Mediterranean—the crucible of Western civilization—was in the process of breaking out into what was called "the Ocean Sea," the Atlantic. It was drawn as into a vacuum by uncharted waters and lands, driven to do so by rivalries, opportunities and technology.

Rivalries involved—but by no means were limited to—the hegemonic conflict between Spain and Portugal for wealth, power and dominion and the competition among the private traders and financiers of Germanic, Flemish, Venetian, Florentine and Genoese origin whose interests and loyalties travelled with their investments. The imperial rivalries of Spain and Portugal were largely bankrolled by the private sector producing enterprises commissioned by one party, financed by a second and led by a third. Columbus's undertaking became just such an enterprise.

Opportunities fueled the imperial and commercial rivalries. They appeared in the form of tempting new sources of wealth. These sources were brought to the attention of Spanish and Portuguese monarchs through the accounts of travelers to the East, especially those of Marco Polo, and of merchants, especially those in contact with Venetian and Moorish traders whose reach extended to what was called the Indies.[2] The new prospective sources of wealth were principally slaves, gold and spices.

At the time of Columbus, technology made it possible to pursue both the rivalries and the riches beyond the confines of the Mediterranean and the coastal waters of the North Sea and of northwest Africa. The technology appeared in the form of new nautical architecture and new water storage methods. The new nautical entrant was the caravel whose design was promoted by Prince Henry the Navigator of Portugal.[3] Its innovations over its predecessors featured a higher freeboard and a rounded keel, offering, respectively, greater protection from the sea and greater carrying capacity. It also featured triangular lateen sails (borrowed from the Arab dhows and feluccas) that enabled the ship to sail close to the wind and even, by tacking, against the wind. The new water storage methods, also learned from the Arabs, employed large watertight casks or "toniels"—from which is derived the contemporary measurement of a ship's size in terms of tonnage or carrying capacity. These new technologies, when fully applied and exploited, would enable European navigators to reach lands which lay beyond the boundaries of the then known world. Columbus was among the first and most accomplished to do so.

Columbus was well equipped by motivation, experience, knowledge, talent and personality to capitalize upon the historic moment created by the rivalries, opportunities and technologies just described. He was quintessentially the right man, in the right place, at the right time.

Columbus's motivation derived from the humble circumstances of his birth in 1450 as the son of a weaver in Genoa.[4] He was intensely driven—to the point of delusions of grandeur—to rise above his lowly origins and achieve fame and fortune for himself and his heirs. In his time and location a means to do so was to go to sea and, through maritime exploits, become both rich and famous. Riches for Columbus meant gold. Fame meant acquiring the title and legacy of a nobleman.

Columbus gained the practical experience required to fulfill his ambition from an early age. In his own words: "From a very small age, I went sailing upon the sea which very occupation inclines all who follow it to wish to learn the secrets of the world."[5] Columbus, who had "very little if any schooling," remained almost constantly at sea for twenty years, between 1465 and 1485.[6] During this period he sailed "every sea so far traversed" which included the full extent of the then known Atlantic Ocean as far north as Iceland and as far south as the Gulf of Guinea. He learned the sea by living on it and the art of navigation by doing it. He then took to the land, in Portugal, and acquired formal knowledge of the world as it was then known or thought to have been known. He read scientific treatises and speculative accounts. He studied charts and globes and made (and sold) his own. Columbus provides a classic example of a person who prepared himself for his destiny through a combination of practical experience and knowledge gained through wide-ranging, if not always disciplined, inquiry. In his case, the former preceded the latter.

Columbus also stands as the archetype of a person who possessed an awesome natural talent. He has been described—even by some of his harshest critics—as history's most talented natural navigator. He had an uncanny ability to read the currents, winds, weather and stars—the natural elements around him. He was unrivaled in his talent for dead-reckoning, relying solely on the mariner's compass and charts for navigation.[7]

Columbus's personality—while complex and even bizarre—suited him to the opportunity and challenge at hand. He was both a loner and an effective persuader. He possessed "gifts of natural rhetoric and tireless eloquence—or at least indefatigable loquacity."[8] Columbus's most powerful and useful personality traits were inexhaustible curiosity and a boundless self-confidence and obstinacy that enabled him to attempt what appeared to be impossible and do what no one had ever done before. "Ambitious, self-taught and self-made, he pursued his ideas with fanatical intensity."[9]

Strategically prepared by his formation and talent and strategically located in time and place, Columbus, at around forty years of age, set about mounting his historic project. It involved sailing west across the Atlantic to Asia, an idea that had been debated for some years by contending schools of thought divided between those who looked eastward and those who looked westward. The former, typified by the Portuguese, Bartholomew Diaz (who was the first European to be blown around the Cape of Good Hope) advocated a passage to Asia via the African Cape and the Indian Ocean, an approach adopted by Portugal. The latter, led by Columbus, advocated a passage to Asia westward across the Atlantic, an approach adopted by Spain. Having unsuccessfully hawked his project in Portugal, Columbus sold it in Spain producing a mission commissioned by Spanish royalty, paid for by Genoese and Florentine investors, and led by himself, a refugee from a weaver's shop in Genoa.

The mission had the clear goal of reaching Asia. While there was speculation at the time about the existence of an antipodal continent and of islands en route, these were sidebars. The great prize being sought was access to the riches of exotic Asia.

What then did Columbus proceed to do? Between 1492 and 1504 he made four epochal Atlantic crossings.

The first and most famous produced the first known direct human transit of the mid-Atlantic Ocean and, effectively, the discovery for the West of the New World. This was accomplished with a modest fleet of two small caravels and a larger carrack (or nao) carrying a crew of ninety at sea for nine weeks.[10] Columbus's sponsors and investors did not put much into the expedition, quite possibly because they expected so little from it. Columbus, by dint of talent and force of character, made up the difference required for success. In the words of one acclaimed biographer: Columbus set forth "with a maximum of faith, a bare sufficiency of equipment and a superabundance of stoutheartedness."[11]

Sailing literally into the unknown, Columbus was unremittingly assailed not only by the elements, for which he was prepared, but by multiple fears, for which there is no preparation; to wit: fear of mutiny, fear of failing to find land and, once found, fear of failing to find a wind that would bear him home.

In the event, the wind was Columbus's friend, primarily because he had an uncanny ability to find and catch the one he needed. His success in transiting the Atlantic on his first attempt was owed almost entirely to his having chosen to embark far south in the then known Atlantic from a Spanish island possession, Gomera. This point of departure enabled Columbus to catch across the Ocean Sea the northeast trade winds that prevail at that latitude. Had he attempted a crossing at a more northerly latitude, the wind would have been in his teeth and his voyage an almost certain failure. As it was, Columbus, on his very first voyage, came within a whisker of running smack into the mainland of North America along the Florida coast (somewhere between the Jupiter Inlet and Cape Canaveral); but in the face of threats from his crew, to which he uncharacteristically bowed, he altered his westerly course at the last minute, sailed to the southwest, and made landfall on one of the small islands guarding the entrance to the Caribbean.[12]

Entering the Caribbean, Columbus explored the islands of Cuba and Hispaniola, establishing a small Spanish garrison on the latter before sailing northwest to find a wind that would take him home. He arrived "home"—actually in Lisbon—on March 4, 1493, seven months after the commencement of his world-transforming voyage. He reported to his sponsors that he had found halcyon islands off the coast of China, one of which he thought might even be Marco Polo's fabled Chipangu, or what is now known as Japan. Columbus had, in effect, stumbled on the New

World; but he did not recognize it as such, nor did he wish to recognize it as such, because his goal—and his promise to his patrons—was the discovery of a westward passage to Asia.

This goal permanently eluded Columbus; but subsequent voyages, in addition to bringing him misery and calumny, added to the historic magnitude of his bold voyages of discovery.

Having achieved immortality on his first voyage by transiting the Atlantic, Columbus made more history on his second voyage. He discovered—on just his second try—the fastest possible route across the Atlantic. This consisted of a straight line to the southwest, in this case between the Canaries and the Caribbean island of Dominica. Using his naked eye, without the aid of reliable navigational instruments or landmarks, Columbus sailed a dead reckoned course straight across the Atlantic, covering the vast Ocean Sea in twenty-one days. This was an awesome feat of navigational virtuosity leading one biographer to put it this way: "No such dead-reckoning navigators exist today; no man alive, limited to the instruments and means at Columbus's disposal, could obtain anything near the accuracy of his results."[13]

This second voyage was devoted to a more detailed exploration of the principal Caribbean islands of Hispaniola and Cuba and the further development, with unfortunate consequences, of the Spanish colony of Hispaniola. On this voyage it became evident—possibly even to Columbus himself—that he was much more in tune with nature than with the human relations required for effective administration. He was a triumph as an Admiral of the Ocean Sea, but a disaster as a Viceroy, as an administrator in the empire his maritime expertise established.

On Columbus's second voyage, he came equipped for colonization with a fleet of seventeen ships, over 1,300 men and multiple trappings of imperial grandeur. It would have been better for Columbus, the Caribbean and the world of discovery if he had stayed lean and efficient, bent solely upon discovery, his forte, rather than on colonization, his nemesis.

During this second voyage a pattern of domination and exploitation of the natives developed which was both inhumane and ultimately unsustainable. Also established was a pattern of dissension among the colonists themselves and between them and Columbus. Columbus returned from this second voyage believing that he could still master the colonial situation and that Cuba, because of its size, must be a promontory of the mainland of Asia. He was dead wrong on both counts.

Columbus was gone on his second voyage for almost three years, from October 1493 to June 1496. He returned effectively empty handed. Riches had not been found and neither, in fact, had Asia. By consequence, Columbus's critics became "emboldened" and his patrons "alarmed." Columbus too became alarmed that the riches, privileges and titles promised him by his royal sponsors were in jeopardy. For two years, he defended himself from his critics, re-ingratiated himself with his sponsors and laid plans for a third voyage. The plan involved sailing further south in hopes of finding a passage to Asia and possibly, en route, an unknown continent, rumors of the existence of which were emanating from Portuguese maritime sources.

It is that continent—and not Asia and its riches—that Columbus found on his third crossing. Setting a more southerly course in June of 1498, he arrived in Trinidad at the end of July and a few days later bumped into America off the coast of Venezuela in the vicinity of the Orinoco River. Columbus explored that vast river basin and the coastline between it and Honduras reaching, in the process, the correct conclusion that the landmass he had encountered was continental in nature. He reported that conclusion in the log of his voyage and thus became the unequivocal discoverer of what subsequently became known as America.

That discovery should not be diminished by Columbus's accompanying insistence that the new continent was located not far from Asia. That insistence, that delusion, was a product of Columbus's obsessive quest for the Orient and his long held Ptolemaic conviction that the world was "small." Columbus persuaded himself that the new continent he had literally stumbled upon was just a stone's throw from the fabled lands of Marco Polo's travels and of the Great Khan.

Having made a world-transforming discovery of a new continent, Columbus returned to the center of the colonial enterprise he had established in Hispaniola and remained there for the better part of three years. He sought to develop the colony as a source of wealth; but it became, instead, a source of misery and shame. Rebellion by the natives, acts of cruelty by the colonists, dissension within Columbus's administrative ranks, and mounting criticism from Spain brought Columbus to his knees. On orders from Castile, he was replaced as colonial administrator in Hispaniola and returned to Spain in chains. It is surely one of history's greatest ironies that the first European to have seen America, and to have correctly identified its continental character, should, on the heels of that accomplishment, be shackled on orders from Spain and returned in ignominy to face his patrons and critics.

Columbus again spent two years in Spain, rehabilitating himself and his reputation. In 1502 he was permitted to embark on a fourth voyage. This one was aimed at finding a passage to Asia that Columbus thought might lie between the islands and the continent of the new world which he had discovered. He sailed in record time directly to Martinique, from which island he deployed to reconnoiter the coast of the mainland from northern Brazil to Honduras. Probing that coast he failed to find a strait or passage to the Orient; instead, he succeeded in demonstrating the staggering length of the continuous coastline from Honduras to Brazil. Discouraged and damaged by attacks from hostile Indians, bouts of malaria, hunger and the deterioration of his vessels and of his own mental state, Columbia sailed for succor in Hispaniola.[14] En route, a storm drove him into Jamaica where his ship was wrecked and he was effectively marooned. There he and the remains of his crew miraculously survived for a year until being grudgingly rescued and returned to Spain by the administrators who had replaced him in the colony he had founded.

Columbus was returned to Spain from his last voyage in 1504. He died two years later at the age of approximately fifty-five, still believing, or professing to believe, that his discoveries in the New World were either the outlying perimeters of Asia or just a stone's throw from them. He spent his declining years, in the words of an acclaimed contemporary biographer, in a mental world that was "incorrigibly self-righteous, implacably defiant and inaccessible to reason."[15]

Paradoxically these personality defects were virtues for Columbus. Had he not been self-righteous, defiant and stubborn, he might not have had the vision, courage and tenacity to do what no man had done before.

Which brings us to the concluding questions; to wit: what did Columbus actually do and how exactly did he change the world?

The magnitude of what Columbus did becomes evident when his multiple accomplishments are tallied. To have achieved one among them would have qualified Columbus for lasting recognition. Combined they qualify him for immortality.

- He was the first person to directly transit the Atlantic.
- He decoded the mid-Atlantic wind systems and discovered the shortest round-trip across the Ocean Sea.

- He discovered for the West the New World and its continental centerpiece, America.
- He was the first person known to transit the Caribbean Sea.
- He charted the Caribbean and the northern coast of Latin America.
- In the course of his Atlantic crossings, he discovered, through observation, that the earth was not perfectly spherical.

Once these achievements were accomplished and recorded, a world transformation was set inexorably in motion. The westward displacement of civilization commenced. A highway to a new world was opened and the civilizations of middle America and Europe were thereby linked. The highway was soon flooded with the traffic of colonizers, adventurers, merchants and refugees from the Old World. A new frontier for European civilization infused that civilization with new sources of nourishment and wealth and a fresh dynamic. Columbus's highway to a new world also placed securely in train a process of girdling the globe, enabling its circumnavigation. That girdling process was soon to be completed by Magellan, creating yet another, and possibly even more powerful, dynamic, that consists of the gravitational pull of Asia, Columbus's destination of choice.

With all the majesty attendant upon Columbus's heroic, world-transforming achievements, it is not possible to reflect upon his life without being struck by its pathos. When the elements of the pathos are combined, they reveal the extraordinarily heavy price that Columbus paid for greatness.

- He failed miserably as a colonial administrator.
- He was pilloried by his critics on land and at sea.
- He was humiliated before his peers and patrons.
- He found refuge in self-delusion and teetered on the verge of madness, "exploring involuntarily the marchlands between genius and insanity."[16]
- Worst of all, he died angry and embittered.

All—or at least most—of this could have been avoided had Columbus been able and willing to do what he did best; namely explore the ocean seas. In this endeavor he had no peers. But he was not able to do so because his patrons were not interested in pure research, but in the production of monetary gain from the research conducted; and he was not willing to do so because he himself sought wealth, not just glory. By consequence, Columbus wasted his time and talent in incompetent colonial administration. Had he foregone those duties and invested himself solely in seaborne discovery, it is quite possible that Columbus would have beat Ferdinand Magellan to Asia.

Columbus was a man within whom burden and glory were in permanent residence. It has been movingly said of him that:

> His sights were always fixed on unmade discoveries, imperfect gains and frustrated crusades. Instead of being satisfied with his achievements, he was outraged by his wrongs; un-assuaged by acclaim, he was embittered by calumnies. This implacable character made him live strenuously and die miserably.[17]

That character also made him challenge conventional wisdom and strike out into the unknown, preferring exploration and experiment to subservience to the status quo. In this light, Columbus stands as an early beacon in the scientific revolution that defines the modern age. When we think of Columbus, we can do his memory greatest honor if we regard him as a summons to "the liberating effects of the progress of exploration."

Columbus's voyages accelerated a westward shift in the world's center of gravity that was, in his time and place, already underway. It did so in ways that could not have been anticipated when his "Enterprise of the Indies" was first conceived and launched. Among the most powerful of the unanticipated consequences were the following:

- In the course of his voyages, Columbus "decoded" the wind systems of the mid-Atlantic. He discovered the easterlies off the coast of the Canary Islands that enabled a quick and relatively safe Atlantic crossing and he discovered, after some considerable trial and error, the westerlies off the coast of Bermuda that facilitated the homeward passage. Once these wind systems were mastered, migration in the age of sail from east to west was inevitably set in motion.
- That migration in turn carried with it the unintended consequences of disease transmission. The advance weapon of western conquest was the Eurasian germ pool. Borne first by the mariners and then the conquistadores, that germ pool struck with devastating conse-

quences a native population unprotected by immunities. Smallpox and measles were the greatest killers. Air borne, these germs had already begun their work among the Incas, for example, before Pizzaro and his shock troops arrived in person. That germ pool not only facilitated conquest, it facilitated conversion of the Amerindians to Christianity inasmuch as the remains of the indigenous populations, observing the immunity of their conquerors, were persuaded that the healthy new arrivals must be protected by a superior God.

- Riches, of course, were anticipated and they materialized. But a nutritional bonanza was not anticipated. In the event, the nutritional bonanza that materialized was extraordinarily significant. The New World yielded crops that substantially augmented the diet and, in consequence, the physical strength of the European population writ large. These included, most prominently, corn and potatoes—crops that quickly supplemented the European diet and helped reduce the endemic cycles of hunger that afflicted the Old World.
- Of course the greatest unanticipated consequence of all was the discovery, denied by Columbus but quickly recognized by his successors, of the western hemisphere. As Samuel Eliot Morison has observed, that hemisphere was not recognized when discovered and then not wanted when recognized.[18] It stood as a massive inconvenience blocking Europe's western access to the riches of the Indies. In the event, that massive inconvenience would turn out to be the most valuable piece of real estate in the world; but that discovery awaited three hundred years and the "Voyage of Discovery" of Lewis and Clark.

NOTES

1. This concept appears often in the writings of Fernández-Armesto. See Felipe Fernández-Armesto, *Columbus* (Oxford: Oxford University Press, 1991), x and 193.
2. See Ibid., 37–39.
3. For descriptions of the caravel, see Samuel Eliot Morison, *The European Discovery of America: The Southern Voyages* (New York: Oxford University Press, 1993), 4–5 and Phillips, William D. and Carla Rahn Phillips, *The Worlds of Christopher Columbus* (Cambridge: Cambridge University Press, 1994), 70.

4. Fernández-Armesto, op. cit., 2.

5. Ibid., 3.

6. Samuel Eliot Morison, *Admiral of the Ocean Sea: A Life of Christopher Columbus.* (Boston: Little Brown, 1942), 15.

7. "Columbus took the course off his mariner's compass, which was the most reliable and the one indispensable instrument of navigation aboard." Morrison, *Admiral of the Ocean Sea,* 187.

8. Fernández-Armesto, op. cit., 64. See also Phillips who puts it this way: "Columbus was one of the greatest salesmen of his time," op. cit., 186.

9. G. V. Scammell, *The World Encompassed: The First European Maritime Empires c. 800–1650* (Berkeley: University of California Press, 1981), 303.

10. Morison estimated the measurements of the caravels as follows: "Overall length about 70 feet, beam about 23 feet, depth of hold amidships about 9 feet." Morison, *Admiral of the Ocean Sea,* 115.

11. Ibid., 6.

12. Ibid., 214.

13. Ibid., 195.

14. Ibid., 306.

15. Fernández-Armesto, op. cit., 180.

16. Ibid., 192.

17. Ibid., 193.

18. Samuel Eliot Morison, *The European Discovery of America: The Northern Voyages,* (New York: Oxford University Press, 1993), 210.

BIBLIOGRAPHY

Fernández-Armesto, Felipe. *Columbus.* Oxford: Oxford University Press, 1991.

Morison, Samuel Eliot. *Admiral of the Ocean Sea: A Life of Christopher Columbus.* Boston: Little Brown & Co., 1942.

———. *The European Discovery of America: The Northern Voyages.* New York: Oxford University Press 1993.

———. *The European Discovery of America; The Southern Voyages.* New York: Oxford University Press, 1993.

Phillips, William D., Jr. and Carla Rahn Phillips. *The Worlds of Christopher Columbus.* Cambridge: Cambridge University Press, 1994.

Scammell, G. V. *The World Encompassed: The First European Maritime Empires c. 800–1650.* Berkeley: University of California Press, 1991.

10

FERDINAND MAGELLAN

"His voyage was the greatest single human achievement on the sea."

—Samuel Eliot Morison, *The European Discovery of America: The Southern Voyages: 1492–1616*

"A man of exceptional energy and courage; his downfall was the effect of two forms of hubris: rashness and over confidence, accumulated in success."

—Felipe Fernández-Armesto, *Millenium: A History of the Last Thousand Years*

Columbus began the European-led process of girdling the earth via a westward passage to Asia. He securely established the Atlantic leg of a circum-navigational ocean highway. Magellan finished the job by putting the Pacific leg in place.

The stories of Columbus and Magellan are those of inspired and intrepid maritime exploration. In the course of that exploration, Columbus achieved multiple firsts. Magellan achieved mighty firsts as well which, for their sheer magnitude, will resound forever in the annals of discovery.[1]

Magellan was a worthy heir to Columbus, whose navigational feats inspired him.[2] Magellan may, in fact, stand above Columbus in terms of raw fortitude. Columbus overcame unfavorable odds. Magellan triumphed over hopelessly unfavorable odds. The story of how he did so is as riveting as his accomplishments themselves.

Like Columbus, Magellan's voyage of discovery was a product of contemporary rivalries, opportunities and technology. And, like Columbus, Magellan was the right man, in the right place at the right time. But Magellan's time was different and so too, of course, was the man himself.

Magellan was thirteen years old when Columbus triumphantly returned from his first Atlantic crossing. Magellan's own global voyage of discovery lay twenty-seven years ahead. In the intervening quarter century, Mediterranean rivalries intensified, opportunities multiplied and nautical technology was substantially fortified.[3]

A survey of Magellan the man, prior to his command of one of history's greatest voyages of discovery, reveals an improbable candidate. That Magellan's name is inscribed on land on a strait, and in the heavens on a constellation, is truly one of history's great stories of redemption.

Magellan was born in northwest Portugal, the son of a low-ranking nobleman. While not rich, the family was comfortable and well connected to the royal court. As a boy, Magellan served as a page in that court and received his education there. This would have included study of map-making, astronomy and celestial navigation as well as some military training.

As a young man, Magellan was employed by the royal family in its colonial and maritime bureau where he served in a clerical capacity keeping records and acquiring maps, globes and nautical instruments in support of an expanding Portuguese maritime enterprise. His own desire to go to sea in search of fame and fortune was frustrated by those in the royal entourage—including King Manuel himself—who, for various factional reasons beyond Magellan's control, disliked him. He was finally liberated from his desk in the royal bureaucracy in 1505 (at the age of twenty-five) and sent to sea in a Portuguese armada commissioned to rout the Egyptian and Venetian maritime forces from their strongholds in east Africa and India. This Magellan proceeded to do for eight years, first as a supernumerary with no specific assignment and subsequently as the captain of an oar propelled coastal raiding craft, as a mounted cavalryman, and finally as captain of his own caravel. Along the way, Magellan fought like a lion, suffered some serious wounds, plundered and massacred like a Portuguese conquistador and accumulated, and promptly lost at sea, several fortunes. After having sailed throughout the Indian Ocean, through the strait of Malacca, to the spice islands of the Molucca Islands and, on an unauthorized cruise, northwest through the South China Sea as far as the Philippines, Magellan returned to Portugal exhausted and penniless, but proud.

Having laid his life on the line as, in effect, a crusading knight for king and country, Magellan expected to be made a knight of the court and properly respected and remunerated. Instead he was ignored, humiliated and insulted by "stay-at-homers" now entrenched in the royal court. His short stature and swarthy, peasant-like appearance worked against him and so did his personality that was taciturn, choleric and undiplomatic.

Like a good knight, Magellan sought to reverse his rejection and reestablish himself by force of arms. He joined an expedition to quell an uprising in Morocco where he once again acquitted himself bravely and once again was wounded. A lance passed through his knee, leaving him partially crippled for life. In the course of this campaign, he was accused of trading with the enemy and was court-martialed. Ultimately the charges were not proven; but he returned to Portugal with a cloud over his head.

Upon his return, Magellan sought permission from King Manuel to lead an expedition to the Spice Islands, specifically to Ternate in the Moluccas where a cousin and former shipmate, Francisco Serrano, was holding sway in grand style over a harem and a cache of spices. Magellan hoped to fortify the Portuguese hold in the Moluccas and establish a direct spice trade between Portugal and Ternate. He chose the wrong time, manner and place to seek permission and his application for an expeditionary commission was rudely rejected by the King.[4]

Thus at the age of thirty-five, Magellan, scarred, broke and spurned, sought an escape from what was, to that point, a courageous, but essentially failed, life.

The way out was hatched in consultation and collaboration with two old friends, one of whom, Ruy de Feleiro, was a noted astrologer and navigational expert and the other of whom, John of Lisbon, was an accomplished explorer. The astronomer provided detailed scientific information on navigating the Atlantic Ocean and the explorer provided a first-hand account of the coast of South America as far south as the Rio Plata estuary, which he speculated might be the gateway to a passage to the oriental sea. Magellan drew this information together and deepened and refined it through exhaustive study of materials in the royal chart-room and maritime library. In that library he discovered a globe crafted by a famous German cartographer which depicted a strait passing through the southern tip of South America, just above Antarctica, leading to another ocean sea. Magellan either pilfered this globe or committed it to memory and replicated it.

Magellan was much impressed with this globe because it depicted a symmetry that was powerfully persuasive. The symmetry consisted of two coast lines, the western coast of Africa and the eastern coast of South America, which, as they were travelled south, receded until a point was reached which formed, in each, a cape. Magellan basically concluded that if there was a cape in Africa (which he, himself, had doubled) there must be a cape in South America that could yield a passage to the Spice Islands.

Magellan had been jilted in his own country, which was fastened on an eastward passage to Asia; so he took his project to Spain, which was, thanks to Columbus, fastened on a westward passage. He did so having never in his life sailed, let alone commanded, a ship in the waters of the western Atlantic.

In Spain circumstances conspired to favor Magellan and his project to find the elusive westward passage. The favorable factors included: increasing Spanish apprehension over Portuguese maritime exploits and conquests; a new, young impressionable king, King Charles, who needed a dramatic achievement—such as breaking the Portuguese spice monopoly in the Indies—early in his reign; and a fortuitous alliance with a Spanish nobleman, Diogo Barbosa, into whose family Magellan immediately married. In petitioning the Spanish king for a commission to find a southwestern route to Asia, Magellan held several trump cards. The first was his certainty that he knew of a strait between the seas, an assertion given credibility by brandishing his trusty globe. The second consisted of his belief, gained from experience sailing among the Spice Islands as far north as the Philippines, and from his study of maps and charts, that the Moluccas, currently being occupied by the Portuguese, were located some degrees on the Spanish side of demarcation laid down by the Treaty of Tordesillas and thus belonged to Spain. Magellan had even had the effrontery to espouse this view when he was in the employ of the King of Portugal! It may be said that what Magellan lacked in diplomacy, he made up for in consistency.

The Spanish king, unlike his Portuguese counterpart, was impressed with Magellan, his presentation and his project. It had taken seven years for Columbus to persuade King Charles's grandparents, Isabella and Ferdinand, to approve his expedition. Magellan got his approved by their young descendant in one month. Where Columbus employed flowery language, Magellan spoke simply.[5] Where Columbus organized an intricate lobbying effort, Magellan laid it directly on the line at the source of power.[6] The King found Magellan to be a gallant knight, a devout Christian crusader and a man of nautical competence. In the King, Magellan found a liege who showed him respect. It was a short courtship (excuse the pun) resulting in an operational marriage.

The King, acting expeditiously and decisively, approved the project and commissioned Magellan, and his partner, Ruy de Feleiro, to co-lead the mission on terms so generous as to immediately arouse jealousy in court circles.[7] The two were to receive, in perpetuity, one twentieth each of the proceeds from all lands and islands discovered, an exclusive right to travel the route and sail in the regions discovered for a decade, twenty percent of the net proceeds of the first voyage and the titles of Viceroy over the lands discovered for themselves and their heirs forever.

These terms, accepted essentially on the spot by the inexperienced king, were not reviewed and approved, as was normal, by his council on Atlantic exploration, the Casa de Antilles. That Casa, headed by the crafty, corrupt and covetous Bishop, Juan Rodriquez de Fonseca, immediately set about, under the Bishop's relentless direction, to wrest authority for the voyage from Magellan and even from the King himself. In the process of doing so, Fonseca set in motion a chain of decisions and actions that fundamentally undermined Magellan's capacity to effectively lead the expedition.

Fonseca conspired to relieve Magellan's compatriot, Ruy de Feleiro, of the co-command; planted his own illegitimate son and trusted agents in pivotal command positions; removed financial control of the voyage from the royal treasury (substituting the private banking house of Jakob Fugger in which he had a stake); and otherwise substantially altered the arrangements agreed upon between Magellan and the King.

Magellan, whose status as a Portuguese refugee in Spain made him suspect and vulnerable, had only the King to whom to appeal for redress. The King's support—that was generally forthcoming—was checkmated behind the scenes by Fonseca. Thus, by the appointed hour of the expedition's departure, Magellan's authority had been effectively compromised and his officer corps and crew infiltrated by appointees who owed their allegiance to Fonseca and to the private bankers who were in league with him.

As Magellan prepared to set sail, he confronted multiple challenges: he first had to cross the Atlantic, still no mean feat especially for someone who had never done it before; then he had to find a strait or cape through or around the South American continent, the existence of which was purely hypothetical; then he had to transit that strait or round that cape and sail through an unknown, uncharted ocean of indeterminate expanse in hopes of bumping into the Spice Islands on the other side of the world. En route, these challenges had to be met and surmounted with the Portuguese deployed at sea to capture him and with co-captains and crew, the composition of which made dissension a certainty and mutiny a palpable possibility.

In such circumstances, it is a wonder Magellan set sail at all let alone overcome the challenges. But set sail he did on September 20, 1517 from the port of San Lucar with a polyglot crew of approximately 300 manning five ships. The crew consisted of 165 Spaniards with the balance comprised of Portuguese (on whom a strict limit had been imposed by Fonseca), French, Italians, Greeks, Irish, English and Moors. It was truly a floating Tower of Babel. The ships, two of 190 tons, two of 90 tons and one of 60 tons, were secondhand naos converted into makeshift carracks, fitted out and supplied for combat. They were presumably provisioned for a voyage estimated at two years but, en route, Magellan discovered that he had been sabotaged by his suppliers who were on the take from the Portuguese Consul in Seville. They had obliged the Consul by falsifying the weights and contents of the ship's stores. In the event the provisions amounted to half of what was purchased and needed, a discovery made only when Magellan emptied his ships for overhauling on the barren coast of Patagonia.

The fleet first stopped in Tenerife in the Canaries for final fitting out and provisioning. There, at a meeting of the five ship captains and their pilots, Magellan's authority as Captain General, as first in command, was directly and openly challenged. He let it pass, preferring to deal with his opposition at sea where he would have a stronger hand.

The strength of Magellan's hand derived from several sources. First, he was highly skilled in combat, quick thinking and completely fearless.

Second, he was the only member of the expedition who presumed to know where the strait to the oriental sea was located. Throughout the voyage to that strait he steadfastly refused to share with the other captains his knowledge of its location and, equally significant, the course he planned to follow to find it. Thus, prospective mutineers had to calculate that deposing Magellan would be the equivalent of losing their guide to the hoped-for strait.

The fleet left Tenerife sailing on a southerly course chosen by Magellan but opposed by the other captains and contrary to the course that had been pre-approved by the Casa de Antilles. Magellan had his own reasons for his course which, it is speculated, involved out-maneuvering a Portuguese fleet that had been sent to intercept him, which fleet could well have known the course favored by the other captains and the Casa. The course Magellan took locked his small fleet into the sweltering doldrums—or horse latitudes—for three weeks, effectively eluding the Portuguese fleet but taking a heavy toll on provisions and shipboard morale. Finding a wind out of the doldrums, Magellan set a course for the coast of Brazil about eight degrees south of the equator.

En route a seaman was sodomized by one of the ship's masters and Magellan convened the fleet's captains to conduct a court martial. At the conclusion of the proceedings, in a meeting in the Captain General's quarters, Juan de Cartagena (the illegitimate son of Bishop Fonseca) captain of the fleet's largest ship, the San Antonio, and the leader of the opposition to Magellan, aggressively declared that he would no longer follow Magellan's orders and summoned the other captains to join him. Before they could do so, Magellan's marines, on a pre-arranged signal, burst into his cabin and held Cartagena at sword's point. Magellan officially pronounced Cartagena a rebel and mutineer and had him hauled off to the stockade. Cartagena was subsequently transferred, in protective custody, to another ship.

After nearly two and a half months at sea, the armada made landfall on the coast of Brazil, precisely at the latitude at which Magellan had aimed. The fleet turned south along the Brazilian coast and in mid-December took refuge in what is now the Bay of Rio de Janeiro. Refreshing and reprovisioning themselves there, the fleet continued south along the coast until it reached the Rio Plata estuary which Magellan hoped was the mouth of a strait between the seas. This vast estuary was thoroughly explored, yielding the devastating news that it was not the pass being sought. Discouraged, the fleet moved further south, hugging the rugged coastline and probing for the hope-for strait in increasingly horrific weather. At the end of March, after two months beating against head-winds, sleet and tempests, a harbor was found which could yield a winter refuge. Magellan, naming it Port St. Julian, announced that the fleet would hole up there for the winter.

Magellan soon faced a rebellion of those who wished to return to the balmy Rio Plata for the winter and then a full-blown mutiny led by deposed captains and disgruntled pilots. They successfully conspired to take over three of Magellan's five ships, including the largest and most heavily armed, the San Antonio. Magellan awoke one morning in the bay of St. Julian to find himself outnumbered and out fire-powered.

It was as if Magellan came out of central casting for the lead role in *Die Hard* to tackle this challenge. He dealt with it swiftly through a combination of artifice, daring and bravery. He sent peace emissaries to one ship who boarded and subdued it. He disguised his own men as sailors from another ship who boarded and subdued it. Facing now a single rebel ship that intended at high tide to run for the mouth of the harbor and the open sea, Magellan artfully arranged to have its anchor lines cut leaving it adrift and at his mercy. In less than twenty-four hours, Magellan ingeniously orchestrated the reversal of a major mutiny without a single loss of life within his own ranks.

What followed next was decisive and brutal. The ring leaders of the mutiny, including the once condemned Juan de Cartagena, were court martialled and sentenced to death by hanging, their bodies then to be drawn and quartered and posted on gibbets erected at the entrances to the harbor. These sentences were executed save for those of Juan de Cartagena and a priest who had collaborated with him. As an act of clemency, Magellan commuted their death sentences and condemned them instead to be marooned in desolate Patagonia.

At the first signs of spring, Magellan's fleet broke camp and resumed its southern crawl along the Patagonian coastline, in the course of which the armada's smallest ship, the *Santiago*, was driven into the cliffs and broke up. Shortly after this disaster, the fleet observed the coastline turning southeast until it ended at a sharp cape behind which was a large bay. In opposition to other captains and pilots, who wished either to sail east around the African cape to the Moluccas or south in hopes of finding the South American cape, Magellan ordered the bay explored. In probing it, a narrow passage was found which opened into a larger body of water. Over a period of weeks, this body of water was thoroughly explored. It yielded the grand prize. It was the pass—the westward passage to the then called "Southern Sea." It was the continental strait that now bears Magellan's name.

The exploration of the strait and the confirmation of its nature as a passage between two oceans came at a heavy price. The fleet's largest and most generously manned, provisioned and armed ship, the *San Antonio*, was shanghaied by its pilot, Esteban Gomez, who cut away from the armada and set sail for Spain. Gomez had competed with Magellan at the royal court for command of the voyage and, having been bested by Magellan there, settled with him in the strait. At the mission's climactic moment, Gomez ran off with the fleet's major asset, returning to Spain to busy himself discrediting Magellan's performance as Captain General. Thus when Magellan emerged from the strait his fleet had been reduced from five to three ships, the *Santiago* having been wrecked just prior to the strait's discovery and the San Antonio having ominously deserted the mission at its apogee.

Also substantially reduced was the vitality of the remaining crew who were weakened by contending with the elements and the unknown at sea for over a year and by the onset of scurvy that was soon to decimate their ranks.

Fortunately, Magellan's fleet in its transit of the 335-mile strait was spared by nature from the worst of that channel's turbulent weather. It was as if having earned his right to be there, mother nature served as a miraculous pilot and guardian, guiding and sheltering Magellan through the strait. Emerging in glorious weather through the western exit of the strait, a limitless blue ocean stretched before the tiny armada. Magellan, hoping the sea would provide a peaceful passage to the Spice Islands, gave it the name it still bears, Mar Pacifico or Pacific Ocean. At the moment of that ocean's christening, it is possible to say that Magellan's luck had peaked.

It is one of the great ironies and tragedies of history that an ocean Magellan called Pacific, because he hoped it would be, would transport him across its breadth to his death in a needless armed conflict. That conflict lay leagues and months ahead. Meanwhile there was an indeterminate expanse of unknown sea to navigate.

As Magellan rounded into the Pacific and contemplated what lay before him, he faced some daunting facts. These included the harsh reality of being in completely uncharted waters whose terminus—if indeed there was one—was equally unknown.[8] He literally had no idea what lay before him. Being in latitudes never before sailed, he did not have the assistance of familiar constellations and simply had to point his depleted armada in the direction he thought was right. Fortunately he had "arrived in the Pacific at just the right moment to get the best of the southeast trade winds that would carry him across the ocean.[9] He then sailed a technically perfect course, making the best possible use of prevailing winds and currents, just as Columbus had done before him in the other ocean sea.[10]

The precision of his course notwithstanding, Magellan's passage across the Pacific featured an almost unbroken string of bad luck. As he sailed northwest, entering and passing through the equatorial latitudes, Magellan's greatest need was to provision his ships with fresh fruit and vegetables to stave off an epidemic of scurvy that was ravaging his crew. There were islands en route where this could have been done; but they either failed to offer adequate anchorages or were beyond the fleet's horizon. These opportunities being missed, Magellan's crew was condemned to withering away under the scorching sun. By the time Magellan reached his first promising landfall—the island of Guam—he had been at sea on the Pacific for three months and had buried in that ocean twenty of his men. Most of the rest were so weakened as to be useless until revived by the needed anti-scorbutics.

When the fleet anchored off Guam, the natives—robust and curious—boarded the ships. Seeing weakened white men lying around the decks, they began helping themselves to whatever they wished, kicking around those in their way. Magellan felt obliged to teach them a lesson and bloodshed followed. The fleet was then forced to secure meager provisions by means of a quick coastal raid instead of bartering for a more ample supply. Magellan moved quickly on to the island of Rota where he established friendly relations with the natives and was able to accomplish some serious re-provisioning and the restoration of his crew.

The fleet soon sailed on, reaching the Philippine archipelago in mid-March, 1521. At that point, personal triumphs were recorded by Magellan, and his slave, Enrique. Some ten years earlier, Magellan, accompanied by his slave, had, on an unauthorized cruise, sailed into the archipelago from the Spice Islands via the South China Sea. Having now reached the archipelago from the opposite direction, Magellan and Enrique became the first human beings to have circumnavigated the globe. Instead of pocketing this triumph and making haste through now familiar waters to the Moluccas, which were "the source of the world's most costly spices (nutmeg, mace and cloves)" and which was the express objective of his voyage, Magellan tarried in the Philippines and began to workup a passion for colonizing and Christianizing the place.[11] This mission, which had manifest imperial dimensions, soon became all-consuming and Magellan metamorphosed from an implacable explorer and Captain General to a maniacal proselytizer and viceroy.[12] Explanations have been given for this transformation including Magellan's naive belief in divine protection and his imperious belief in the invincibility of a Spanish armada; but, at the end of the day, the reasons may be reduced to vaingloriousness, hubris and religious zealotry bordering on madness.

In this frame of mind, Magellan, throwing all caution to the winds, personally choreographed his certain fate. Having befriended and baptized the chieftain and tribe of the island of Cebu, Magellan ordered all neighboring chieftains and tribes to embrace Christianity or face the consequences of having their villages put to the torch. Here was Magellan, thousands of miles from Castile, behaving like the Grand Inquisitor himself. One chieftain who occupied the nearby island of Mactan refused to bow to Magellan and his god and prepared himself for war, mobilizing a formidable, albeit naked, force of native warriors. Magellan's armada with its overpowering weaponry and armor, could have put such a force to rout; but Magellan insisted—in contravention of royal rules of engagement which forbade the Captain General from placing himself at risk on land—on leading the charge himself with a small group of volunteers. And lead it he did with a ragtag group of sixty untrained and ill-equipped volunteers, twenty from each ship. Magellan led this motley crew ashore without any preparation and in a tide which left them floundering on coral reefs in light armor exposed to the lances, spears, scimitars and poisonous darts of a land-based force of upwards of 2,000 enraged natives. The timing and terrain were disastrous and the odds overwhelming. After a gallant but failed assault, Magellan and his men were driven back into the surf where Magellan was essentially hacked to death. Half of his men were lost, including two of his most loyal and noble lieutenants.

An attempt was made to ransom Magellan's corpse, but to no avail. The fleet then weighed anchor for the Moluccas; but not before the chieftain of Cebu decided that with his friend, Magellan, dead, and Spanish armed might thwarted by a pack of naked natives, he should cut his losses. He did so by inviting those who succeeded Magellan in command of the fleet to dinner and killed them.

Thus it was that an essentially leaderless armada slunk its way to Molucca, having consolidated what was left of the crew on two ships, the *Trinidad* and the *Victoria*, scuttling the *Concepcion*. Once in the Moluccas they found that the legendary Francisco Serrano had died and that his equally legendary cache of spices amounted to less than had met the ear. Loading up what was available, the ships were about to set sail for the Cape of Good Hope and Seville when a mishap delayed the departure of the Trinidad. The Victoria sailed on alone, reaching Seville on September 8, 1522, just three years after it had left home. On board were twenty shrunken men and a cargo worth roughly three quarters of a million dollars. The Trinidad, having, on account of its delay, lost the monsoon winds that would carry it across the Indian Ocean, decided to double back across the Pacific but was stalled by headwinds. It eventually sailed back to the Moluccas and surrendered itself to Portuguese authorities there.

In the end, only about ten percent of the men who had shipped with Magellan returned from the entire trip alive. Their treasure was barely adequate to reimburse the investors in the mission. And soon after their return, the Spanish King renounced all claims to the Moluccas, it having been determined that—contrary to Magellan's belief—the Spice Islands lay on the Portuguese side of the line of demarcation agreed upon at Tordesillas.

The immediate human consequences of Magellan's voyage were tragic. But its contributions to history were monumental. These were, in the order achieved, as follows:

- Magellan was the first to sail and chart the South American coastline south of the Rio Plata estuary.
- He discovered and transited the southern passage between the two great oceans through a strait that now bears his name.
- He discovered and transited the great southern sea that he named the Pacific Ocean, whose southern constellations now bear his name.

- He became the first person to circumnavigate the globe, thus providing the first empirical evidence that the world was round and could be girdled at sea.
- He discovered the Philippines which became a Spanish possession and which remain the only Christian nation in all of Asia.

After accomplishing all of this, Magellan lost it. He became a religious fanatic and a victim of his own irrational belief in his invincibility. Few men have paid a higher price for going berserk. He was denied the completion of his voyage and recognition in his own time. But it must be observed that qualities of character that figured in his own self-destruction were the very same that had led him around the globe; to wit: a defiant belief in his own convictions coupled with dauntless courage.

Withal, what kind of man emerges from the historical record?

Physically, Magellan was unprepossessing. A contemporary chronicler described him as "not of imposing presence, since he was small in stature and did not appear to be much."[13] His towering character was in inverse proportion to his size. The hallmarks of that character were honor, intensity, bravery and spirituality.

Magellan's conception of honor derived from the traditions of knight-errantry and featured passionate devotion to his liege. Once having promised King Charles that he would find the southwest passage to Asia and secure Spanish interests there, Magellan was honor bound to do so. From the moment of that commitment to his liege, he could, in the words of the historian, William Manchester, "endure disappointment and frustration with an almost inhuman patience, but he could never submit to defeat."[14]

The handmaiden of his honor was uncommon intensity. Magellan was a driven man. He pursued the southwest passage with the monomaniacal intensity of Ahab pursuing the White Whale. Once having found "the paso," he moved on to Asia where he became a messianic missionary with an intensity bordering on hysteria. Magellan was the pit bull of everything he tackled.

Magellan's bravery was legendary, ultimately to the point of foolhardiness. He was totally fearless, partly because he believed in divine protection and partly because he was just plain tough. This bravery was accompanied by an iron-will and, for his adversaries, an iron fist.

Magellan was a deeply religious man. In his personal life he was austere and puritanical. In his professional life he was a courageous, valiant Christian crusader. He placed his life at the disposal of that crusade. His belief in divine protection may explain why Magellan never calculated risk. He continually threw it to the winds in the tradition of heroic knighthood. As William Manchester has written of his hero, Magellan: "The hero acts alone, without encouragement, relying solely on conviction and his own inner resources."[15] For Magellan these inner resources were strengthened by spirituality.

Magellan saw things by his own lights and steered an uncompromising course in keeping with them. And so it was with Magellan to his final hour.

In a sense, however, Magellan's feats were so world-transforming that his final hour will never arrive. By "taking the full measure of the oceans," by providing the first empirical evidence that the world was round, Magellan liberated intellectual inquiry into cosmology. In doing so he "provided a linchpin for the men of the Renaissance" who challenged received wisdom about the universe and man's relation to it.[16] Magellan helped mightily to release a big genie from its bottle, the genie of empirical inquiry that energized a scientific revolution.[17]

In conclusion, it is appropriate to give one of the greatest historians of seaborne exploration, Samuel Eliot Morison, the last word on Magellan: "Magellan is to be ranked as the first navigator of ancient or modern times and his voyage the greatest single achievement on the sea."[18] That achievement completed the globe encompassing circuit of ocean highways, initiated by Columbus, which provided the gateway to the continuation of the world's westward march.

NOTES

1. Samuel Eliot Morison called it: "The greatest voyage in recorded history." Samuel Eliot Morrison, *The European Discovery of America. The Southern Voyages* (New York: Oxford University Press, 1993), 303.
2. William Manchester, *A World Lit Only by Fire* (Boston: Little Brown and Co., 1992), 236.
3. For a description of the benefits of new ship technology see Charles McHew Parr, *So Noble a Captain* (New York: Thomas Crowell, 1953), 41–42.
4. In the words of Morison, Magellan lived "under the shadow of royal displeasure." Morison, op. cit., 318.
5. Manchester, op. cit., 83.

6. Laurence Bergreen, *Over the Edge of the World* (New York: William Morrow, 2003), 33.

7. Magellan demanded "a handsome price for the voyage," Parr, op. cit., 157–58.

8. Manchester, op. cit., 167.

9. Felipe Fernández-Armesto, *Pathfinders: A Global History of Exploration* (New York: W. W. Norton & Co., 2006), 199.

10. Manchester, op. cit., 168.

11. Fernández-Armesto, op. cit., 195.

12. See Manchester, op. cit., 185.

13. Parr, op. cit., 212.

14. Manchester, op. cit., 226.

15. Ibid., 288.

16. Ibid., 323.

17. Bergreen, op. cit., 414.

18. Morison, op. cit., 320.

BIBLIOGRAPHY

Bergreen, Laurence. *Over the Edge of the World.* New York: Harper Collins, 2003.

Fernández-Armesto, Felipe. *Pathfinders: A Global History of Exploration.* New York: W. W. Norton & Co., 2006.

Manchester, William. *A World Lit Only by Fire.* Boston: Little Brown, 1992.

Morison, Samuel Eliot. *The European Discovery of America: The Southern Voyages.* New York: Oxford University Press, 1993.

Parr, Charles McHew. *So Noble a Captain.* New York: Thomas Crowell, 1953.

11

SIR FRANCIS DRAKE

"Three of the greatest navigators in history: Columbus, Magellan and Drake."

—Samuel Eliot Morison, *The European Discovery of America: The Southern Voyages 1492–1616*

"Drake was at his prime, as his successes demonstrated and even his opponents agreed, one of Europe's greatest seamen."

—G. V. Scammell, *The World Encompassed: The First European Maritime Empires c. 800–1650*

"Sir Francis was the first Englishman that did ever compasse the World."

—Admiral Sir Robert Mansell as quoted by John Cummins, *Francis Drake*

Columbus and Magellan have had their turn. It is now Drake's turn.

Sir Francis Drake was a legendary English sea captain and pirate whose exploits, modus operandi and personality capture the essence of the Elizabethan maritime era. A rendering of his career provides—in vivid color—a dramatic portrait of the dangers and the glories of challenging—and preying upon—the rich and far-flung Spanish empire in the 16th century. It reveals the assets and liabilities of maritime expeditions in which private and national interests sometimes converged, sometimes clashed and almost always were blurred. A review of Drake's life adds formidable evidence to the claim that real life is stranger than fiction.

Francis Drake was born in the county of Devon, England in 1542, fifty years after Columbus's first, history-making voyage. Like Columbus he was born into modest circumstances, though he had kinfolk, most notably the Hawkins family, who were wealthy, established participants in the powerful Devonshire seafaring enterprise. Drake, like Columbus, went to sea "from an early age" and learned his craft in coastal seaborne trade between England and continental Europe. He sailed on small cargo barks midst the currents, tides, shoals, fog and unsure anchorages of the English Channel and the Baltic Sea. This was ideal preparation for the maritime challenges which lay ahead of him in the "coves, estuaries and islands" of the Spanish West Indies and the coast of the Spanish Main.[1]

Drake, who, at the age of twenty, inherited a coastal bark from the owner/master whom he had served, was introduced to Spanish waters in the Western hemisphere by his relative, John Hawkins.[2] Hawkins was among the first of the English sea captains who sought to profit from trade with Spain's new world. The route of this trade ran between the coasts of Africa and Central America. Its cargo consisted of Negroes purchased from African tribal chieftains or independently abducted. These Negroes were sold by English privateers to Spanish colonists who essentially defied their country's prohibition against such trade in order to replenish their depleted work force. Having first enslaved the natives who died from disease and their conditions of servitude, the Spanish colonists enslaved imported laborers.

This Spanish trade with the English was sometimes carried on willingly and sometimes at the point of guns mounted on English privateers. It was a kind of gunboat trade in which sometimes reluctant Spanish colonial administrators found it the better part of valor to purchase the chattel offered by the well armed and threatening English privateers.

John Hawkins figured prominently and successfully in this trade and his younger kinsman, Francis Drake, cut his mature seafaring teeth in company with Hawkins in slave trading. On one such expedition, in 1568, a small fleet commanded by Hawkins on board his flagship the *Jesus of Lubeck*, put into a Spanish colonial port on the Isthmus of Central America called San Juan de Ulua. Apparently promised safe harbor by the resident Spanish authorities, the fleet was then mercilessly attacked at anchor and Hawkins's flagship was sunk with substantial loss of life.[3]

Survivors boarded two small ships, the *Minion* and the *Judith*, the former captained by Hawkins and the latter by young Drake. The *Judith*, never looking back, sailed swiftly to safety but the *Minion* struggled and, in the absence of the *Judith*, was forced to fend for herself. Ultimately she too sailed to safety, begrudging both the Spanish treachery (which cost Hawkins three quarters of his men and one thousand tons of shipping) and her seeming abandonment by the *Judith*. Henceforth, relations between England and Spain would never be the same as Hawkins—and especially Drake—sought every opportunity to avenge the Spanish perfidy at San Juan de Ulua. For Drake, revenge became a life-long and monomaniacal obsession—akin to Ahab's enraged pursuit of Moby Dick.

Drake mounted the first installment of his revenge in 1572 when he organized a West Indian expedition consisting of two ships—the *Swan* and the *Pascha*—and a crew of seventy men to raid the Spanish warehouses in Nombre de Dios in what is now the country of Panama on the Spanish Main. Nombre de Dios, located on the east coast of the Isthmus of Panama, was the staging area for the transshipment of Spanish treasure from the rich west coast of South America (especially from Peru) across the Caribbean and Atlantic to Spain. Drake aimed to sack this imperial emporium and carry its treasure back to England. His attempt to do so was incredibly audacious, consisting of an assault by a small landing party of lightly armed men whom he led. The assault came within a whisker of succeeding. It ended, however, with a wounded Drake capturing, instead of gold and silver bullion, a Spanish ship laden with wine from the Canaries.

Drake, having narrowly missed his first objective to sack Nombre de Dios, immediately set upon another even more daunting mission that aimed to rob the mule trains hauling Spanish treasure from the city of Panama on the west coast of the Isthmus, across the Isthmus to Nombre de Dios. In this endeavor, Drake's contingent was fortified by the Canary wine and a fortuitous alliance with the Cimarrons, who were African slaves who had escaped from their masters and were living in the Panamanian jungle. With their eager and indispensable help, Drake undertook an overland assault on the trans-Isthmus mule train. A failed first attempt was followed by a partially successful second attempt (in league with some French corsairs). Drake succeeded in ambushing a mule train and both burying and carrying off some of its gold and silver bullion. The eventual transport of this treasure to England, however, required still more heroics. Drake had to build a raft to sail in search of his ships that were being hemmed-in by the Spanish fleet and he then had to return to the mule trail to recover the buried treasure. Miraculously he succeeded in doing both and ultimately returned to England, raiding en route for provisions and plunder, with treasure worth 20,000 pounds. Drake's share, after providing his investors (including the Queen) with their shares, left him, now barely in his thirties, an "abundantly rich" man.[4]

Drake was not, however, left sated in his quest for fame, riches and revenge. Over the next five years his planning pointed to a Pacific adventure which would begin with plundering raids along the southeast coast of the Spanish Main, transiting to the west coast via the Strait of Magellan, where plundering would continue and a search would be made for the western entrance to the illusive Northwest Passage, returning home via the Moluccas and the Indian Ocean, thus completing a circumnavigation of the globe. This enterprise was supported by prestigious investors, including the Queen herself, her favorite, the Earl of Leicester and John Hawkins.[5] Drake's fleet of five ships carrying a crew of 164 sailed in mid-November 1577, following a course similar to that of Magellan. In fact the similarities, including threatened mutinies, executions of accused ringleaders and abandonment by ships en route, are striking. So too are the personality traits of the two mariners, both ruthless in exercising authority and ready with their anger.

Suffice it to say that by the time Drake transited the Strait of Magellan and survived his first encounter with the fury of the southern Pacific, his fleet had been reduced to his flagship, the *Pelican*, which, at the entrance to the Strait of Magellan, he had renamed the *Golden Hind*.[6] Alone and undaunted Drake undertook with awesome daring and equal success the pursuit of his multifaceted mission.

First on his agenda was the plundering—south to north—of the Spanish ports in South America. This he proceeded to do—beginning in Valpariso—with virtual impunity and stunning effect. Swooping in on unsuspecting, largely undefended and hitherto tranquil coastal towns, Drake absconded with Spanish treasure at will, leaving resident Spanish authorities dumfounded, impoverished and quaking in their boots. Drake's arrival, literally from out of the blue, had an impact on Spanish colonial administrators "akin to that in a modern emerging nation by news that its unfriendly neighbor has just developed a ballistic missile."[7]

A Drake biographer sums up his breathtaking and incredibly lucrative series of raids along the coast as follows:

> He seized ships, retained them when he needed them, dispensed with them when they were no longer of use . . . took up and released local Indian and Spanish pilots for successive stages of the voyage, apparently killed nobody, lost only one or two men, and gradually filled the Hind with a massive quantity of plunder. It was a time of euphoric success, self–congratulation, jokes at the Spanish expense, and affordable magnanimity.[8]

For their part, the Spanish were spread thin defensively and astonishingly complacent. In the case of Drake's biggest prize, the treasure ship *Cacafuego,* taken off the coast of the Cape of San Francisco, its captain did not resist because he simply did not have the means to do so. The ship, with its cargo of "thirteen chests of silver coin, approximately twenty-five tons of silver bars, and eighty pounds weight of gold," carried no cannon or even small arms.[9] In such incredible circumstances, with his prey so vulnerable, Drake enjoyed easy pickings. In the process he loaded up his *Golden Hind* with tons of gold, silver and jewels, conveniently using them as ballast for an ongoing voyage.

That voyage took him unmolested along the coast of California where apparently he made a desultory search for the hoped-for western entrance to the illusive Northwest Passage. Somewhere along the coast of central California, Drake, who was more interested in wealth and revenge than in exploration, abandoned the search for the passage and headed west for the Moluccas to gather a cargo of spices which would be worth their weight in gold. This he succeeded in doing, sailing almost without incident to the Philippines and the Moluccas and thence across the Indian Ocean, rounding the Cape of Good Hope and arriving in England in late September 1589, two years and ten months after his departure. He returned home not only with fabulous riches on board, but with the historic distinction of being the first person to accomplish an unbroken circumnavigation of the world. Both literally and figuratively, Drake's globe girdling voyage through sea-lanes which were supposedly under Spanish and Portuguese monopolistic control, laid the oceans open to daring mariners courageous enough to run the Spanish and Portuguese gauntlets. His voyage around the world laid, as well, the conceptual basis for the subsequent British Empire.

While Drake returned "massively rich," the Spanish for their part demanded the return of their stolen treasure. Queen Elizabeth (who, after all, was one of the leading investors in Drake's enterprise and whose coffers were bare) not only summarily rejected this but went so far as to attend a banquet hosted by Drake on the *Golden Hind* at which she knighted him for his exploits at Spain's expense. Such were the extent and humiliation of Drake's depredations and robberies on the Spanish Main, that Spain's King Philip II launched new defensive and offensive measures against England, the latter leading to the eventual deployment of the formidable Spanish Armada. Meanwhile, King Philip, in retaliation for the sacking of his treasure ships and emporia, detained, and impounded the assets of, English merchants in Spain.

The contest now escalated as Drake and his erstwhile compatriot, Martin Frobisher, organized a full-scale English raid on Spanish outposts in the Caribbean. What had started out as gunboat trade led by John Hawkins had, under Drake's obsessed leadership, become first a pattern of opportunistic plundering of Spanish treasure ships and outposts, now followed by an audacious plan to seize, sack and ransom entire settlements. This Drake, as Admiral and, Martin Frobisher, as General, set out to do in 1585 in a veritable armada of thirty-three vessels carrying close to two thousand men, the vast majority of whom were soldiers. Theirs was not an expedition, it was plainly "an invading fleet."[10]

The fleet departed in September 1585, sailing toward Spain, thence to the Canaries and the Cape Verde Islands, requisitioning ships and pillaging en route. From the Cape Verdes, Drake sailed for a crown jewel in Spain's West Indian Empire, and its first outpost there, Santo Domingo. In the transit of the Atlantic, Drake began to lose an alarming number of his men to sickness, probably at first to the plague and, later in his voyage, to yellow fever. Their ravages would progressively sap the fighting force of the armada; but Santo Domingo was the first stop and Drake arrived fully prepared to seize it. And seize it he did, overwhelming a premier and allegedly impregnable Spanish entrepot through a "straightforward combined operation which demonstrated the ideal balance between sailors and soldiers in Drake's force."[11] Drake's forces sacked Santo Domingo and then held it for ransom. In the ransom negotiations that followed, Drake was described by his Spanish opposite number as follows: "A man of medium height, fair, tending toward stockiness; he is merry but careful. In command he is forceful, is feared and obeyed by his men. He is firm in punishing. Alert, restless, well spoken, ambitious, vainglorious but generous and liberal; not a cruel man."[12]

The restless and ambitious Drake next sailed his armada to Cartagena on the Spanish Main that, with all odds overwhelmingly in its favor, succumbed to a brilliant "Drakian" land and sea operation. Once again the town was plundered and held for ransom.

While a brilliant military success, the sacking of Cartagena and the negotiations for its ransom yielded a disappointing harvest of treasure. Meanwhile, Drake's men were dropping like flies to the fever. With the strength of his fleet eroding, Drake sailed for Cuba, passing it by in favor of pillaging along the Florida coast. He sailed as far north as the settlement founded in Roanoke, Virginia by Sir Walter Raleigh, where he picked up the remnants of the "weary residents" of that settlement and transported them back to England, arriving home just short of a year after his departure.

This so-called "Great Expedition of the West Indies" resulted in high human cost and low material gain; but it struck a "stunning blow" to Spanish pride. In doing so it stiffened and hastened Catholic King Philip's determination to strike directly against Protestant England. This he chose to do by means of an amphibious assault staged from a massive armada. As this plan, and its attendant ship construction, became known to Queen Elizabeth, she commissioned Drake to lead a preemptive first strike against ships in Spanish ports. This he proceeded to do in 1587, striking first at Cadiz where the harbor was "teeming with ships." With audacity and arrogance, Drake's fleet swept in upon the anchored vessels, "like a hawk among dozing chickens" and unleashed "an unprecedented storm of destruction" sending 10,000 tons of Spanish shipping to the bottom.

Drake then sailed on to raid the Spanish controlled southeast coast of Portugal, first attacking, and failing to take, Lagos and then attacking Sagres, the historic capital of Portugal's advanced and immensely profitable maritime industry. Personally leading a bold assault on the formidable fortress at Sagres, Drake took possession of this strategic stronghold and used it as a base for capturing and destroying ships supplying the construction of King Philip's fleet in Lisbon. Ever anxious to capture treasure ships, Drake then sailed on to the Azores and captured an enormous Portuguese ship, the *Sao Philipe*, the holds of which were packed with silks, spices and jewels worth over 100,000 pounds!

Drake returned to England with the majority of his missions impressively accomplished and his reputation elevated to mythic proportions. He had bought England time by laying waste to Spanish shipping and he had handsomely augmented the Queen's treasury (and his own) with valuable plunder. But the day of reckoning with a Spanish armada still awaited and would require, in the event, a substantial, technologically advanced and well-organized English naval capability. Queen Elizabeth, who had long taken an interest in the navy—both in the construction of ships and in the maintenance of their crews—entrusted the development of that capability to John Hawkins.

Hawkins, appointed Treasurer of the Navy in 1578, essentially mounted a revolution in naval tactics and ship design. The tactics involved reliance on long-range naval gunnery in place of close quarter combat and boarding; the ship design featured "race built" vessels that were smaller and had a greater proportion of length to beam. These ships were more mobile (and cheaper to build and operate) than the large Spanish galleons and carried, per ton, a greater number of heavy guns. They were built not to transport armies (as were Spanish ships); but to operate in defense of England in the close ocean quarters of its island home. A substantial fleet of these ships was at the ready when the allegedly invincible Spanish Armada was sighted off the Cornish coast on July 30, 1588. The English hand has been described as follows: "Everything indeed favored the English. On the day she mustered more fighting ships. In general they were better armed than their opponents, and enjoyed a crushing superiority in firepower, both by range and weight of shot. They were also smaller, handier and livelier craft than the Spanish."[13]

What the English beheld was an armada carrying 19,000 men forming "an arc of great ships (130 in total) two to three miles wide."[14] The Armada's assault plan involved a joint land and sea attack, the former to be mounted by amphibious forces led by the Flemish Duke of Parma whose landing craft were to be escorted across the channel by the Armada led by the Spanish Count Medina Sidonia. The achilles heel of that plan lay at the intersection of the forces of Parma and Sidonia. In the event, that intersection was seriously flawed.

The English, led by Drake, who, as always, favored a preemptive strike, launched their "race built" fleet in an attack on the Armada. The efficiency and firepower of the English fleet astonished the Spanish and chipped away at their formidable but not agile Armada. The Armada, modestly diminished, sailed across the channel to rendezvous with the forces of the Duke of Parma, only to find him unprepared for the amphibious assault and themselves cornered by the English in the channel. Having essentially trapped the Armada in the channel, the English ships, commanded in squadrons by Drake, Hawkins and Frobisher, cut into it and effectively dispersed it.

Drake returned to England a hero, having played a leading role in the defeat of a towering threat to England that has only been equaled in magnitude since by the Nazi airborne assault in 1940.

The Armada for its part returned to Spain, weakened "but basically sound and reparable."

It can be said that Drake reached his apogee in the defeat of the Spanish Armada. Thereafter his actions show evidence of bad judgment and his fortunes deteriorated.

The English were slow and inept in following-up on their stunning defeat of the Spanish Armada. An expedition led by Drake consisting of 180 ships and 23,000 men sailed in April of 1589 with the purpose of attacking Spanish shipping in its ports, seizing Spanish treasure ships and reinstalling a Portuguese prince as the ruling monarch of Portugal. The expedition suffered from a combination of rashness, indecision and excessive scope and ended up an utter failure on all counts, costing the English heavily in ships and in the loss of rank and file soldiers. As the expedition proceeded, Queen Elizabeth saw the handwriting on the wall and desperately but fruitlessly warned Drake against "an humour of vainglory which will obfuscate the eyes of your judgment."[15]

The eyes of Drake's judgment were plainly obfuscated but his passion for fame, plunder and revenge against the Catholic Spanish burned as intensely as ever. Two years after his failed expedition against Spain, Drake set forth with Hawkins on a mission that had the incredible objective of taking the Isthmus of Panama from the Spanish. A fleet of six royal galleons and twenty private vessels, under the joint command of Drake and his elder kinsman, Hawkins, sailed in August of 1595 to attack the Spanish Main at its jugular. The expedition was ill-fated from the start. It met with military setbacks, first in the Canaries and then in Puerto Rico. Drake and Hawkins, visibly shaken by unaccustomed defeat and by now being closely monitored and harassed by beefed-up Spanish land-based and seaborne defenses, set upon their main target, the Isthmus of

Panama. Hawkins, himself, then age 63, died en route and was buried at sea before the main target had been reached.

The plan was to take Nombre de Dios and then march overland on the mule trail to capture Panama itself. Nombre de Dios was taken easily but then Drake was taught a bitter lesson by the Panamanian jungle (a lesson which subsequently and repeatedly was taught to those with schemes to subdue the Panamanian elements). His fever ridden and inadequately shod troops got mired in the rainy season en route to Panama and were literally brought to their knees by the terrain, weather and pestilence of the Isthmus. Their painful progress along the mule route was easily blocked by the Spanish. Drake's forces—if that is what they could then be called—limped back from whence they had come. A disheartened Drake made some desultory efforts to salvage the expedition by plundering the theater; but evidently his spirit was broken, his will weakened and his health sapped. He died in his cabin a few weeks later (at age 54) and his body, instead of being transported to his beloved England for burial as per his wishes, was placed in a leaden casket and consigned to Davey Jones's locker.

Drake's last fleet—depleted and miserable—returned to England with "the news of the death of Drake and Hawkins and with a dispirited, acrimonious and impoverished crew." The wheel of fortune had turned and Drake's final mission had taken him to the very depths of frustration and failure. Having once lavished glory and riches upon his country, he departed leaving England and himself with neither.

Drake was a seaborne knight in shining armor. For decades he was a blade runner, challenging fate face-to-face and miraculously surviving. He repeatedly snatched victories from the jaws of defeat and lived what can only be described as a charmed life. Luck played its part. But "audentes fortuna invat" (fortune favors the brave). Drake was brave, always precariously balanced on the fine line that separates audacity from foolhardiness. He, like Columbus, had the arts of navigation on his fingertips. And, like Columbus, he had the "ambition and naked greed . . . of a poor man's son."[16] He, like Magellan, was a crusader with a burning, albeit Protestant, piety. And, like both Columbus and Magellan, his personal interest and the national interest frequently converged. When they did not, and Drake sought, out of greed or hubris, to line his pockets and burnish his image, he exposed himself to valid criticism and progressively blotted his copybook.

What manner of man emerges from the pages of Drake's life? This is not easy to sort out because Drake's exploits were for the English so heroic and for the Spanish so devilish that an objective summation is hard to draw. It can, however, be said with confidence that Drake was brave, tough, resourceful and lucky. He was, as is the case with most leaders, "a willing hearer of every man's opinion, but commonly a follower of his own."[17] And, as with all great leaders, he was a bundle of contradictions. He was "brutal and devious" but also "charming and generous." He was severe and quick to anger but also "courteous, magnanimous and liberal." He was, in many ways, a mirror image of his Queen ("who tried to turn him into a gentleman") and of his times.[18] He was a harbinger of England's future as his maritime exploits had opened "new horizons for trade, exploration and the 'planting' of colonies."[19]

Drake's story cannot be considered complete without recounting an especially entertaining and eventually significant episode. En route to his awesome, unbroken circumnavigation of the world, Drake sailed through the Moluccas—the Spice Islands—and befriended the Sultan of Ternate, the spice island Magellan had sought to reach. From these initial contacts, the English secured their own spice island—an island named Rum—the possession of which broke the monopoly on the spice trade that the Dutch had by then established. The Dutch were so eager to restore that monopoly that later—when they had settled New Amsterdam in what is now Manhattan—they traded Manhattan for Rum, placing what later became the world's financial capital in English hands.[20] The world's "main axis of commerce and communication" eventually moved there!

NOTES

1. John Cummins, *Francis Drake* (New York; St. Martin's Press, 1997), 13.
2. Frank Sherry, *Pacific Passions: The European Struggle for Power in the Great Ocean in the Age of Exploration* (New York: William Morrow and Co., Inc., 1994), 124.
3. Ibid., 124.
4. Cummins, op. cit., 65.
5. Sherry, op. cit., 125.
6. Ibid., 130.
7. Cummins, op. cit., 92.
8. Ibid., 92.

9. See Sherry, op. cit., 133.

10. Cummins, op. cit., 137.

11. Ibid., 148.

12. Ibid., 149.

13. G. V. Scammell, *The World Encompassed: The First European Maritime Empires c. 800–1650* (Berkeley: University of California Press, 1972), 469.

14. For a description of the action see: Christopher Hibbert, *The Virgin Queen* (New York: Addison-Wesley Publishing Company, Inc., 1991), 223–24.

15. Cummins, op. cit., 211.

16. Ibid., 304.

17. See Cummins, op. cit., 305.

18. Harry Kelsey, *Sir Francis Drake: The Queen's Pirate* (New Haven: Yale University Press, 1998), 399.

19. John Hampden, *Francis Drake: Privateer* (Alabama: University of Alabama Press, 1972), 14.

20. This episode is delightfully recounted in: Milton Giles, *Nathaniel's Nutmeg* (New York: Penguin Books, 1999).

BIBLIOGRAPHY

Cummins, John. *Francis Drake.* New York: St. Martin's Press, 1997.
Giles, Milton. *Nathaniel's Nutmeg.* New York: Penguin Books, 1999.
Hampden, John. *Francis Drake: Privateer.* Alabama: University of Alabama Press, 1972.
Hibbert, Christopher. *The Virgin Queen.* New York: Addison-Wesley Publishing Company, 1991.
Kelsey, Harry. *Sir. Francis Drake: The Queen's Pirate.* New Haven: Yale University Press, 1998.
Morison, Samuel Eliot. *The European Discovery of America: The Southern Voyages.* New York: Oxford University Press, 1993.
Scammell, G. V. *The World Encompassed: The First European Maritime Empires c. 800–1650.* Berkeley: University of California Press, 1981.
Sherry, Frank. *Pacific Passions: The European Struggle for Power in the Great Ocean in the Age of Exploration.* New York: William Morrow and Co., Inc., 1994.

12

CAPTAIN JAMES COOK

"The greatest explorer of the eighteenth century, perhaps of any century."

—Lynne Withey, *Voyages of Discovery*

"Over a period of some ten years, Cook's explorations enlarged the known world far more greatly and more suddenly than in a thousand years before."

—Daniel Conner and Lorraine Miller, *Master Mariner: Captain James Cook and the Peoples of the Pacific*

Roughly two hundred years elapsed between the English voyages of Sir Francis Drake and those of Captain James Cook. In the intervening years, the objectives of maritime expeditions had moved on from piracy (as classically pursued by Drake) to discovery (as classically pursued by Cook). Scientific inquiry gained ground as a motivation for exploration and the voyages of Captain Cook showcased this emergent dimension of exploration. "His voyages, full-fledged scientific expeditions dedicated to 'discovery' in it broadest sense, established a model that would be followed by explorers for decades to come."[1] They also established the Pacific Ocean as an identifiable "geographic unit," setting the stage for its creation as an economic zone in the course of the world's westward march.[2]

Captain Cook's most famous arena of exploration was the Pacific Ocean. It is a vast arena. The Pacific Ocean is the largest, most formidable geographic feature of our earth. It stretches ten thousand miles between the American and Chinese coasts and nine thousand miles between the polar seas. Its daunting size can be summed up as follows:

> The Pacific is the greatest physical unit on earth. From pole to pole, from shore to shore, the Pacific is larger than of all the dry lands of the earth put together. It comprises more than a third of the surface of the world and is almost twice as large as the great Atlantic, three times the size of the Indian Ocean, which in itself is larger than the continent of Asia.[3]

Not only does the sheer size of the Pacific challenge comprehension, it is occupied—and sometimes ravaged—by variable winds, dangerous reefs, monumental ice flows, suffocating heat, bone chilling cold, dense fogs, and, in the time of Captain Cook, unknown lands of disparate shapes and sizes and of native peoples of disparate demeanor and behavior.

When Captain Cook began to sail and chart the Pacific in 1768, it was, for all practical purposes, unknown to the western world. The strong, resourceful and humane Vasco Balboa had blazed a trail across the Isthmus of Panama and "discovered" the Pacific Ocean, claiming it on behalf of Spain in 1513. This discovery was soon followed by the voyage of Ferdinand Magellan in 1519, which sought a path between the ocean Columbus had transited and the one Balboa had sighted. Magellan's voyage had found a path between the seas that lies at the tip of South America and produced the first known transit of the Pacific and the first known circumnavigation of the globe.

Bits and pieces of the Pacific were subsequently placed—though rather roughly—on the world map by the voyages, for example of: the Dutchman, Abel Tasman, who discovered New Zealand and the west coast of Australia; the Dane, Vitus Bering, who discovered the sea and straits that bear his name; and the Englishman, Sir Francis Drake who sailed along the west coast of South and North America from the Strait of Magellan to Northern California which he named New Albion. But when Captain Cook set forth in 1771, no more was known of the Pacific than was known of the vast interior of Africa or, for that matter, the interior of the North American continent itself.

Cook's voyages would make the Pacific essentially completely known and would lead almost directly to the exploration of the North American continent. In fact his instructions from the Royal Society governing his first voyage are comparable to those Thomas Jefferson issued to Lewis and Clark; to wit: "on finding land, examine it in detail, and establish friendship and alliance with the inhabitants."[4] Cook's voyages, directly and indirectly, filled in the map of what was then the world's largest void. They qualify as a monumental feat and a world-transforming event. In the words of one of Cook's recent biographers, "Cook made history by making geography."[5]

Cook stands today widely recognized as the greatest explorer of all time. Biographies on him continue to multiply; they now number in the hundreds. And his image appears on stamps, coins, bank notes, wine labels and tea towels. His image has come to be considered the personification of the names of the two Whitby colliers on which he sailed through largely uncharted waters for over 200,000 miles (roughly the distance to the moon); to wit: the *Endeavor* and the *Resolution.*[6]

What were the essential features of Cook's voyages and of the man responsible for them? First, to the features of the voyages; then, to the features of the man himself.

Cook's three voyages—beginning in 1768 and ending in 1779—were often exercises in what the late historian Daniel Boorstin calls "negative discovery." The first two voyages—each lasting roughly three years and each covering distances several times the circumference of the earth—were aimed principally at finding the fabled southern continent—a landmass that was presumed to exist in order to balance the weight of the landmasses in the north. This antipodal piece of real estate was supposed to harbor untold sources of wealth and new species of fauna and flora. The problem was that the vast antipodal continent was not, for all practical purposes, accessible. It took Cook two harrowing voyages, including months of cruising among the ice flows of the Antarctic circle, to definitively prove that that was the case.

Along the way, however, Cook: established, an astronomical station in Tahiti to measure the rare transit of Venus across the sun; charted the entire New Zealand coast (a country which he felt "was the most beautiful that nature unassisted by art could produce") and the eastern coastline of Australia; discovered the Great Barrier Reef; and placed multiple Pacific islands and their peoples on the world map.[7] In not finding what he was sent to search for, Cook discovered enormously important real estate and filled in, on accurate maps, substantial areas of "terra incognita."

The same exercise in "negative discovery" can be said of his third voyage that was commissioned to find the elusive Northwest Passage to Cathay. Ever since Marco Polo wrote of his travels, the West sought quick routes to the riches of the Great Khan. The Spanish thought they were the first to do so in 1492, with Columbus's voyage that arrived in what he called the Indies, which he fancied were islands off the coast of Cathay. But the Portuguese were the first to actually get to where Columbus thought he was with the voyages of Vasco da Gama in 1498, and his immediate successors. These voyages rounded the Cape of Good Hope, transited the Indian Ocean and opened a route to the South China Sea.

Next up was Magellan, who started off on Columbus's western route and actually got to where Columbus thought he was via a strait that bears his name. But Da Gama's eastern route and Magellan's western route were both long, arduous trips. Perhaps there was a northern route that would avail a faster passage to the Orient.

The English were the first and most persistent to explore this possibility, beginning with the voyage of John Cabot in 1497. Some sense of the difficulty of probing the North Atlantic for a passage to Cathay can be gained from Cabot's experience. His first voyage, on which he rediscovered Newfoundland and the waters off the Newfoundland Banks teeming with codfish, was speedy and apparently uneventful. On his second voyage, which followed hard on the heels of his first, he disappeared without a trace, apparently in a fierce North Atlantic storm. There followed numerous "Voyages of Delusion" searching for a passage through what is now the eastern coast of Canada to the vast ocean lying to the west. These voyages—at least fifty before Cook sailed—failed for the simple reason that, for all practical purposes, there was no such passage. But hope springs eternal and Cook—having volunteered to replicate in the north Pacific what he had bravely and laboriously done in the south—was dispatched on his third voyage to find the entrance to the fabled passage, this time on the northwest coast of North America.

This he failed to do, because (until the ice melts!) the passage does not exist. But in making that negative discovery, he found additional Pacific islands including Tonga and Hawaii. He also meticulously charted the northwest coast of the North American continent, eventually enabling Starbucks and Microsoft to settle there!

The late Daniel Boorstin was a great fan of the process of negative discovery.[8] And rightly so. He refers to a saying that "It ain't what a man knows that makes him a fool; but what he knows that ain't so."[9] Put another way, this time in Boorstin's own words, "The great menace to progress is not ignorance, but the illusion of knowledge."

In Cook's time, leading lights believed that there was a southern continent and a northwest passage. They had already drawn them on maps. Cook, through methodical, arduous and meticulous maritime research, proved that both were beyond reach.

Cook's voyages not only made negative discoveries and, along the way, filled in the map of the Pacific Ocean, they made dramatic contributions to maritime technology and to human health on the high seas. In doing so, Cook shifted the outcome of the age-old contest between the oceans and the mariner in favor of the latter. That, all by itself, produced a world transformation. Henceforth, man, not nature, was, in the main, in charge of the high seas.[10]

Cook's voyages were launched in the face of two mighty challenges that had confronted mariners from time immemorial. The first was the conundrum of fixing longitude. The second was the scourge of scurvy. The former left you lost on the high seas. The latter left you dying. Cook's voyages mounted breakthroughs on both fronts.

With respect to the fixing of longitude, Cook experimented with, and tested, John Harrison's famous new chronometer (the invention of which, chronicled in Dava Sobel's classic book *Longitude*, is a story that rivals Cooks' with respect to challenges overcome). Cook essentially field tested a new, highly promising technology and became the first "commander of a ship in history to know almost precisely where he was for most of his time at sea."[11] In the process of doing so, he enabled the fixing of longitude as calculated in minutes distant from Greenwich meantime. Mariners, long able to fix their latitude based on the declination of the sun by day and the Pole Star at night, could now fix their longitude. The intersection of a vertical and horizontal line now fixed their position—and their discoveries—on the vast seas of the world. To paraphrase the famous Southwest Airlines ad, mariners were now "free to move about the world."

As Cook was experimenting with Harrison's chronometer to fix longitude, he also was experimenting with nutrients to stave off scurvy. This disease has been described as "an ugly affliction resulting in debility, depression, loss of teeth, hemorrhaging and death."[12] His experimental nutritional kit consisted of everything from sauerkraut to lemon juice. With "iron discipline" he forced his crew to consume the needed nutrients.[13] By doing so, he not only saved their lives, but revealed the essential ingredient that his antiscorbutics had in common, namely Vitamin C. He effectively conquered the scourge of scurvy and was so recognized by the Royal Society with its award for reaching "the summit of intellectual achievement." It was the only time the medal was awarded for advances in nutrition. Cook accepted it with characteristic modesty saying: "It is with real satisfaction and without claiming any merit but attention to duty that I accept this award."[14]

Cook's negative discoveries and applied research breakthroughs hold important lessons. And they are not comforting ones. They point in the direction of not only pressing the outer edge of the envelope but stretching it. In his search for the fabled southern continent, Cook crossed into the Antarctic Circle and sailed further into its icebound waters than any man had gone before or would go again for a hundred years. Here is one of Cook's most memorable lines which dramatically captures what is required to prove what people think is true is actually false. Cook wrote that his ambition to find the fabled southern continent led him "not only further than any man before me, but as far as I think it possible for man to go."[15] In recognition of this feat, King George had emblazoned on Cook's coat of arms "Nil itentatum reliquit." "He left nothing unattempted."

The same stretching of the envelope was replicated in the northwestern waters as Cook probed for the entrance to the mythical Northwest Passage. He entered domains that would later entomb explorers, most notably Sir John Franklin, whose entire party found itself icebound and ultimately froze to death in a search for the Northwest Passage in 1847.

Now onto Cook the man who has been described as "tall and spare, with piercing blue eyes, sharply defined features and a serious almost stern demeanor."[16] He was born in modest circumstances in 1728, the son of a Scottish laborer.[17] His formal education was limited to a couple of years in a one room Quaker schoolhouse. He went on to teach himself the science and math of hydrography and became one of history's greatest surveyors and cartographers.

His early career featured some false starts. He started as an apprentice to a grocer's clerk. At age eighteen he became a mate aboard an English coastal collier, transporting coal from Newcastle to London. He sailed the North Sea which—with its shoals and tides and "ill-lit headlands"—was "an extremely exacting nursery for 18th century seamen."[18] "Off watch he applied himself to his books, sweating over the mathematics of navigation in the dim light of the crews' quarters."[19] At age twenty-seven he was offered command of his own collier. This he declined and, instead, joined the Royal Navy as a common seaman. From this lowly position (normally occupied by those in their teens who had been impressed into service from bars and brothels) and relatively late in life (at that time), Cook "starting below decks," rose like a rocket, commanding "the respect of his men by sheer competence and force of personality."[20] Thirteen years later, at age 40 (late middle age in his time) he was commanding England's most important voyage of discovery.

Cook's career was powered by his skill as a chart maker. In this craft he had no peer. He painstakingly developed that skill, largely on his own, and applied it with telling effect on board English ships in the Seven Year War with France in the mid-18th century. Cook meticulously plotted the coastlines of the Gulf of St. Lawrence which were as "jagged as an awful wound" providing the English with the geographic intelligence that enabled them to capture Quebec and defeat the French. Cook's talent as a cartographer set him apart and became his ticket to fame.

Cook was a neat freak. He was constantly preoccupied with the cleanliness and orderliness of his vessels and their crews.[21] His ships—first the *Endeavor* and then the *Resolution*—were routinely scrubbed down with vinegar. His crew was subjected to the functional equivalent of regular physical examinations. As a result of these measures—and his antiscorbutic regimes—Cook rarely lost a man to sickness at sea. On his second voyage that covered 60,000 miles, two and a half times the circumference of the earth, Cook lost only one crew member to sickness. It was an amazing feat given the length and climatic challenges of his voyage.

Cook was a severe taskmaster but, at the same time, a benign autocrat.[22] He pushed his crew hard, but not over the brink. He had them lashed when they stepped out of line. But his men could count on him to be fair and to look after their requirements of both food and alcohol. The normal daily ration of the latter was either a gallon of beer or a half pint of rum.[23] It was a fact of life in those times that a ship could only sail as far as its supply of alcohol permitted. At every landfall that offered appropriate ingredients, Cook set his crew to work brewing beer! He knew that "a tight ship was a happy ship!"

While a severe taskmaster with his crew, Cook qualifies, in the main, as a kinder/gentler explorer. He knew that his contact with native peoples disrupted and sometimes damaged their lives. He actively sought to minimize these effects. At the same time, he sought to learn as much about the people he encountered as he could. He generally treated the native peoples with respect, even with empathy, and with the hope that somehow their contact with English civilization would benefit them.

Cook was not flashy. He was sober (literally), prudent and methodical. What he lacked in terms of showmanship, he gained in the way of seamanship and survival. His boring qualities of reserve, attention to detail and apparent equanimity, won for him the respect and admiration of his crew and, when applied to his craft of cartography, produced the meticulous rendering of both physical and demographic maps that charted the lands and peoples of the Pacific. His boring qualities also won him an unrivaled record for returning home, not only alive and with the vast majority of his crew, but in the same ship in which he departed.

Cook sailed three times around the world in two Whitby colliers, 110 feet long, 30 feet wide and shallow drafted. They were like hollowed out corks, bobbing and weaving on the unpredictable surface of the deepest and largest body of water on the planet. On his second voyage—that has been classified as "the greatest single voyage in the history of the world"—Cook and his crew "experienced hardships never before experienced by mortal man."[24] Two legs of his second voyage involved 122 and 117 days at sea and a leg of 10,000 miles over vacant seas without sighting land. The odds of a safe return were monumentally stacked against Cook. But his unspectacular qualities of vigilance, patience and attention to mind-numbing detail allowed him to survive the vicissitudes of nature in the course of three globe-girdling voyages.

Fortunately, Captain Cook was a diarist. Writing did not come naturally to him, but he practiced and became proficient in it. It was a very good thing that he did, because without his personal, authentic account of his voyages, the history of them would be left almost entirely to historians fond of "deconstruction" who believe that there are no historical facts, only interpretations. Historians of this stripe, bent on "political correctness" and, essentially, "the killing of history" accuse Cook of all manner of things from spreading syphilis (which he mightily tried to prevent) to misrepresenting the native peoples (whom he earnestly tried to understand and even to succor). Had Cook been left without a diary, the facts of his voyages would have been left to "interpretations" possibly robbing him of his iconic stature as a seaman and explorer.

Cook's last journal entry appeared on January 7, 1779 when he returned to Hawaii from a voyage to the Pacific Northwest. Roughly a month later, on Valentine's Day, Cook was killed and mutilated in Hawaii. Why? What happened?

Accounts differ, but this much is clear. When Cook arrived in Hawaii for the second time in early January of 1779, he had been well received and treated like a great chief, even like a god. After a fortnight's stay, he departed to further explore the islands but was almost immediately forced to return to Kealakeua Bay to repair a broken mast. By then Cook had worn out his welcome and the islanders gave him the cold shoulder. One of them stole a large cutter—a kind of tender attached to the *Resolution*. Cook sent a party ashore to hunt for the thief and the stolen cutter while he himself went to the house of the local chief to take him on board the *Resolution* as a hostage to the return of the cutter. While Cook was returning to the shore with the chief in tow, a crowd gathered, led by the chief's wife. At the same time word arrived that the scouting party had, in the course of their search, killed another local chief. The crowd then feared for the life of their own chief and pressed in on Cook. He fired his musket—which was loaded with grape shot—to scare them off. But the crowd closed in on Cook and he was stabbed. His body was carried to a sacrificial area where he was ceremoniously deboned. Pieces of his flesh were then returned to the *Resolution* whose officers proceeded to perform their own ritual, burying Cook's remains at sea.

Did Captain Cook over-react to the theft of his cutter? Did he lose his legendary cool? It is quite possible he did because in the course of his third voyage, "he had been showing increasing signs of strain and irritation."[25] The only thing that is certain is that he lost his life. Perhaps the losing of it in such a grim way has made him more of a legend than he would otherwise be. But in reading and thinking about Captain Cook, one ends up wishing that he had lived on to enjoy a well-earned retirement and the accolades of his countrymen in England and of mariners everywhere.

Captain Cook's voyages opened up a new era of maritime opportunity, essentially providing those who followed him with a safety kit. The safety kit consisted of meticulous charts of Pacific Ocean highways and the islands and coasts to which they led, and answers to a scourge and a problem that had plagued mariners for centuries—the scourge of scurvy and the problem of fixing longitude. Cook's voyages achieved breakthroughs in both fields, enabling an explosion of maritime activity that, in short order, placed his country in command of the high seas and in the van of imperial powers that featured prominently in the world's westward march.

NOTES

1. Lynne Withey, *Voyages of Discovery: Captain Cook and the Exploration of the Pacific* (Berkeley: University of California Press, 1989), 10.
2. Felipe Fernández-Armesto, *Pathfinders: A Global History of Exploration* (New York: W. W. Norton & Company, 2006), 303.
3. Felix Riesenberg, *The Pacific Ocean* (New York: McGraw Hill Book Company, Inc., 1942), 3.
4. Daniel Conner and Lorraine Miller, *Master Mariner: Captain James Cook and the People of the Pacific* (Seattle: University of Washington Press, 1978), 10.
5. Nicholas Thomas, *The Extraordinary Voyages of James Cook* (Canada: Penguin Books, 2003), xx.
6. Ibid., xxxi.
7. Ibid., 169.
8. See: Daniel Boorstin, *Cleopatra's Nose* (New York: Random House, 1994), ix.
9. Ibid., 65.
10. Thomas, Nicholas, op. cit., 8.
11. Conner and Miller, op. cit., 17.
12. Ibid., 17.
13. Fernández-Armesto, op. cit., 297.
14. Conner and Miller, op. cit., 19.
15. Thomas, op. cit., xvii.
16. Withy, op. cit., 16.
17. Conner and Miller, op. cit., 3.
18. Ibid., 3.
19. Ibid.

20. Salmand, Anne *The Trial of the Cannibal Dog: The Remarkable Story of Captain Cook's Encounters in the South Seas* (New Haven: Yale University Press, 2003), 29.

21. Conner and Miller, op. cit., 43.

22. Ibid., 43.

23. Ibid., 17.

24. Ibid., 13.

25. Glyndwr Williams, ed., *Captain Cook's Voyages: 1768–1779* (London: The Folio Society, 1997), xxvii.

BIBLIOGRAPHY

Boorstin, Daniel. *Cleopatra's Nose.* New York: Random House, 1994.

Conner, Daniel and Lorraine Miller. *Captain James Cook and the Peoples of the Pacific.* Seattle: University of Washington Press, 1978.

Fernández-Armesto, Felipe. *Pathfinders: A Global History of Exloration.* New York: W.W. Norton & Company, 2006.

Riesenberg, Felix. *The Pacific Ocean.* New York: McGraw Hill Book Company, Inc., 1942.

Salmand, Anne. *The Trial of the Cannibal Dog: The Remarkable Story of Captain Cook's Encounters in the South Seas.* New Haven: Yale University Press, 2003.

Thomas, Nicholas, *The Extraordinary Voyages of Captain James Cook.* Canada: Penguin Books, 2003.

Williams, Glyndwr, ed. *Captain Cook's Voyages: 1768–1779.* London: The Folio Society, 1997.

Withey, Lynne, *Voyages of Discovery.* Berkeley: University of California Press, 1989.

13

THOMAS JEFFERSON AND THE LOUISIANA PURCHASE

"In the history of the United States, the acquisition of Louisiana is an event that ranks in importance below only the achievements of independence and union."

—Robert Tucker and David Hendrickson, *Empire of Liberty*

"There are few occasions in history when a single decision may assure the future greatness of a nation. In the course of American events the Louisiana Purchase must be ranked as one of these."

—Patrick C. T. White, (ed.), *Conducting the Diplomacy of the New Nation: 1793–1815*

The world's westward march was enabled by newly discovered sea-lanes running both east, around the Cape of Good Hope, and west, through the Strait of Magellan. Once discovered these sea-lanes became ocean highways which connected previously sundered continents and over which a succession of western powers travelled, most notably the English, the French and the Dutch, followed ultimately by Europe's offspring, the United States. The combination of motivations for transiting these ocean highways—and exploiting what lay along the way and at their end—evolved over time. But essential elements included, in varying degrees (according to historic circumstances): a quest for wealth; a search for religious converts; an ambition for power; a yearning for discovering the unknown; a thirst for freedom, adventure and glory.

The gravitational pull—indeed, the intoxicating effects—of these forces proved irresistible to western countries. One by one they succumbed to them and placed their imprint on the globe as if propelled by a natural force mounted on a steamroller. Imperialism and its handmaiden colonialism were the operational expressions of this movement to which no western country of consequence was immune.

From the very beginning, America looked west and coveted the lands that lay there. And no one of the founding fathers looked west more intently, expansively and resourcefully than did Thomas Jefferson. He envisaged a bicoastal "empire of liberty."[1]

Thomas Jefferson was a great—if flawed and contradictory—man. Today we stand on his shoulders as the inheritors of principles for which he stood. The most notable of these principles are anchored in the idea of freedoms—freedom of religious practice, freedom of speech, freedom of trade, and faith in education as the foundation and salvation of freedom. Much is owed to Jefferson, not least the wording of the Declaration of Independence itself. The fluency and economy of his writing alone earned him immortality.[2] But what interests us is Jefferson's role in the westward expansion of the United States, his centrality to the continental movement west from the Atlantic to the Pacific and his place in the primordial shift of the world's center of gravity from East to West.

Jefferson had a story to tell. The story involved a continental America possessed of an abundance of cheap land, available in a seemingly inexhaustible frontier, which would provide the space required for freedom and prosperity to flourish. Jefferson not only told this story, he implemented it; and in so doing he became a great leader of America's (and the world's) westward migration.[3] He did so by playing a leading role in events which led to a quadrupling in the size of the United States and the subsequent charting of a transcontinental route to the Pacific.

The story came naturally to Jefferson. He was born—on April 13, 1743—on America's frontier in a simple farmhouse in Albemarle County, Virginia. His father, Peter, whom he revered, was a "rising planter . . . an explorer, and a map maker on the frontier."[4] His father was "in the vanguard of western settlement" and Jefferson, though he never traveled farther west than what is now West Virginia, saw the world (as many of us do) through his father's eyes. Throughout his life, Jefferson "always honored, even romanticized, western explorers."[5]

Jefferson grew up on the back of a horse and had instilled within him from infancy an essential requirement of freedom—the ability to roam. His father taught him the skill of surveying, which Jefferson later passed on to his nephew, Meriwether Lewis. His father also taught him the importance of physical conditioning, believing that the individual who was strong in body was also "strong and free in mind."[6] Intellectually, Jefferson was a philosopher; but physically and conceptually he was a frontiersman.

Jefferson lost his father—a pioneer, a frontiersman, and substantial land, slave and livestock owner—when he was fourteen. As with other great men in history who lost their father's before becoming men (Theodore Roosevelt and Winston Churchill, for example), Jefferson's life became a mission to take up where his father had left off. In his case, his father had left off exploring, mapping and laying claim to western lands that led across the Appalachian Mountains to the Mississippi. Later in his life, in two successive diplomatic triumphs, Jefferson would figure centrally in the acquisition for the United States first of land between the Appalachian Mountains and the Mississippi and then of lands stretching from the Mississippi to the Rocky Mountains.[7] Seldom in history have a son's deeds so magnificently extended a father's profession and vision.

Jefferson prepared himself for his destiny by being one of history's most conscientious students. In this he was like our most admirable Captain Cook. As a student he adopted "a marathon routine of studying" devoting himself to his books—in philosophy, political theory and law—sixteen hours a day. In his own words, he "was bold in the pursuit of knowledge."

Jefferson emerged from his prodigious immersion in the classic texts, much of it spent in independent study, as a magnificently prepared lawyer. While constitutional law would become his hallmark, the young Jefferson, admitted to the Virginia bar in 1766, devoted himself tirelessly and resourcefully to the practice of frontier law. Jefferson philosophically and physically always faced west (indeed Monticello faces west), turning his back on the old world that he disliked. It was the frontier that summoned his attention and framed much of his grand strategy.

During Jefferson's college and postgraduate years of study, the frontier had literally changed hands. When Jefferson rode off to the College of William and Mary in 1760, "much of North America from the St. Lawrence basin to the Gulf of Mexico was still in French hands."[8] By the time he had graduated, Britain (with one hundred and fifty-six ships of the line to France's seventy-seven) had drubbed France in the Seven Year's War and taken possession of all French real estate from the Arctic Circle to the Falkland Islands. Thus, when Jefferson began his practice as a "land tenure lawyer in the fluid upland region" of Virginia, the frontier, which he loved, was in British hands, which he loathed.

The British exerted their authority over the frontier by issuing a royal proclamation in 1763 "closing the west between the Appalachian Mountains and the Mississippi River to white settlers and protecting it as an Indian reserve."[9] This "massive extension of British authority" especially challenged Virginians who claimed land to the banks of the Mississippi and who, among all the colonists, were, when it came to land, the most "aggressive" and "greedy." For his part, Jefferson could literally see from his Monticello hilltop the British line delimiting white settlement and he "had long been privy to a Virginia scheme to capture from Britain the country between the Appalachian Mountains and the Mississippi River."[10] He was determined to breach the line drawn by the British and so too were George Washington and Benjamin Franklin "both of whom sought at this very time vast personal claims to western land so recently wrested from French domination."[11]

Britain, however, was, at least temporarily, in the driver's seat. In this position it formally established in 1774 a governing authority based in Quebec with power to administer all North American lands captured from the French running as far south as the Ohio River. The famous Quebec Act of 1774 cut Virginia off from "much of her claimed western territory" and incited the wrath of "stock holders of major land companies including Jefferson and his neighbors, the Walkers, George Washington and several of the Lees, Benjamin Franklin of Philadelphia and other investors from Massachusetts to South Carolina who had been pressing claims to western lands for up to a quarter of a century."[12]

With this act, the British unwittingly forged a formidable American coalition of frontiersmen, merchants and planters determined to make good their frontier claims. Thus did British arbitrary control of the frontier become a summons to revolution on a par with the more famous outcry against "taxation without representation." For his part, Jefferson's "interest in the West was as active as any war hawk's."[13]

Jefferson was soon in a personal position to deliver a counterblow. As a revolutionary war Governor of Virginia, Jefferson clandestinely supported in 1777 an expedition led by George Rogers Clark (older brother of the famous William Clark) to capture the old French forts in the Northwest Territory and to chart and effectively claim this territory for Virginia.[14] Clark's army of several hundred, augmented by alliances with the French en route, marched 1,000 miles, rowed their way up rivers, shot treacherous rapids in flat boats and succeeded in capturing strategic outposts. The success of the Clark campaign, vigorously, almost fanatically, supported by Jefferson, laid the basis for American claims to the Northwest Territory in negotiations in Paris which ended the Revolutionary War. The Treaty of Paris in 1783 moved America's boundary to the Mississippi, doubling its pre-revolutionary war size, incorporating the Northwest Territories and much of what was subsequently referred to as the Midwest. Jefferson, who has been characterized as being "mesmerized" by the West, had, from his expansive base in Virginia, figured centrally in preparing the ground for the doubling of his country's geographic dimensions.

Fifteen years later, he would have an opportunity, this time as President of the United States, to do it again. This time the territory involved lay west of the Mississippi, in a vast, vaguely defined area, known as Louisiana. Jefferson coveted this immense property as a kind of promised land in which an American republic would find the space he believed was required for the practice of democracy and the generation of prosperity. Jefferson's political philosophy was rooted in the requirement of *lebensraum*.

While Ambassador in Paris in 1788, Jefferson had talked with John Ledyard, an American from Connecticut who had accompanied Captain Cook on his third voyage. On that voyage, Ledyard was the first American to set foot on the Pacific Northwest. Jefferson urged him to lead an expedition west from the Mississippi to the Pacific. Ledyard decided to explore Africa instead; but Jefferson tucked the idea away and carried it with him to Washington when he became president of the United States in 1801.

When Jefferson assumed office, Louisiana was nominally in Spanish hands. This suited Americans fine since Spain was perceived as the weakest of the European powers and its control of Louisiana was essentially rhetorical. On the ground, America was taking over Louisiana, steadily penetrating it with migration and commerce. It was assumed that Louisiana would simply fall to the United States by the push of demographics and the pull of economics and that Spanish dominion would essentially be swept away by an irresistible American tide. That process was well underway when the tables suddenly turned. In October of 1800, Spain entered into a secret agreement with Napoleon, offering to recede Louisiana to France in return for a kingdom in northern Italy (the magnificent Tuscany region) that was a French possession. When word of this secret retrocession reached Jefferson in Washington in the spring of 1801, his reaction was historically akin to President Kennedy's reaction to the Cuban missile crisis. It was as if France—that was, at the time, Europe's premier military power—intended to emplace ballistic missiles in New Orleans. He announced that France in possession of Louisiana would be America's enemy and that in response America would be obliged not only to mobilize for war, but to "marry itself to the British fleet and nation."[15] This was a remarkable policy stance for a man who was a rabid Francophile and Anglophobe.

A series of events made war—which became a bipartisan rallying cry—unnecessary. The famous Thomas Paine suggested to Jefferson that Napoleon, whose treasury was bare, might be willing to sell Louisiana to the United States. Jefferson thus followed a two-track policy; to wit: mobilizing for, and threatening, war while dispatching James Monroe to Paris to join the U.S. Ambassador there, Robert Livingston, the former Minister of Foreign Affairs under the Confederation, to negotiate the sale of Louisiana. It is likely that this negotiation in the old world would have failed had not events in the new world come to the rescue.

Napoleon wanted Louisiana as a breadbasket for a western empire. The crown jewel of that empire was to be—of all places—Santo Domingo, on the island first discovered, and then essentially destroyed, by Columbus. At this time Santo Domingo was in the hands of descendants of black slaves who had been imported to work the island's plantations as the Amerindians died off. The blacks had successfully revolted and controlled the island under the leadership of the charismatic Toussaint L'Ouverture. Napoleon was determined to reoccupy the island and establish it as a hub of a western trading empire.

As the retrocession of Louisiana was in train, Napoleon sent the largest armada ever dispatched to the Caribbean to wrest Santo Domingo from black control. The effort was a gigantic failure, enormously costly to France in blood and treasure. In a failed siege of Santo Domingo, an estimated 50,000 French soldiers were either killed in the guerilla war or lost to yellow fever.[16] This debacle, which materialized as negotiations for the sale of Louisiana unfolded, removed a lynchpin from Napoleon's imperial plans in the western hemisphere and robbed Louisiana of much of its strategic significance to him. Facing a likely war with Britain, needing to restore a treasury drained in part by his Caribbean debacle, and seizing an opportunity to befriend America (and moot an Anglo-American alliance), Napoleon agreed to part with Louisiana for $15,000,000, or roughly three cents an acre. The United States, which did not have $15,000,000 at the time (it was an amount twice the existing Federal budget), agreed to pay in bonds bearing interest of 6% and maturing in 15 years. With this agreement in hand, Jefferson had in his pocket his "greatest presidential triumph"—the peaceful acquisition of one third of a vast continent for pennies on the acre.

On October 20, 1803, Jefferson "proclaimed the Louisiana treaty the law of the land."[17] The territory was formally delivered by France to the United States on December 20. With that acquisition, America then possessed land "the size of all Europe."[18] A wave of extravagant imperial celebrations ensued, crowned in late January 1804 "with a ball for 500 in Georgetown."[19] Jefferson's coup was widely viewed as "the greatest diplomatic success recorded in American history."[20]

Throughout the crisis precipitated by Spain's retrocession of Louisiana to the French, Jefferson acted brilliantly. He was at the top of his game because the prize—a vast new frontier—transfixed him. His blending of the threat of force, and of opportunistic strategic alliance, with diplomacy was masterful. The adoption of the idea of purchasing Louisiana was a stroke of genius and its implementation deftly handled. His exploitation of the bipartisan character of the cause of western expansion was brilliant. And his finessing of all constitutional barriers to the unilateral acquisition by the Executive branch of territory that doubled the size of the country, demonstrated that America's foremost democrat would act like an autocrat—and assume broad extra-constitutional powers—when western expansion was at stake.

Autocracy did not stop with the ratification by the Senate of the treaty conveying Louisiana to the United States. It extended to the arrangements for governance of the new territory. The territory, which stretched from the Mississippi in the east to the Rockies in the west, and from Canada's southern border in the north to New Orleans in the south, was, at the time of its purchase, occupied by roughly 60,000 inhabitants: Indian, French, Spanish, German and American. Jefferson—the author of American self-government—announced these people unfit for self-rule and essentially placed them under a trusteeship. In other words, Louisiana became an American colony. It was so administered partly—perhaps largely—because Jefferson feared that a self-governing Louisiana might secede from the United States.[21] Once possessed of the promised-land, he had no intention of letting it go.

Holding it fast would be facilitated by knowing what was possessed. In anticipation of this requirement, Jefferson had projected and set in motion an expedition to transit Louisiana from the Mississippi to the Pacific Ocean even before it was formally acquired by the United States. Jefferson wished to find a navigable river to the West—a functional equivalent of the elusive Northwest passage—that could carry American trade along its route "and to the Pacific and Asia."[22] In conceiving of the expedition, and then assigning it to a "Corps of Discovery" led by Meriwether Lewis and William Clark, Jefferson explicitly sought "to discover the way by which Americans may some day extend their population and their influence to the coasts of the South Sea."[23] With Louisiana now formally in American hands, this expedition and its hoped-for results assumed even greater urgency and importance.

The Jefferson led acquisition of the Louisiana territory (which proved to have impressively elastic boundaries), moved America dramatically toward the shores of the South Sea, first claimed for Spain by Balboa and first transited for Spain by Magellan. It set the stage for America to "grow in gulps."[24]

> Other chapters modeled after the 'affair of Louisiana' would follow in 1819 (the acquisition of Spanish held Florida), 1845 (the annexation of Texas), and 1848 and 1853 (the acquisition from Mexico of the Pacific southwest and California) until the flag of the American republic flew over a continental empire that spread unbroken from the Atlantic to the Pacific.[25]

Once on the shores of the two great seas, America, in the later words of Theodore Roosevelt, clasped the crescent of an ocean in either hand. With the coasts of two oceans in its hands—and the world's most fertile land lying between them—America inexorably rose to a position of global preeminence. That rise was confidently predicted by Robert Livingston, co-negotiator of the Louisiana Purchase, who, upon the successful conclusion of the negotiations, announced that: "from this day the United States take their place among powers of the first rank." Taking possession of that exalted rank in turn moved the main axis of world communication and commerce further west, from the North Atlantic to North America itself. For his part, Jefferson, two centuries ago, "pushed the United States to the Pacific Rim." That Rim, in its turn, is poised today to pull the world's center of gravity even further west.

NOTES

1. Robert W. Tucker and David C. Hendrickson, *Empire of Liberty* (New York: Oxford University Press, 1990), 101.
2. Jefferson possessed "a peculiar felicity of expression" noted for its "simplicity and elegance." See Tucker and Hendrickson, op. cit., 3–4.
3. Ibid., ix.
4. Willard Randall, *Thomas Jefferson: A Life* (New York: Henry Holt & Co. 1994), 6.
5. Ibid., 7.
6. Ibid., 13.
7. "The central figure of early American diplomacy was Thomas Jefferson." Tucker and Hendrickson, op. cit., viii.
8. Randall, op. cit., 69.
9. Ibid., 72.
10. Lawrence F. Kaplan, *Thomas Jefferson: Westward the Course of Empire* (Wilmington: Scholarly Resources, Inc. 1999), 20.
11. Randall, op. cit., 99.
12. Ibid., 219.
13. Kaplan, op. cit., 147.
14. For Jefferson's support of the Clark mission, see: Kaplan, op. cit., 21.
15. Ibid., 126.
16. For a description of the debacle, see: Kaplan, op. cit., 139.
17. Alexander DeConde, *The Affair of Louisiana* (New York: Charles Scribner, 1976), 219.
18. Dale Van Every, *Ark of Empire: The American Frontier: 1784–1803* (New York: William Morrow & Co., 1963), 356.
19. DeConde, op. cit., 207.
20. Kaplan, op. cit., 150.

21. See Kaplan, op. cit., 80.

22. Randall, op. cit., 568.

23. DeConde, op. cit., 130.

24. Gerald F. Kreyche, *Visions of the American West* (Lexington: University of Kentucky Press, 1989), 5.

25. DeConde, op. cit., 240.

BIBLIOGRAPHY

DeConde, Alexander. *The Affair of Louisiana*. New York: Charles Scribner, 1976.

Kaplan, Lawrence S. *Thomas Jefferson: Westward the Course of Empire*. Wilmington: Scholarly Resources, Inc., 1999.

Kreyche, Gerald F. *Visions of the American West*. Lexington: University of Kentucky Press, 1989.

Randall, Willard. *Thomas Jefferson: A Life*. New York: Henry Holt & Co., 1997.

Tucker, Robert C. and David C. Hendrickson. *Empire of Liberty*. New York, Oxford University Press, 1990.

Van Every, Dale. *Ark of Empire: The American Frontier: 1784–1803*. New York: William Morrow & Co., 1903.

White, Patrick C. T., ed. *Conducting the Diplomacy of the New Nation: 1793–1815*. New York: Jerome S. Ozer, Publisher Inc., 1971.

14

THEODORE ROOSEVELT AND THE PANAMA CANAL

"Speak softly and carry a big stick, you will go far."

—Theodore Roosevelt

"The Panama Canal would not have been started if I had not taken hold of it."

—Theodore Roosevelt

Before turning to TR and his canal, let us briefly review the road we have thus far traveled.

As ocean highways were opened by intrepid mariners, a process of world transformation unfolded—driven by merchants and missionaries, explorers and exploiters, conquerors and colonizers—and power gradually shifted from East to West. From the eastern Mediterranean (Istanbul and Venice), to southwestern Europe (Spain and Portugal), from southwestern Europe to northwestern Europe (the Netherlands, England and France), and from northwest Europe to the western hemisphere—to the New World itself.

A primary impetus for all this derived from a quest for the riches of the East. Thus, the search for ocean routes to the Indies. In the early 19th century, these routes stood very much as they did at the end of the 16th century. They consisted of the route east around the Cape of Good Hope and through the Strait of Malacca (the Vasco da Gama era) and of the route west, across the ocean sea and through the Strait of Magellan (the Columbus/Magellan era) or around Cape Horn (discovered and named by the Dutch). Both routes—both east and west—were long, tedious, dangerous and costly. From the very beginning—from Columbus's third voyage—the search was on to find a short-cut to the Indies—via a pass through the Isthmus of Central America or a northwest passage through the continental United States or Canada.

The breakthroughs—both literally and figuratively—to more direct—and thus faster and cheaper—ocean routes to Asia came in the mid-19th and early 20th centuries. And they were made, not by mariners, but by engineers. Not by the Portuguese and Spanish; but by the French and the Americans. Not by ships and guns; but by mechanical devices and medical discoveries.

The first of these breakthroughs was the Suez Canal which shortened the eastern routes to Asia by 6,000 miles. Built between 1859 and 1869 by a French syndicate led by the legendary Ferdinand de Lesseps, the Suez Canal, cut from the Mediterranean to the Red Sea at sea level, obviated, for those who chose to transit it, the long and perilous passage around the African cape. It telescoped the distance between the West and the East and intensified the commercial and cultural contact between the Occident and the Orient. The canal itself—as an engineering feat—and as a financial bonanza—testified to European world supremacy, to European world dominance in the middle of the 19th century.

The baton of that supremacy, that dominance—which was wrought of both ingenuity and money—was soon to pass to American hands. And the symbol of that transfer of power, that transfer of predominance, was no less than the construction, by American means, of the Panama Canal. Suez marked a pinnacle of European world hegemony; Panama marked the preview of American world hegemony. And both marked the man-made completion of faster routes to the riches of Asia over unfettered, defensible sea lanes.

A canal through the Isthmus of Central America was a dream since Columbus discovered that a continent lay between him and Asia, since Balboa hacked his way across the Isthmus to become the first European known to have laid eyes on the Pacific, since Magellan fought his way through the tempestuous waters of the strait that bears his name.[1]

The fulfillment of that dream simply awaited a concerting, a conjoining, of ambition, resources and leadership. America provided a unique convergence of all three factors at the end of the 19th century. And Theodore Roosevelt, a cross between a Yankee blueblood and a Western cowboy, embodied, expressed and acted upon that convergence.

Much was awry in the world as it transited from the 19th to the 20th century. Some of what was awry is magnificently captured and chronicled in Barbara Tuchman's best-ever book, *The Proud Tower.*[2] It portrays a decadent, complacent, arrogant Europe and a crude, boisterous, confident America. Indeed, an American Heritage history book of fin d'siecle 19th century America is entitled *The Confident Years*. Tuchman's book dramatizes the seemingly hopeless class disparities in wealth and power that fueled the anarchist movement—a movement which—when an anarchist assassinated President William McKinley—ushered Theodore Roosevelt into the White House.

Whatever else—for better or worse—was going on in the world in the late 19th century, it can be argued that the main event underway at the time was the completion of continental America—from sea to shining sea—and the search for what to do next.

That continental completion had the attributes—in retrospect—of a steam roller. Starting with the Louisiana Purchase in 1804 and ending with the Alaskan purchase in 1867, the people who came to the United States on the ocean highway established by Columbus, settled the expanse of the continent and stitched it together—coast to coast—with a network of canals and railroads. By 1869 (the same year the Suez Canal was completed) a transcontinental railroad running from the Missouri to the Pacific was christened. Not long after, the Census Bureau was forced by demographic realities to declare that an American frontier no longer existed. At that point, the burning question became: "what next?" As Woodrow Wilson exclaimed in 1897—as a professor at Princeton: "The nation is made. Where do we go from here?"

Wilson did not venture an answer. But a small group of confident and determined men were all too eager to respond. They were, most conspicuously, Theodore Roosevelt, Henry Cabot Lodge and Alfred Thayer Mahan—all born in the middle of the 19th century, all exhibiting the hallmarks of those who came to their maturity in the "confident years."

Mahan was the guru of the triumvirate. He provided the conceptual framework. That framework was articulated between the covers of his enormously influential book, published in 1887, entitled *The Influence of Sea Power on History.*[3] That book argued that no great nation could long endure without the protective arm of a great fleet, globally deployed and supported with forward bases. Mahan's thesis was a logical extension of the discovery made by the Portuguese and implemented by the shipboard cannon of Vasco de Gama and Alfonoso de Albuquerque in the early 16th century.

It would be impossible to exaggerate the influence of Mahan's book.[4] It was adopted as the gospel by foreign powers who honored him—most conspicuously England and Germany—and by incipient imperialists in the United States who quoted him—most conspicuously Theodore Roosevelt and Henry Cabot Lodge.[5] For aggressive Americans, Mahan's thesis provided the answer to Woodrow Wilson's question of "where do we go from here?" We should go west beyond the water's edge to plant the American flag on a new frontier of commercial activity protected by an American fleet and accompanying bases. Should some justification beyond the need for America to exert herself to maintain her dynamism be needed, then that would be provided by Rudyard Kipling who wrote a convenient sidebar to Mahan which read as follows: "Take up the white man's burden; send forth the best ye breed; go bind your sons to exile; to serve your captives' need."

The missing ingredients needed for the United States to follow the summons of Mahan and Kipling were threefold: a navy, an inter-oceanic canal through which to deploy it, and bases abroad from which to provision and protect it. All three absent but essential ingredients were provided to a large degree by that bull in a china shop, that irrepressible adolescent, that champion of the big stick, that explorer, warrior and statesman, Theodore Roosevelt.[6]

Theodore Roosevelt was born in New York City in 1858. His father was strong, handsome, wealthy, philanthropic and devoted to his family. His mother was a beautiful, but neurotic, southern bell. Teddy for his part was a frail, near-sighted odd-ball whose youth featured regular asthmatic attacks and a compulsion to collect and dissect insects, reptiles and birds.[7] By the time Teddy was eleven "he had collected over 1000 stuffed animals and birds."[8] He was tutored at home, read "omnivorously," taken on grand tours of Europe by his resourceful and indefatigable father, placed on a regimen of exercise to build himself up and finally sent off to Harvard.[9] Arriving at Harvard, a classmate observed "I wonder whether he is the real thing or only the bundle of eccentricities which he appears."[10] While there, his hero (whom he called "Brave Heart")—his loving and seemingly indestructible father—died. His example and his inspiration were henceforth young Teddy's constant companions.[11]

Teddy graduated from Harvard *magna cum laude,* standing 21st in a class of 177. He then immediately married a Boston Brahmin girl—Alice Lee Saltonstall (whom he had zealously courted) and almost as immediately got himself elected (at age 27) to the New York state Assembly.[12] En route, he wrote a book on *The Naval War of 1812* which became a classic in its field.

He rose rapidly to prominence and influence in the New York Assembly; but while doing so his bright and shining life was dealt a double blow. His beloved wife died in childbirth and his precious mother died a day later, in the very same house, of typhoid fever. Soon thereafter, Teddy left his young daughter, Alice, in the care of his elder sister and dropped out, packing himself and his broken heart off to the Bad Lands of the Dakotas. He rarely mentioned his wife's name again.

In the Dakotas, Teddy admired and acquired the "manly virtues" of which he was such an ardent advocate and exemplar. They were the virtues of a frontiersman: fearlessness, toughness, resourcefulness. He plunged wholeheartedly into the life of the frontier, purchasing a cattle ranch, hunting buffalo and bear and tracking down thieves. He became a frontiersman, lock, stock and barrel. Later in life, TR (as he will now be called) said: "If it had not been for my years in North Dakota, I would never have become president of the United States."[13]

After several years in the Wild West, TR returned to New York, ran unsuccessfully for Mayor, married a childhood friend, Edith Carrow, and devoted himself, with some success, to writing. Soon his ambition for public service was requited with an appointment to the U.S. Civil Service Commission and TR moved himself and his family to Washington. There he became a figure of some prominence, leading the charge for civil service reform (which involved challenging the entrenched and corrupt system of patronage) and joining a distinguished social circle which included John Hay, Henry Cabot Lodge, Henry Adams and, sometimes, Rudyard Kipling.[14]

From his fight in Washington against patronage, TR moved back to New York where he was appointed to, and became chairman of, the Police Commission. There he led crusades against graft—often prowling the streets at night, sometimes on a bicycle, to find policemen in league with gangsters and prostitutes—and against serving beer in bars on Sundays.[15] (The latter crusade earning him a reputation as a spoilsport and a "prude on the prowl.")

Meanwhile, TR's cherished frontier had disappeared. The Census Bureau announced as much and TR became preoccupied—some would say obsessed—with the question of what next. He came under the sway of Alfred Mahan who argued for blue water sea power, of Henry Cabot Lodge who believed that the United States should join the march of countries acquiring real estate abroad, and of the historian, John Fiske, who had revived the concept of "manifest destiny" (first articulated in 1845) and argued that the English-speaking peoples were equipped and obligated to run the world.

Embracing and elaborating upon these ideas, TR sought a position from which to implement them. This he found with an appointment as Assistant Secretary of the Navy in 1897, in the first McKinley Administration. From that position, in a burst of feverish activity, he extolled the virtues of combat, beefed up the navy, readied the Asian fleet commanded by Admiral George Dewey to blockade the Spanish fleet in the Philippines and called for a war with Spain over the insurrection in Cuba.[16]

Thanks to an explosion on the warship *Maine* while anchored in Havana harbor, the loss of 250 sailors and the fervor of a jingoist press, TR got his war with Spain in 1898 (notwithstanding the fact that there wasn't then, and isn't now, conclusive proof that the Spanish were responsible for the explosion).[17]

The war with Spain placed America in charge of Cuba (which had been discovered by Columbus), Puerto Rico and the archipelago of the Philippines (which had been discovered by Magellan). These possessions, and the recent acquisition of Hawaii, made it inevitable that America would build an inter-oceanic canal to connect them. The only questions remaining were where and when.

TR not only got his war with Spain he got to fight in it. He enjoyed the fight immensely and emerged, rather miraculously, as a war hero after his legendary charge up San Juan Hill (which TR later called "the greatest day in my life").[18] His post-war notoriety as the commander of the colorful and fearless Rough Riders, catapulted him first into the governorship of New York in 1998 and then the Vice-Presidency of the United States in 1900. An assassin's bullet placed him in the presidency in September of 1901. He then blew into Washington "like a tornado off the Great Plains."[19]

From his "bully pulpit" in what he named the "White House," Theodore Roosevelt, whom the leading Republican kingmaker of the day, Mark Hanna, had variously called a "madman" and a "damned cowboy," moved decisively and, when necessary, unilaterally, to have a transoceanic canal built. In rapid succession he made key decisions and took bold action.

First, he decided to advocate a Panamanian rather than a Nicaraguan route, persuaded on engineering grounds that the Isthmus was preferable, reinforced by the fact that the French had left a big ditch there in a failed attempt to build a sea level canal. This attempt was led by Ferdinand de Lesseps, the legendary impresario of the construction of the Suez Canal. His project to replicate his feat in Suez foundered in the face of his decision to try to dig a sea level canal in a zone plagued by Yellow Fever. Both challenges overwhelmed the French effort, leaving behind a catastrophic bankruptcy but also "a navigable water passage 25 feet deep and 70 feet wide for a distance of 11 miles."[20]

Prevailing in his choice of Panama, TR then arranged to buy the French interests for $40,000,000, the largest real estate transaction in American history up to that time. Then, failing to establish a right to the route through treaty negotiations with Columbia, he aided and abetted a comic opera of a revolution in Panama which paved the way, so to speak, for the acquisition of the desired route. This has been described as "the most controversial act of his presidency" but the one of which he was most proud![21]

With the route and the French ditch in hand, Roosevelt then made the crucial decision—against prevailing opinion—to opt for a lock canal rather than a sea level canal. The latter scheme had brought the French to their knees. The former would help assure American success.

There then unfolded a massive public works project and a formidable public health project aimed at conquering Yellow Fever. As the work progressed on both projects, TR paid a visit to Panama in 1906 (becoming the first American president to leave the country while in office) and climbed into the driver's seat of a bulldozer. It provided a perfect image of the man at the controls of a world transforming undertaking. (He then, curiously enough, never visited the canal again, not even for its opening in 1914.)

TR's canal—a towering engineering accomplishment—had multiple powerful ramifications. It helped get the U.S. on its feet industrially and served as a "standing monument to its constructive ability."[22] By cutting 9,000 miles off a seaborne east-west trip, it connected the country's two coasts and helped to make "the giant of the West" an operational unit. It immeasurably facilitated trade on a global basis. And it served as the essential vehicle to make good upon the "large policy" advocated by Mahan, enabling the U.S. to project its gathering strength abroad.[23]

The spirit of TR's enterprise, and his modus operandi, were captured by a statement made by him and another made by Joe Cannon, the then Speaker of the House. TR said he "built the canal and left Congress to debate him, not the canal." Cannon said, TR "has about as much regard for the constitution as a tomcat has for a marriage license."

TR's canal, constructed under the banner of "A Continent Divided—A World United," was opened (on budget!) in 1914, ironically on the very day World War I broke out.

Looking back, it is possible to see that World War I and the construction of the Panama Canal converged to place the United States in the driver's seat of world affairs. The political, financial and physical carnage of World War I demoted European powers to second rank as the United States emerged practically unscathed and with new industrial and maritime strength developed in the course of the war. For its part, the Panama Canal facilitated the deployment of that strength through the sea lanes of two great oceans on a global basis. The war and the canal combined to shift the main axis of world commerce and communication to America.

TR did not wait for the completion of the canal to signal that that shift already was well underway. Instead, in 1907, he decided to showcase America's emergent power by sending a "Great White Fleet" of sixteen battleships, numerous escort craft and 8,000 uniformed personnel on an east-west cruise around the world.[24] Doing so would display the muscle of the giant of the West; remind the Japanese, with whom we were then at odds, of America's naval superiority; impress the world with our newly developed and deployable strength; and build popular support for the Navy's continued expansion. The "Great White Fleet" returned in 1908 with all objectives fully achieved and the "Giant of the West" in clear forward motion.

NOTES

1. "The resolution of a dream as old as the voyages of Columbus." David McCullough, *The Path Between the Seas: The Creation of the Panama Canal 1870–1914* (New York: Simon and Shuster, 1977), 12.

2. Barbara Tuchman, *The Proud Tower: A Portrait of the World Before the War 1890–1914* (New York: The Macmillan Co., 1965).

3. A. F. Mahan, *The Influence of Sea Power on History* (New York: Dover Publications, Inc., 1887).

4. Mahan's book "planted the poisonous seed of the Anglo-German naval rivalry that became a root cause of WWI." Ivan Musicant, *Empire by Default: The Spanish American War and the Dawn of the American Century* (New York: Henry Holt and Co., 1998), 10.

5. See R. W. Brands, *T R: The Last Romantic* (New York: Basic Books, 1997), 309.

6. McCullough puts it this way: "Rarely had there ever been so neat and effective a practice of all that Captain Mahan had preached." McCullough, op. cit., 379.

7. Kathleen Dalton, *Theodore Roosevelt: A Strenuous Life New York* (Alfred A. Knopf, 2002), 21.

8. Ibid., 41.

9. Ibid., 7–10.

10. Brands, op. cit., 68.

11. See Dalton, op. cit., 34 and Brands, op. cit., 78–84.

12. At an early age, TR announced that "he intended to be one of the governing class." Brands, op. cit., 126.

13. Edmund Morris, *The Rise of Theodore Roosevelt* (New York: McCann and Geohagen, Inc., 1979), 374.

14. See Brands, op. cit., 221.

15. Ibid., 279.

16. Brands puts it this way: "TR worked ardently" to bring about U.S. interference in Cuba. Op. cit., 324.

17. Secretary Long thought that TR "came very near to causing more of an explosion than happened to the Maine." Brands, op. cit., 320.

18. Ibid., 257.

19. Ibid., 419.

20. McCullough, op. cit., 440.

21. Brands, op. cit., 586.

22. Ibid., 429.

23. See Musicant, op. cit., 329–330.

24. Brands, op. cit., 611.

BIBLIOGRAPHY

Brands, R. W. *T R: The Last Romantic.* New York: Basic Books, 1997.

Dalton, Kathleen. *Theodore Roosevelt: A Strenuous Life*. New York: Alfred A. Knopf, 2002.

Mahan, A. F. *The Influence of Sea Power on History*. New York: Dover Publications, Inc., 1987.

McCullough, David. *The Path Between the Seas: The Creation of the Panama Canal 1870–1914*. New York: Simon and Schuster, 1977.

Morris, Edmund. *The Rise of Theodore Roosevelt.* New York. McCann and Geohagen, Inc., 1979.

Musicant, Ivan. *Empire by Default: The Spanish American War and the Dawn of the American Century*. New York: Henry Holt and Co., 1998.

Pringle, Henry F. *Theodore Roosevelt.* New York: Harcourt Brace & Co., 1984.

Tuchman, Barbara. *The Proud Tower: A Portrait of the World Before the War 1890–1914.* New York: The Macmillan Co., 1965.

15

WINSTON CHURCHILL

"A small, befreckled, under-sized, ginger-haired runt of a boy, who came to his first English school possessed of a lisp and few friends."

—John Charmley, *Churchill: The End of Glory*

"It was the nation and the race dwelling all round the globe that had the lion's heart: I had the luck to be called upon to give the roar."

—Sir Winston Churchill, Prime Minister, speech in Westminster Hall

We left off with the completion of the Panama Canal, built under the banner of "A Continent Divided—A World United." Its grand opening in 1914 coincided with the outbreak of the First World War. World War I—often referred to by the Europeans as "The Great War"—then raged on for four and a quarter dreadful years.

With respect to the Great War, memory of it has, in the words of historian Niall Ferguson, fallen into the "historical void" between the American Civil War and World War II. This is most unfortunate inasmuch as the Great War spawned a chaotic and bloody 20th century and continues to condition the world we live in today.

George Kennan has called WW I "the great seminal catastrophe of the 20th century." In his book "The Pity of War," the historian Niall Ferguson calls WW I "the greatest error in modern history."[1] However it is described, the war was cataclysmic across-the-board. It first buried and mutilated vast numbers of soldiers and civilians. Ten million soldiers were killed (sometimes upwards of 100,000 in a single battle and on average 6,000 a day for four and a quarter years), another twenty-one million were seriously wounded, eight million of whom returned home permanently disabled. Twenty-two million civilians were killed or maimed. Eight million horses were killed. The war from hell (fought with terrible new weapons—the machine gun, poisonous gas, the submarine and from 6,000 miles of trenches in which "the unknown killed the unseen") wiped out a generation (France lost a quarter of its male population between the ages of eighteen and thirty), wrecked entire countries and empires, threw the Middle East into disorder and then spawned an early twentieth century featuring communism, fascism, totalitarianism, revanchism, civic and social violence, class conflict and yet another world war.

One looks back on all the pain and finds absolutely no gain. The world was infinitely better off before the war than in its aftermath. Which supplies a powerful argument for those who argue that the war should never have been fought in the first place.[2]

WW II was another matter. It had to be fought because the world faced a dark threat from Nazi Germany which, had it not been confronted and thwarted, would have turned the clock back on civilization.

On the ramparts of the western world, fearlessly confronting the threat, was Winston Churchill. He stood as "the standard bearer" and the sole defender of the Western democracies at their hour of greatest peril.[3] If a single man can be credited with saving the day for the West, it was a man who, as a youth, struggled to get out of the starting gate.

Winston Spencer Churchill was born into "the highest echelon" of British society November 30, 1874.[4] His mother, Jennie Jerome, was a promiscuous American beauty. His father, Lord Randolph Churchill, was a prominent English orator and politician.

Winston admired his parents but they essentially neglected him. His father, whom he worshipped, remained aloof and critical. Winston could account for no more than "three or four long intimate conversations with him."[5] Young Winston was on the receiving end of letters from his father that expressed "the bleakest view" of his educational career and warned that he was on his way to becoming a "social wastrel."[6] Sent off to boarding school at an early age, Winston was deprived of the satisfaction of getting to know his father. It was a deprivation that drove him through life as he sought to live up to his father's expectations and disprove his father's predictions.

His father had substantial grounds for fearing for the future of his son because Winston was wayward from the start. He slouched to his own drummer. And right from the start he showed a proclivity for what one critic has called "jay walking through life."[7] Put another way, Churchill showed early signs of being a crank, an eccentric—a label he wore as a kind of badge of honor.

Ample evidence of his waywardness was provided in his early boarding school education, that he stoutly resisted. In his own words:

> How I hated this school, and what a life of anxiety I lived there for more than two years. I made very little progress at my lessons. . . . I counted the days and hours . . . when I should return home from this hateful servitude. . . . My teachers saw me as at once backward and precocious . . . reading books beyond my years and yet at the bottom of the Forum. They were offended. They had large resources of compulsion at their disposal, but I was stubborn. Where my reason, imagination or interest was not engaged, I would not or I could not learn."[8]

As one biographer has put it: "The little Churchill was a tough proposition for any organized system of education."[9]

Where his interest was engaged, and what he did learn, ultimately came to the rescue of the Western world, namely the English language. On account of his refusal to learn Latin and Greek, he was, at Harrow, retained in the lowest Forum. In consequence, as his classmate went on to learn the classic languages, Churchill was taught English. In his own words:

> We were considered such dunces that we could only learn English. . . . As I remained in the Third Forum three times as long as anyone else. I had three times as much of it. I learned it thoroughly. Thus I got into my bones the essential structure of the ordinary English sentence—which is a noble thing.[10]

Save for mastering the English language and for fencing (in which he won the Public School championship!) his schooling was a "somber patch" consisting of "an unending spell of worries that did not seem petty, and of toil uncheered by fruition; a time of discomfort, restriction and purposeless monotony." The experience left him feeling "completely outclassed and left behind at the start of the race."[11] Perhaps this initial handicap provided the incentive to win the race later in life, which he most surely and dramatically did. Looking back, he offered the following advice: "No boy or girl should ever be disheartened by lack of success in their youth, but should diligently, and faithfully, continue to persevere to make up for lost time."[12]

In many ways, Churchill was an improbable character to play a pivotal role in the history of Western civilization. His childhood was essentially dysfunctional as his parents spent most of their time complaining about him.[13] They wrote to him as follows: His mother: "Your work is an insult to your intelligence." His father upon his son having failed an exam for entry into the British infantry: "In this failure has been demonstrated beyond refutation your slovenly, happy-go-lucky, harum scarum style of work for which you have always been distinguished."[14] Given this degree of parental disapproval and accompanying neglect, it is rather astonishing that Churchill grew up essentially spoiled and expecting "to live as he pleases, doing exactly what he wanted to do when he wanted to do it."[15]

Churchill's schooling was largely a failure thanks to his stubbornness, cocksureness and mind-boggling idiosyncrasies. His early professional life exhibited flashes of brilliance as a colonial soldier and sometimes journalist; but it also featured a shameless exploitation of his mother's liaisons in his quest for public recognition and a path to power. His political career—beginning in 1900 with his election to Parliament at age 26—was sometimes brilliant but always turbulent. It featured energy, arrogance and combativeness, qualities that sometimes consigned him to the political wilderness. "Controversy accompanied him everywhere."[16] One fellow MP put it this way: "He is rash, impetuous, tactless, contentious, inconsistent, unsound and forever out of step." He complained to Lady Astor that: "We don't know what to make of him." She had a ready reply: "How about a nice rug?"[17]

Churchill's involvement in military affairs as a sometimes First Lord of the Admiralty exhibited a combination of conceptual brilliance and operational naivety. With respect to the latter quality, it has been said of him that he "was readily able to convince himself that any military operation he favored would be attended with speedy success and momentous consequences."[18] Unfortunately, as the debacle at Gallipoli so painfully demonstrated, that was not always the case.

Overall it would be possible to say that Churchill's extraordinary talents—that would be on full and effective display in 1940—had been, throughout his life, hampered by flaws in judgment and temperament.

This having been said, Churchill in 1940 held in his personal and professional quivers the arrows needed to become the war Prime Minister of Great Britain and from this position lead the defense of the democracies safely through their darkest hour. It was, in fact, as if Churchill had been "preparing for a crisis like 1940 his whole life."[19]

Churchill's singular endowments and assets consisted of the following:

- He was absolutely fearless and actually looked forward to war. In his own words:

> From very early youth I had brooded about soldiers and war, and often I had imagined in dreams and day-dreams the sensations attendant upon being for the first time under fire. It seemed to my youthful mind that it must be a thrilling and immense experience to hear the whistle of bullets all around and to play at hazard from moment to moment with death and wounds.[20]

- Beyond his youth, as an adult, he believed "that the great issues of his time would be decided on the battlefields."[21]
- Churchill had been an early and ardent critic of Neville Chamberlain's policy of appeasement, observing at one point that while Britain's ruling class continues "to take the weekends in the country, Hitler takes his countries in the weekends."[22] He also had been an early advocate of a British defense build-up and a harsh critic and outspoken opponent of Hitler's from the mid 1930's forward.
- He had been an earnest and eloquent advocate of organizing a collective security system to contain Germany and had even proposed an alliance with Russia to this end.
- Across the decades, Churchill had served with bravery boarding on foolhardiness in the British colonial armed forces attached as a regimental officer to, seriatim: the Fourth Hussars, the 31st Punjab Infantry, the 21st Lancers, the South African Light Horse, the Oxfordshire Yeomanry, the second Grenadier Guards, the Royal Scots Fusiliers and lastly with the Oxfordshire Artillery. He had "pioneered the switch from coal to oil in the Royal Navy;" practically

invented the tank and was an early advocate of air power (as well as being an amateur pilot himself). He had fought in the trenches in the Great War. He also had served most prominently as the First Lord of the Admiralty in WW I and on the eve of WW II. He was admired—if not always trusted—by the officer corps of Britain's most powerful military asset, the Royal Navy.

- Added to these assets, and crowning them, were Churchill's rhetorical powers. These powers, acquired as he pursued his "ambition to be master of the spoken word," had been painstakingly polished through disciplined practice "including spending long hours of practicing in front of a mirror, declaiming speeches he had committed to memory."[23] And those powers had been rigorously tested and honed over the years in the formidable British House of Commons.

On May 10, 1940, with the Germans at the gates of Paris and the British forces about to be swept into the sea at Dunkirk, Churchill succeeded Neville Chamberlain as Prime Minister. The very first thing he did was to arm the English language and send it to war.

First he spoke to the House of Commons:

> I would say in this house, as I have said to those who have joined this Government, I have nothing to offer but blood, tears and sweat. . . . You ask what is our policy? I will say it is to wage war by sea, land and air with all our might and with all the strength God can give us. That is our policy. You ask what is our aim? I can answer in one word, it is victory. Victory at all costs, victory in spite of all terrors, victory however long and hard the road may be; for without victory, there is no survival.[24]

Then he spoke to the nation and, in effect, to the world:

> Side by side, the British and French peoples have advanced to rescue not only Europe but mankind from the foulest and most soul-destroying tyranny which has ever darkened and stained the pages of history. Behind us, behind the armies of Britain and France, gather a group of shattered states and bludgeoned races: the Danes, the Dutch, the Belgians. Upon all of whom a long night of barbarism, unbroken by even a star of hope, unless we conquer, as conquer we must; as conquer we shall.

> Upon this battle depends the survival of Christian civilization. Upon it depends our own British life, and the long continuity of our institutions and Empire.
>
> Hitler knows that he must break us on this Island or lose the war. If we can stand up to him all Europe may be free and the life of the world may move forward into broad, sunlit uplands. But if we fail, then the whole world, including the United States, including all we have known and cared for, will sink into the abyss of a new Dark Age, made more sinister, and perhaps more protracted, by the lights of perverted science.
>
> Let us therefor brace ourselves to our duties, and so bear ourselves, that if the British Empire and its Commonwealth last for a thousand years, Men will say "This was their finest hour."[25]

Churchill believed that wars were won by superior will power. His speeches were designed to "wrest the initiative from the enemy and impose our will on him."[26] In the words of the British philosopher Isaiah Berlin: Churchill "imposed his imagination and his will upon his countryman idealizing them with such intensity that in the end they approached his ideal and began to see themselves as he saw them. In doing so he transformed cowards into brave men, and so fulfilled the purpose of shining armor."[27]

Churchill's rhetoric was powerful and effective not only because it was skillfully crafted and dramatically delivered, but because it welled up from the depth of his convictions. In an unpublished essay found among his papers—entitled *The Scaffolding of Rhetoric*—Churchill had argued at an early age that the efficacy of rhetoric derived from fundamental, passionate belief in what was being expressed.[28] Churchill merged his convictions with his masterful command of the English language. The combination produced a powerful force.

Churchill did not sugarcoat the challenge Britain faced. Instead he promised that "death and sorrow will be the companions of our journey, hardship our garment, constancy and valor our only shield."[29] He believed that telling the people the truth would summon their greatness. "In an hour of peril such as none had ever known, Churchill's vision of the destiny of England began to fill the stage."[30]

Two horrendous years would then pass with Germany ascendant on every front before the tide would be turned and Churchill vindicated in his heroic resistance, against overwhelming odds, to a long, seemingly endless, night of barbarism.

For a year and a half—from June 1940, when the Battle of Britain was launched, until the end of 1941, when the American's entered the war—Britain was under siege at home and abroad. The defense of freedom was hanging by a thread. America's entry into the war—long sought by Churchill as the only hope for saving the democracies—and Hitler's strategic blunder in invading the Soviet Union and thus splitting his forces to wage a two-front war, inexorably turned the tide of the war. The outcome, however, remained in doubt throughout 1942, during which the Axis powers were still advancing on all fronts. Then, in mid-1943, the tide turned in three strategic theaters.

- The Allied powers, thanks chiefly to American shipbuilding capacity, regained control of the vital shipping lanes of the Atlantic.
- The British and American forces—with heroic help from New Zealand and Australian divisions—defeated the German forces in North Africa.
- Simultaneously, the Russian army first starved and then captured the German army deployed in Stalingrad.

Thus, by mid-1943, the Allied forces were in the ascendance, making Hitler's defeat now a matter of time. Tough fighting lay ahead; but from mid-1943 forward the outcome could not be in serious doubt. At that point, Churchill's decision to defy Hitler's military machine and risk reducing Great Britain to rubble, was fully and triumphantly vindicated.

Viewing World War II through the lens of the world's westward march, it is clear that Hitler's primary objective was to move it in the opposite direction—to gain living space (or *lebensraum)* in the East. Had he concentrated his awesome firepower on Russia and the Caucuses, he might well have secured vast eastern dominions. The world's center of gravity would then have been lodged powerfully there. Instead, he split his firepower between east and west. And Churchill's singlehanded defiance of that power in the West, gave the giant of the West, the United States, the time it needed to enter the war. Once it did so, the potential movement of the world's center of gravity eastward was prevented. The tide created by Columbus, Magellan and their successors resumed its course.

In 1940, during the Battle of Britain, as the Royal Air Force staved off the Luftwaffe over the British homeland, Winston Churchill famously declared that never in history had so many owed so much to so few. By 1943, it could be said of him that never before in history had the liberty of so many been owed to the fearlessness and defiant rhetoric of a single man.

As the war ground to a halt, with Germany totally defeated, the challenge of constructing a viable peace presented itself. The failed peace that followed the Great War was a haunting prospect to be avoided at all costs. Churchill was anxious to take his hand at crafting a peace that would reflect his belief "in victory magnanimity, in peace good will." But electoral defeat in 1945 would send him, visibly shaken, to the sidelines. His wife, Clementine, tried to console him in opining that his electoral defeat "may well be a blessing in disguise." To which Churchill responded: "At the moment it seems quite effectively disguised."[31]

In the course of the war, Churchill had wanted American and British forces to beat the Soviets to the occupation of major central European countries and their ancient capitals. As he put it, "I deem it highly important that we should shake hands with the Russians as far to the East as possible."[32] The Americans refused to participate in this race, which the Soviets then easily won. Once militarily installed in central Europe, the Soviet communist system was imposed upon the peoples of the captured nations and, in Churchill's famous words, an "iron curtain" descended on a divided Europe.[33] As it did, Churchill mounted the barricades again. In a history-making speech, introduced by President Truman at Westminster College in Fulton, Missouri in 1946, Churchill called for "an international armed force for the United Nations" and "a special relationship between the British Commonwealth and Empire and the United States." Once again, Churchill was summoning the New World to come to the rescue of the Old. It was a summons to which, over a period of two years, the United States, step by step, creatively responded. The statesman profiled in the next chapter was a leading architect of that response which—by conjoining the resources of America and Western Europe—securely anchored the world's westward march.

NOTES

1. Niall Ferguson, *The Pity of War: Explaining World War I* (New York: The Penguin Press, 1998).
2. See an article by Tim Stanley on the Opinion page of *The Telegraph,* November 6, 2018.
3. William Manchester, *The Last Lion: Alone 1932–1940* (New York: Bantam Doubleday Dell Publishing Group, Inc., 1989), 346.
4. Andrew Roberts, *Churchill: Walking with Destiny* (New York: Penguin Random House, 2018), 27.
5. Ibid., 26.
6. Ibid., 27.
7. William Manchester, *The Last Lion: Visions of Glory 1874–1932* (New York: Bantam Books, 1983), 21.
8. Winston Churchill, *My Early Years* (New York: Touchstone, 1958), 11.
9. John Charmley, *Churchill: The End of Glory* (New York: Harcourt Brace & Co., 1993), 12.
10. Churchill, op. cit., 161.
11. Ibid., pp. 38–39.
12. See Martin Gilbert, *Churchill: A Life* (New York: Henry Holt and Co., 1991), 64–65.
13. Charmley, op. cit., 11.
14. Roberts, op. cit., 26.
15. Manchester, *Visions,* 645.
16. Ibid., 755.
17. Ibid., 861.
18. Charmley, op. cit., 10.
19. Roberts, op. cit., 975.
20. Churchill, op. cit., 76.
21. Manchester, *Visions,* 12.
22. Manchester, *Alone,* 481.
23. Charmley, op. cit., 16.
24. Manchester *Visions,* 681.
25. Ibid., 681.
26. Gilbert, op. cit., 682.
27. Manchester, *Alone,* 682.
28. See Manchester, *Alone,* 208.
29. Ibid., 683.
30. Charmley, op. cit., 35.
31. Gilbert, op. cit., 855.
32. Ibid., 834.

33. "Those who think that Churchill had with some foresight spotted the onset of the Cold War, might be inclined to praise him for trying to alert the Americans to what was afoot; those who think that such warnings were a contributory factor in the causes of the Cold War take a different view." Charmley, op. cit., 621.

BIBLIOGRAPHY

Charmley, John. *Churchill: The End of Glory.* New York: Harcourt Brace & Co., 1993.
Churchill, Winston. *My Early Life.* New York: Touchstone, 1958.
Ferguson, Niall. *The Pity of War: Explaining World War I.* New York: The Penguin Press, 1998.
Gilbert, Martin. *Churchill, A Life.* New York: Henry Holt & Co., 1991.
Manchester, William. *The Last Lion: Visions of Glory 1874–1932.* New York: Bantam Books, 1983.
———. *The Last Lion: Alone 1932–1940.* New York: Bantam Doubleday Dell Publishing Group, Inc., 1989.
Roberts, Andrew. *Churchill: Walking with Destiny.* New York: Penguin Random House, 2018.

16

DEAN ACHESON

"The most important figure in American foreign policy since John Quincy Adams, Dean Acheson was the quintessential American realist who most fully understood and mastered the exercise of American power in the American era."

—James Chace, *Acheson: The Secretary of State Who Created the American World*

"Perhaps only with the transatlantic partnerships of the world wars in the twentieth [century], did the weight of America wrench the centre of gravity of western civilization away from its European heartlands."

—Felipe Fernández-Armesto, *Columbus*

Were this book to be devoted to American presidents who figured prominently in the world's westward march, particular attention would be paid not only to Thomas Jefferson and Theodore Roosevelt, but also to more contemporary figures including Franklin Roosevelt, Harry Truman and Richard Nixon.

Franklin Roosevelt played a decisive leadership role in saving the West in WW II which, had it been lost, would have rolled the world's center of gravity eastward and placed the world in dark and menacing hands. Harry Truman, so ably assisted by his principal foreign policy lieutenants, George Marshall and Dean Acheson, presided over the institutionalization of a western led world. Finally, Richard Nixon, backed-up by the redoubtable Henry Kissinger, oversaw the reentry of China into the family of nations, setting the stage for a Chinese renaissance, which has pulled the commercial center of the world's gravity further west to the Pacific Rim.

Each of these statesmen had a vision, which is the indispensable requirement for the exercise of leadership of historic proportions. Franklin Roosevelt's vision blended those of his hero (and uncle), Theodore Roosevelt and of his mentor, Woodrow Wilson. It envisaged a decolonized world, nourished by liberalized trade and supervised by the allied great powers, assembled at a kind of family table, at the head of which the United States would be seated. Harry Truman's vision imagined a world in which the vast resources of the United States—that had been mobilized to win a World War—would be deployed—generously and creatively—to win the peace. Richard Nixon, for his part, envisaged a world in which the global balance of power was configured in America's favor through a rapprochement with the world's most populous country, China.

Each of these figures is, in his own way, a great American statesman. Each is worthy of detailed attention. But so too is someone who might be considered a second-tier statesman—a secretary of state rather than a president. In this category, Dean Acheson, that "blade of steel" who—in the words of his biographer, James Chace—was not only present at the creation of "the American world" but was the principal architect of it, rises to the fore.[1]

Dean Gooderham Acheson was born into an upper-middle class family in Middletown, Connecticut. His father, an Episcopal minister, and his mother were of English heritage by way of Canada. His early childhood was idyllic until he was sent away to boarding school. There the tide turned in his own colorful words as follows: "The organization of boarding school, like the wolf, in Icelandic saga, which ran up the sky and devoured the sun, devoured my early freedom. I found it necessary to erect defenses for the last citadel of spiritual freedom."[2] While erecting these defenses, young Acheson performed poorly in school. At Groton he graduated at the bottom of his class. At Yale, he scraped the bottom. He was only distinguished in school by: his rebellion against authority; his wit; the courage of his convictions; his natty dressing; and his social popularity. In fact his early education was reminiscent of Winston Churchill's; which is to say that it was unremarkable.

Fortunately for Acheson (and his country) he blossomed in graduate school. There, at Harvard Law School, he discovered that "magnificent mechanism" called a brain; and there he distinguished himself, graduating near the top of his class and being elected to the editorial board of the Harvard Law Review.[3] At Harvard he came under the influence of mentors—most prominently Felix Frankfurter—later a Supreme Court Justice—who literally changed the course of his life. Frankfurter's interests in law and society pointed Acheson in the direction of public service.

Following graduation (and marriage), Acheson moved to Washington to clerk first for Justice Louis Brandeis and then for the legendary, Oliver Wendell Holmes. Under their exacting tutelage an already fine mind was even more finely honed. A flavor of his clerkship experience is imparted in Acheson's later account of working under Justice Louis Brandeis: "Justice Brandeis' standard for our work was perfection as a norm, to be bettered on special occasions."[4]

Acheson then found fortuitous employment with the prestigious Washington law firm of Covington and Burling, practicing law and arguing cases before the Supreme Court and the International Court of Justice in The Hague. Then, in 1933, Acheson joined the first administration of Franklin Roosevelt as Under Secretary of the Treasury. He did not at first like, or work well with, Roosevelt. He found him condescending and behaving as if he were royalty.[5] (Acheson was a committed foe of snobbery and pomposity, though he himself could be arrogant.) Acheson believed Roosevelt to be expedient and challenged him when Roosevelt, on his own authority, decided to change the price of gold to which the U.S. dollar was pegged. Acheson believed the President did not have the legal authority to do this. Showcasing the courage of his convictions, Acheson submitted to the President a respectful letter of resignation that was promptly accepted.

Returning to the practice of law, Acheson worried as war clouds gathered over Europe and was among the early advocates of American rearmament and alliance with the democracies. His speeches on these topics were practically mirror images of those of Winston Churchill.[6] He saw, ahead of his time, the need, in the aftermath of the war, for "a free trading system undergirded by a stable monetary system as a central building block in the postwar order."[7] Those views on international economic policy won him a return to the Roosevelt administration in 1941, as Assistant Secretary of State for Economic Affairs. From this position, and later as Assistant Secretary of State for Congressional Relations and International Conferences, Acheson provided leadership for the forging and congressional approval of the historic Lend-Lease Program in 1941, the United Nations Relief and Rehabilitation Agency (UNRRA), and the world-transforming Bretton Woods agreements in 1944. He was responsible for steering the United Nations charter through the Senate where it passed on a vote of 89 to 2.

Lend-Lease brought the New World to the rescue of the Old as it teetered on the brink. The Bretton Woods Agreements, which established the World Bank and the International Monetary Fund, provided the economic and financial underpinnings of the American led post-war world. The agreements also established the U.S. at the epicenter of the world economic system with one-third of the votes, based on the level of its subscriptions, in both the Bank and the Fund. And the United Nations provided a basis for universal collective security.

Acheson's leading role in the origins of the Lend-Lease Program, UNRRA and the Bretton Woods agreements, and his successful congressional lobbying for the United Nations, would, by themselves, have earned him a place of honor in the annals of American foreign policy. It would become, however, just the first of a series of initiatives that qualify Acheson for the title of architect of an American led world. The subsequent initiatives read like a litany of achievements in what is widely regarded as the finest hour of American diplomacy.

Before that hour arrived, American foreign policy struggled to find its feet in 1945 and '46. Harry Truman succeeded Roosevelt as president without experience in foreign affairs. Acheson immediately recognized Truman's admirable qualities of frankness, honesty and decisiveness. But before these qualities could be constructively applied, the right foreign policy team had to be put in place and the nature of the post-war world had to be figured out. This was done roughly simultaneously in 1946 when George Marshall succeeded James Byrnes as Secretary of State and when Winston Churchill visited the United States to announce that an Iron Curtain had descended in Europe. That visit was followed a year later by the formal British announcement that it could no longer sustain anti-communist aid to Greece and Turkey. This blockbusting news coincided with the dawning of a recognition in Washington that an entire world structure and order that had been inherited from the 19th century lay in ruins and that a new world structure and order had to be built with American intellectual and physical resources.

Acheson moved to the forefront in the building of it, first as Under Secretary of State to General Marshall, and then, after Truman's election as President in '48, as Secretary of State in his own right throughout the four years of Truman's elected presidency.

Acheson moved to the forefront riding a powerful premise that he, above all others, was the most effective, the most forceful and the most colorful in articulating. The premise was that the United States would be interned on its own continent, and its way of life would gradually wither, if the values and resources of Western Europe were lost to it. He set to work to obviate that outcome by binding America and Western Europe together—across Columbus's ocean highway—economically, politically and militarily.

He began, as Under Secretary, by staffing the proposal for aid to Greece and Turkey. He followed that by providing the rationale for what became the Marshall Plan and the rhetoric that sold the Plan on Capitol Hill and to the country at large. He then moved, as Secretary of State, to reinforce political stability and economic development in Europe with a collective security system, NATO, that would securely bind the U.S. to Europe. He followed this up with successful efforts to stimulate European integration, a Franco–German rapprochement and the integration of West Germany itself into NATO. The sum of these achievements amounts to no less than the creation of a new international structure featuring active and sustained American engagement and leadership. It is an awesome record, generally regarded as unrivaled in the annals of 20th century American diplomacy.

Why was Acheson so successful? What can be learned from him, his experience, his qualities, his modus operandi and his character?

With respect to experience, Acheson's preparation for his role as Secretary of State, as architect of what his biographer calls "the American world," was perfect. He was, to say the very least, properly apprenticed. He served twice in the Roosevelt administration, first in Treasury and then at State. In those positions: he observed the ill-effects of disarray as Roosevelt tried to be his own secretary of state; established a circle of colleagues at home and abroad with whom to work through problems; and gained invaluable experience in the conduct of negotiations, congressional relations and of international conferences. He then served as Under

Secretary of State under James Byrnes, who, for his part, tried to be his own president in the foreign policy field and who clashed with Truman, resulting ultimately in his resignation. Acheson learned again of the necessity for harmony and unity between the president and his secretary of state. That harmony and unity was established under General George Marshall, who served as a highly influential role model for Acheson.

This rich, hands-on experience in government service, practically uninterrupted, over eight years, through tumultuous times, helped forge and temper a "blade of steel." The blade itself was a composite of formidable intellectual and personal qualities.

Intellectually, Acheson was extraordinarily self-confident—to the point of arrogance. He was sure of himself—sometimes cocksure. And he had ample reason to be. He had a broad and synthetic mind—a finely tuned generalist's mind—that seemed to have been both a natural endowment and the product especially of his Harvard Law School education, his clerkships and his self-education as an avid reader (mostly of histories and biographies).

His son, the late David Acheson, said that his father had an uncanny ability to see all aspects of a problem, and their interrelationships, and to hold a clear picture of a multi-dimensional problem in his mind until he had precipitated a policy response.

Accompanying his formidable intellect was a carefully cultivated and maintained aura.[8] Tall, erect, mustached, impeccably groomed, affecting a European style and air, he looked like a statesman out of a classical mold.[9] Acheson believed that leadership required not simply "the direction of great affairs, but the creation and development of personality." His persona clearly reflected that conviction.

And he wrote and spoke like a statesman.[10] He had read deeply into great European statesmen and had mastered the written and spoken style of the best of them. His eloquence sometimes tripped him up when he shot from the hip or with disdain for his opposite number; but it more often rose brilliantly to the occasion and provided the persuasive rationale—the lucidity coupled with conviction—that turned the tide at watershed moments in policy making.[11]

Acheson's writing and rhetoric were buttressed by preparedness. He took time to learn what he was talking about. He did his homework and he almost always did it more thoroughly, more meticulously than those with whom he dealt. In this, he was enormously assisted by a first-rate circle of colleagues, each of whom is a household name in their own right. Acheson understood that it would be his "ability to choose and handle those under him that would be crucial to the successful conduct of foreign policy."[12] And he chose and handled extraordinarily well. A handful of his associates go by the moniker, The Wise Men, and included George Kennan, Chip Bohlen and Averell Harriman.[13] There was another handful of nearly equal stature. Acheson drew upon their capacities with extraordinary skill: orchestrating, delegating, inspiring and steadfastly supporting each one of them. His was a case study in leadership by example, by trust, by loyalty. As he put it: the Secretary of State

> Must be their protector and inspirer, their center, the appreciator of excellence, harsh toward shoddiness or conclusions contrived to comply with the currently accepted notions. He cannot be aloof. He must share and guide their thoughts, partake of their complexities . . . so that the productivity of their common work is advice which the government of this nation can wisely and practically put into execution in the world as it is.[14]

Loyalty reached a legendary level of perfection in the bond between Acheson and the "the captain with the mighty heart," Harry S Truman. The two men were as one. There was no daylight between them. Acheson had observed at close quarters and over six years the damage done to the conduct of our foreign affairs when the President and the Secretary of State were estranged or competing. He understood the power and effect that could flow if the two were joined at the hip, presenting a united front to all comers, all challengers, each discharging the different but complimentary duties of their respective offices. The joining derived from mutual admiration and was cemented by genuine devotion and affection. Of Truman, Acheson said: "One could not ask for a commander with more directness, understanding and courage."[15]

Truman and Acheson met alone a minimum of twice each week, and frequently three times each week. These meetings were conducted with a clear understanding of the respective roles and responsibilities of the two men. As Acheson put it, Truman did not want to make foreign policy from the White House; what he wanted was "respect, consultation and the right to make final decisions."[16] For his part, Acheson never forgot "who was President" and "the President most punctiliously remembered who was Secretary of State." Truman's regard for Acheson was such that he granted more power to him than was possessed by any preceding or succeeding secretary of state in the twentieth century.[17]

Truman and Acheson were, literally, inseparable and, on that account, ultimately invulnerable. Their friendship transcended the offices they held, reached into their personal and family lives and maintained its intimacy to the very end. For Acheson, Truman was "the best friend in the world."

Acheson's achievements as Secretary of State were sometimes equaled by the calumny that was heaped upon him—by Senator Joe McCarthy (who accused Acheson of harboring Communists in the Department of State and of "losing China" on his watch to the Communists), by the supporters of General Douglas MacArthur (whom Acheson had participated in firing), and by the critics of the conduct of the Korean War. Somehow Acheson was able to not only endure this calumny, but to rise above it in a most admirable way. He was able to do so, I believe, because he saw himself as superior to his critics, as more knowledgeable, correct and decent.[18] And because he led a balanced life, apportioned admirably among his work, his family, his friends, his hobbies, and his books. Acheson worked hard, but he was not a workaholic. He walked leisurely to work (with Justice Felix Frankfurter) circa nine in the morning and returned home in time to romp with his children and enjoy the cocktail hour. He almost invariably read himself to sleep, usually absorbed in histories and in biographies of "dashing statesmen, like Disraeli."[19] On the weekends he headed for his farm in Maryland where he busied himself with the making of furniture. In sum, Acheson was well grounded and well balanced. That grounding and balance enabled him to maintain clarity of thought and decisiveness of action in the midst of tumult, crises and criticism.

Acheson's security resided ultimately in his absolute integrity of character. No less an authority than George Kennan has pronounced definitively on that character. He has described Acheson as "the soul of honor."[20]

Acheson approached the conduct of American foreign policy as a realist. He believed that "the balance of power" was "the best international sheriff the world has ever had."[21] He was fully aware of the "limitations of American power and purpose." He understood that his country could not direct and control or remake the world. He felt that the requirement was the "search for limited ends," adjuring the search for absolutes.

What was essential was to determine what it was within America's means to do and how it could be done with the "materials at our disposal." Acheson believed that the materials at our disposal were sufficient to secure America's vital interest, which he felt resided in binding together the Old World and the New. The doing of that, he felt, would prevent Soviet hegemony in Europe and restore a 20th century balance of power on the European landmass. That, as James Chace, points out "was his long term strategy" and "his lasting legacy."

Acheson pursued his realist objectives openly but shrewdly. He has characterized the diplomacy of the Truman Administration as follows: "Our whole purpose was to talk anywhere at anytime with anybody, but never stop acting at all and never allow the talk to get us maneuvered in any field which would stop us from acting."[22]

The last word on Dean Acheson as the creator of the American world can be left to his biographer, James Chace. He wrote as follows: "The measure of greatness is the ability to seize the moment and create out of chaos the enduring structures of success."[23] This is what the greatest statesmen have done in centuries past. This is what Dean Acheson did in the second half of the twentieth century. The structures that he created—including most prominently and importantly the Marshall Plan, the Bretton Woods institutions and NATO—underpinned and secured the world's westward march in his time and beyond.

NOTES

1. James Chace, *Acheson: The Secretary of State Who Created the American World* (New York: Simon and Schuster, 1998), 442.
2. Dean Acheson, *Morning and Noon* (Boston: Houghton Mifflin Company, 1965), 24.
3. See Chace, op. cit., 38.
4. Acheson, op. cit., 78.
5. Ibid., 165.
6. Ibid., 217.
7. Chace, op. cit., 78.
8. See Acheson, op. cit., 132.
9. See David McCullough's description of Acheson in: David Acheson, *Acheson Country* (New York: W. W. Norton & Co., 1993), 15.
10. Ibid., 18.

11. For splendid samples of "Achesonian" writing see: *Dean Acheson, Present at the Creation* (New York: W. W. Norton & Co., 1969), 71, 89 and 90.

12. Chace, op. cit., 359.

13. See Walter Isaacson and Evan Thomas, *The Wise Men: Six Friends and the World They Made* (New York: Simon and Schuster, 1986).

14. Chace, op. cit., 359.

15. Ibid., 226.

16. Ibid., 256.

17. Ibid., 441.

18. See Isaacson and Thomas, op. cit., 494.

19. Chace, op. cit., 199.

20. Ibid., 307.

21. Ibid., 42.

22. Ibid., 332.

23. Ibid., 439.

BIBLIOGRAPHY

Acheson, David. *Acheson Country*. New York: W. W. Norton & Co., 1993.

Acheson, Dean. *Morning and Noon.* Boston: Houghton Mifflin Co., 1965.

———. *Present at the Creation.* New York: W. W. Norton & Co., 1969.

Chace, James. *Acheson: The Secretary of State Who Created the American World.* New York: Simon & Schuster, 1998.

Isaacson, Walter and Thomas, Evan. *The Wise Men: Six Friends and the World They Made.* New York: Simon & Schuster, 1986.

17

DENG XIAOPING

"Deng Xiaoping may be seen as one of the greatest political leaders of the 20th century, a man who set underway the biggest improvement in the living standards and personal freedoms of the largest number of people in human history."

—*The Economist*

"China today is largely of his making."

—Michael Dillon, *Deng Xiaoping: The Man Who Made Modern China*

"All the maritime empires founded in the world in the last 500 years have crumbled. China is still there."

—Felipe Fernández-Armesto, *Pathfinders: A Global History of Exploration*

Deng Xiaoping's life spans the most remarkable century in China's multi-millennial history. It is a century that witnessed the most profound revolutions in the history of mankind. And Deng himself both made and contributed to much of that history. He was the grand survivor of a tumultuous era, whose accomplishments place him securely in the top rank of 20th century leaders. In the words of his German biographer: "In our century, I have not seen in either the East or the West such a statesman as Deng Xiaoping who has traversed so tortuous a path in life and accomplished so much."[1] The emergence of a Pacific Century, the accelerating movement westward of civilization's main axis of commerce and communication, is owed powerfully to the decisive actions of this diminutive man.

The story of Deng's life, and of the actions he took to catapult China into the 21st century, is a saga of mythical proportions. It is an illustration of the fact that real life can be more arresting than fiction.

Deng's entire life was a contest against seemingly overwhelming odds. He stands out, for his sheer grit and resilience, as a giant in a pantheon of 20th century leaders. He emerged from the searing crucible of a Japanese invasion, a civil war and revolutionary struggle unbowed, undaunted and as the widely acknowledged architect of China's greatest ever leap-forward.

Deng was born in relatively prosperous and supportive circumstances in the Sichuan Province of southwestern China in 1904.[2] As a young student, he read the classics—and biographies. He was said to be able to recite an entire book from memory after having read it three times.[3] He took a special interest in language—in words, sentences and phrases—for which he was later to become famous.[4]

At age sixteen Deng was sent by his extended family to France on a work-study program designed to introduce a core of young Chinese to the methods of the West. France was, in the immediate aftermath of World War I, on its knees. To new arrivals from abroad it could not offer much. Deng was unable to support himself while studying and was obliged to drop out of school and take up menial factory work. He remained in France for five formative years experiencing (and somehow weathering) long stretches of "indigence and insecurity."[5] Along the way it is not surprising that Deng (and his Chinese confreres) became Marxists and political revolutionaries. As such, they were under constant surveillance.[6]

Practical experience as an impoverished laborer in the vineyards of capitalism was topped-off with a year of political indoctrination and revolutionary training at the Sun Yat-sen University in the Soviet Union. There, Deng received "practical training for a revolutionary career" and was singled out for a "promising future in propaganda and organizational work."[7]

Deng (and his colleague Zhou Enlai) returned to China in the late 20's as zealous Communist Party cadre. They immediately set to work to liberate China from bourgeois and foreign influences and oppression.

That work involved: broadening the base of the Chinese Communist Party and its handmaiden, the People's Revolutionary Army; fighting the Nationalist Kuomintang forces in the first phase of China's 20th century civil war; then turning to fight the Japanese for eight years—from 1937 to 1945 (at a cost of 20 million military and civilian casualties); and finally returning to the struggle with the Kuomintang in China's great civil war—for four years from 1945 to 1949.

Through this quarter century, Deng served as a political operative, a propagandist and a soldier. In all capacities he was almost daily under threat of being captured or killed. He lived a largely clandestine life, a fugitive's life, a warrior's life while he organized, indoctrinated and led cadre so that his cherished Communist Party would grow, prevail and ultimately govern a unified and foreigner-free China. In his work for the Communist Party he was "the efficient organizer, the administrator who made things happen; he was never a charismatic leader or a theorist man."[8]

Deng was built for what he faced. Short, stocky and broad shouldered, he was quick, energetic and tough.[9] Drawing on these physical resources he helped lead the legendary Long March from southeast to north central China over 12,500 kilometers of forbidding terrain—a strategic retreat from October '34 to October '35 which salvaged the Liberation Army and positioned it to ultimately prevail.[10] He fought against the Japanese alongside Mao Zedong and Zhou Enlai and lived with them in mountain caves. He helped lead the daring attack against Kuomintang forces across the presumably impassable Yellow River, delivering a strategic blow to those forces. Along the way, Deng was a principal articulator and disseminator of the political propaganda which mobilized and galvanized the Communist fighting force and persuaded masses of peasants to succor and support the People's Liberation Army. He tried to stay aloof from "the factional and ideological disputes within the Party, preferring to make judgments on a pragmatic basis."[11] For a quarter century, working his way slowly, surely and quietly from the bottom up, Deng invested himself, heart and soul, in the Chinese Communist revolutionary movement and literally placed his life at its disposal.

Once that movement finally prevailed in 1949, Deng—then aged 45—served as an architect of a new Chinese state ruled by the Chinese Communist Party. He also served as a troubleshooter and as a utility infielder, assigned to fix problems wherever they appeared. His early career featured "practical economic work at the grassroots level that conditioned his outlook on what was pragmatically required to boost the peasantry's quality of life."[12] He ranged the country in the process and rose through the ranks to the top of the second tier of Communist Party leaders, just below the daunting and doctrinaire Mao Zedong and the intellectually formidable and less doctrinaire Zhou Enlai.

These leaders had achieved initial success in unifying China, in ending foreign privilege, in implementing wholesale land reform and in restarting the Chinese economy after two decades of civil and foreign war.[13] Unfortunately for the Chinese people, Mao adopted a Soviet model of political control featuring the omniscience and omnipresence of the Chinese Communist Party. And just as unfortunately, he adopted the Soviet model of economic development featuring central planning, state enterprises and collectivized farming.

In 1958 Mao went further to emulate the Soviet emphasis on heavy industry, launching the then famous (and now infamous) "Great Leap Forward." This crash program (which Deng supported at the time) aimed to propel China into the ranks of the industrialized economies. It produced instead an economic and humanitarian disaster. The skewing of state investment toward heavy industry starved the agricultural sector and, as a result, the Chinese people. The ill-advised "Great Leap Forward" was soon abandoned but not before an estimated 20 million Chinese peasants and workers had died from hunger—the greatest toll from famine in the 20th century.[14]

"The Great Leap Forward" exposed Mao's fallibility. It was followed a decade later by another colossal blunder; to wit: The Cultural Revolution. This rabid, anti-intellectual movement sponsored by Mao aimed to create the fabled classless society. It sought to do so by first humiliating and then re-indoctrinating China's intellectual and managerial elite. The goal was to eliminate the distinction between mental and menial labor.[15] A campaign of persecution and reeducation unfolded that was unbridled in its zealotry and brutality. A minimum of a half million members of China's scientific and administrative corps were killed and millions more relocated to perform menial tasks, to confess their errors and to be reeducated. Deng Xiaoping, who at that time occupied the position of Vice Chairman of the Communist Party, was a victim as was his family. In 1967, Deng was required to make a "humiliating statement of self-criticism," placed under house arrest as the country's "number two capitalist roader" and subsequently sent to the hinterland to work part-time in a tractor repair factory for three years. His eldest son, a student at the time, was thrown out of a second story window by the shock troops of the Cultural Revolution—the Red Guards—and left as a paraplegic.

The Cultural Revolution drove China into chaos and set it back at least a decade. As it played itself out, Mao, on the recommendation of Deng's greatest friend and political ally, Zhou Enlai, restored Deng to his former positions in 1973. But not for long. In early 1976, Zhou Enlai died. Zhou had come to disagree fundamentally with Mao on China's macroeconomic philosophy and policy. Mao, in consequence, wished to have Zhou pass unnoticed from the scene. But a spontaneous popular memorial tribute to Zhou was convened in Tiananmen Square in which Deng was thought to be associated. Soon after, Mao, encouraged by the notorious "Gang of Four" (led by his wife) once again stripped Deng of his offices and sent him into the political wilderness.

Mao died shortly after Zhou and there then ensued an all-out power struggle between the Gang of Four dedicated to a radical leftist reformation and Mao's hand-picked successor Hua Guofeng who was dedicated to the restoration of Mao's mainline political legacy. Hua prevailed and the Gang of Four was arrested. On the heels of petitions from key party members, and a silent popular demonstration of support accomplished by placing little bottles (xiao pings) around the streets and monuments in Peking, Deng Xiaoping (after professing loyalty to Hua Guofeng) was, once again, resurrected.[16] This time, at age 74, he returned to stay and to ultimately lead China on a path of fundamental economic reform and modernization.

The story of Deng's ascension (between 1977 and 1979) to the effective position of China's supreme leader was "a slow and tortuous affair" involving "delicate negotiations and bitter battles."[17] It is one of the most dramatic in the annals of political history. Suffice it to stay that Deng prevailed by means of a carefully crafted political coup d'etat. The coup was a *tour de force* underpinned by Deng's seniority, his record of bravery throughout the struggle for liberation, his popularity with the army, his encyclopedic memory, his awesome administrative, analytical and communication skills, and the basic correctness and popular appeal of his platform of reform. Ultimately it was reform that was needed and would matter most. It is the content of that reform—which effected the greatest socio-economic revolution in the history of the world—to which we now turn.

In 1979 when Deng displaced Hua Guofeng as Mao's successor, China was politically divided, economically backward, technologically obsolete and internationally marginalized.[18] In the words of Deng's daughter, her father "inherited a disaster ridden country."[19] The country was being left behind the march of history while other Asian countries and city states—most notably Japan, South Korea, Taiwan, Hong Kong and Singapore—were surging ahead. Any objective reading of China's circumstances would lead to the inescapable conclusion that much—and much of Mao—was fundamentally wrong. It took Deng Xiaoping to bring the needed objectivity to China's leadership and to change China's course by, in his own inimitable phrase, "seeking truth from facts."[20]

Deng had started out as a communist doctrinal purist and he had long been an obedient servant of Chairman Mao. He served as Secretary General of the Chinese Communist party from the mid-fifties until the Cultural Revolution. But along the way—as a trouble-shooter and utility-infielder—Deng had become closely familiar with the real—vice rhetorical—world of Chinese life at the grassroots. His views shifted during the course of the "Great Leap Forward" and were further modified by his painful personal experience with the Cultural Revolution. He emerged from that experience "with a new vigor and new vision to ensure that a catastrophe like the Cultural Revolution could never happen again."[21] He came out into the open as an avowed pragmatist—within the overarching confines of the dictatorship of the Communist Party. This pragmatism evolved into a personal philosophy that was captured in Deng's most famous aphorism: "Whether white or black, a cat is a good cat so long as it catches the rat."[22] This fundamental pragmatism led Deng to progressively reverse "almost all of Mao's economic policies in the face of opposition from those who were determined to adhere firmly to Mao's every word."[23]

Mao had collectivized agriculture. Deng de-collectivized it through the endorsement of the family responsibility system. That system returned collectivized land to peasant families and allowed them to sell their over-quota production on the free market.[24] That decision alone unleashed enormous productive capacity while liberating 600 million peasants from the yoke of regulation and surveillance. Had Deng stopped there, he would already have implemented—in terms of lives affected—the most liberating revolution in history.

Mao had placed disproportionate emphasis on heavy industry. Deng shifted the emphasis to light industry and basic manufactures, providing more jobs, more consumer goods and more exports. The agricultural reform won Deng the support of the peasants. The industrial reform won him the support of the urban workers. And both reforms combined won China at large rapid improvements in standards of living and quality of life.

Mao had placed emphasis on the quantity of production and equality of economic rewards. Deng placed emphasis on quality and on economic incentives to spur and reward productivity.

Mao had focused on class struggle as the primary preoccupation of Communist Party leadership. Deng opposed "theatricality, mass movement and perpetual revolutionary rhetoric which were Mao's stock in trade."[25] Deng jettisoned that approach and replaced it with a priority concentration on economic development and on China's "modernization."[26]

Mao had been an anti-intellectual. Deng placed a premium on education and championed scientific and technological progress.

Mao had held the reins of political control tightly, maintained an intrusive security apparatus based on masses of police informers, and nourished a cult of personality. Deng loosened the reins, withdrew much of the surveillance apparatus, and opened up the system for more consultation and decentralized decision-making. He moved China "from 'strong man politics' to a politics that was closer to the man and woman on the street."[27] Simultaneously, he eschewed the cult of personality and forbid portraits of him to be displayed.[28] He systematically relinquished key positions, ultimately exercising power from behind the scenes (most notably as Honorary Chairman of the Chinese Bridge Association!). His power flowed from his heroic record of national service, his earned popularity and from his clarity and decisiveness.

Mao had held the world at arm's length. Deng actively embraced the world—its resources and its technology—in the interests of China's modernization. He established the legendary Special Economic Zones in southeast China that replicated Hong Kong as centers of manufacturing and trans-shipment and as magnets for foreign investment. He encouraged and facilitated study abroad for China's successor generation. And he effectively represented China to a world that he knew held the financial and technological keys to the door marked "economic development." In the words of his daughter, Deng "took the bright road of reform and of opening to the outside world and started a new revolution and a new long march."[29]

Today, Deng's legacy is clouded by his armed suppression of the democracy demonstration in Tiananmen Square in 1989 and ongoing Western concern with human rights abuses in China. But that incident and those concerns should not obscure—and cannot discredit—the revolutionary improvement in China's quality of life, and standing in the world, presided over by Deng Xiaoping. In appraising Deng's display of an iron fist against the democracy demonstrations, it is worth reflecting on his point of view as expressed in the following quote:

> Democracy can develop only gradually, and we cannot copy Western systems. If we did, that would only make a mess of everything. Our socialist construction can only be carried out under leadership, in an orderly way and in an environment of stability and unity. That's why I lay such emphasis on the need for high ideals and strict discipline. Bourgeois liberalization would plunge the country into turmoil once more.[30]

Deng was a subcompact. In his prime he stood only a fraction over five feet. But his accomplishments are, by any historic standard, large enough to qualify him for immortality. Under Deng, China cast off the chains of centralized, Soviet-style economic control and invested economic power in the people. That power may gradually be transformed into political power, a process which, at the local level already is underway.[31]

Perhaps it is best to end, not with Deng's vital statistics, but with China's vital statistics achieved under Deng's leadership. In the last fifteen years of the 20th century—the Deng Xiaoping years—China's national income quadrupled and its share of world trade trebled. Foreign direct investment into China poured in at the rate of $40 billion annually and China's foreign exchange reserves topped $100 billion. Literacy rates soared, life expectancy dramatically increased and infant mortality rates plunged. Private life—and its accompanying dignity—returned to China. Using the people's welfare as an index, nothing short of a historic humanitarian revolution took place in China during the Deng Xiaoping era.

Deng's revolution set China in clear forward motion. More and more of Asia—and the world at large—is being caught in its draft. China was awakened and is becoming a giant. In consequence, the relative location of the world's assets and action, commerce and communication, is shifting to Asia. The diminutive, Deng Xiaoping, led the giant, China, onward and upward and, in doing so, accelerated the westward shift in the world's center of gravity. That shift, starting a half millennium ago, is now bent on coming full circle.

NOTES

1. See Richard Evans, *Deng Xiaoping and the Making of Modern China* (London: Penguin Books, 1995), 220.
2. Evans, op. cit., 1.
3. Ibid., 5.
4. Maomao Deng, *Deng Xiaoping: My Father* (New York: Harper Collins, 1995), 73.
5. Evans, op. cit., 4.
6. Michael Dillon, *Deng Xiaoping: The Man Who Made Modern China* (London: L. B. Taurus & Co., Ltd., 2015), 23.
7. Ibid., 27–29.
8. Ibid., 35.
9. See Evans, 86.
10. See Dillon, op. cit., 64.
11. Ibid., 42.
12. Ibid., 51.
13. See Harry Harding, *China's Second Revolution: Reform After Mao* (Washington: Brookings Institution Press, 1987), 12.
14. See Evans, op. cit., 153.
15. Ibid., 169.
16. See Harding, op. cit., 59.
17. Dillon, op. cit., 205.
18. Harding, op. cit., 36.
19. Deng, op. cit., 469.
20. See Evans, op. cit., 33.
21. Dillon, op. cit., 255.
22. Evans, op. cit., 164.
23. Dillon, op. cit., 145.
24. See Harding, op. cit., 71.

25. Dillon, op. cit., 188.
26. See Evans, op. cit., 231.
27. Dillon, op. cit., 281.
28. Evans, op. cit., 245.
29. Deng, op. cit., 469–70.
30. Evans, op. cit., 281.
31. Ibid., 320.

BIBLIOGRAPHY

Deng, Maomao. *Deng Xiaoping: My Father*. New York: Harper Collins, 1995.

Dillon, Michael. *Deng Xiaoping: The Man Who Made Modern China*. London: L. B. Taurus & Co., Ltd., 2015.

Evans, Richard. *Deng Xiaoping and the Making of Modern China*. London: Penguin Books, 1995.

Harding, Harry. *China's Second Revolution: Reform After Mao*. Washington: Brookings Institution Press, 1987.

CONCLUSION

As this book on the world's westward march draws to a close, the question of what fundamentally drove the westward movement should be addressed. Here the wheel does not necessarily have to be reinvented. There are at least two outstanding books that have done this, one by David Landes that offers an economic and cultural perspective, the other by Jared Diamond that takes an environmental and geographical explanatory route. I have summarized these excellent books as Appendix A and B. I have also included a reflection written by one of my former students that offers a unique and compelling perspective, entitled *The Hungry Spirit: How Fear and Yearning Drove World History* (Appendix C). In addition, I should like to add a perspective that emerges from the events and individuals surveyed in this book. That perspective highlights the role of ideas and individuals.

When a formidable individual embraces a powerful idea and is prepared to make an intensive life commitment to it, the world can be transformed. Let us take the cases in point covered in this book.

Genghis Khan had an idea of a unified Mongol people who would take possession of a group identity and exert a hegemonic influence on the Eurasian landmass, creating in the process a secure turnpike that facilitated East-West trade and the transfer of "resource portfolios" that later helped to enable the rise of the West.

Mehmet the Conqueror had the idea of a powerful central Eurasian tribe establishing a capital in Constantinople and leveraging that extraordinarily strategic location to create an empire that would span the then known world. While coming close to doing so, he boxed the West in and sent it off into a seaborne age of exploration.

Christopher Columbus had an idea for a short western route across the Atlantic to reach the "riches of Cathay." He sold the idea, acted upon it and then discovered a landmass that has been the subsequent epicenter of the world.

Ferdinand Magellan believed that there was a passage between the ocean Columbus had transited and the great sea Balboa had first sighted. He found it, navigated it and, in the process, took the first full measure of the earth providing impetus to further Western exploration and expansion.

Captain Cook believed that science should be advanced as discovery was pursued and, in the process, accurately charted the world's greatest ocean and new lands therein while assisting in defeating the age-old scourge of survey and the maritime mystery of longitude. Once accomplished, the mariner then became master of the ocean highways.

Thomas Jefferson envisaged a new republic liberated from the Old World and nourished by vast open spaces to the west. With a vision of "an empire of liberty" in hand, he proceeded to double the size of the new country and to commission its exploration from coast-to-coast.

Theodore Roosevelt then viewed a country "clasping the crescent of two oceans in its hands" and resolved that those crescents be connected by a path between them. He moved decisively to do so, creating in the process a continental behemoth that anchored the world's center of commerce and communication.

Winston Churchill saw clearly the looming threat from the East led by Hitler and rallied his countrymen to rise up against it at the eleventh hour. By doing so, he enabled the maintenance of a western led world.

Dean Acheson believed that western leadership could only be secured if the resources of the Old World and the New were firmly conjoined. He moved decisively to assure that they were by creating institutions providing for the defense and prosperity of the western democracies within the overarching framework of American international leadership.

Deng Xiaoping believed that pragmatism, not a rigid ideology and class warfare, should guide China's path to modernization and the recovery of its greatness. "It does not matter if a cat is white or black. If it catches the rat, it is a good cat." Deng Xiaoping turned China loose on that basis and it surged forward.

For those interested in finding the key to the ingredients of transformational leadership, they may find it in the coupling of a powerful idea and a formidable individual driven by it.

Which brings us, finally, to the question of what makes a renowned leader. Generalizations are risky. There is no ironclad recipe for baking a leader. Nevertheless, it is useful to inventory the characteristics that reappear with frequency among individuals who have stood center stage at watershed moments in history and turned the tide in the direction of their visions.

The first characteristic is possession of a vision itself. According to Howard Gardner, a foremost student of leadership, the only common denominator of leadership that he has been able to identify with certainty, is the possession of a vision, or, in his words, possession of a "story to tell." If you walk through the individuals featured in this book, each had a story to tell, as briefly summarized above.

A corollary to the requirement of possessing a vision is that a leader must live that vision intensively both personally and professionally. They must vividly personify their deep commitment to their vision, placing themselves on the line in its pursuit. Each of the explorers, warriors and statesmen profiled in this book did so, often placing themselves in peril along the way. Genghis Khan and Mehmet the Conqueror led their armies in battle. Columbus piloted his ships and their crews into the unknown. TR led the charge up San Juan Hill. Churchill personally defied the vaunted German Luftwaffe, arming the English language and sending it to war. They all walked their talk.

Beyond the requirement of possessing a vision and a deep commitment to it, other characteristics appear with frequency in the profiles of leaders. Here, in no particular order of importance, is a partial list:

- The ranks of leaders are heavily populated by individuals who were rebellious, nonconformist and independent from day one. Mehmet defied his teachers and submitted to education only when it was forced upon him. Columbus bolted his home in Geneva, went to sea at an early age and never looked back. Theodore Roosevelt grew up an odd ball and did not submit himself to formal education until he attended Harvard at age seventeen (where he continued to be an odd ball). Winston Churchill refused to submit himself to the regimen of British public schooling and proceeded to "jay walk" through life.

Dean Acheson also slouched to his own drummer in his early life, scraping the bottom at both Groton and Yale. Insubordination and defiance of convention make frequent appearances in the early lives of leaders.

- Some leaders—and some of the very best—never "grow up." They remain as rambunctious, as headstrong and, yes, as spoiled as they were as children. Theodore Roosevelt and Winston Churchill are prime examples. Perhaps Beaudelaire got it right when he observed that "genius is no more than childhood captured."
- Whether leaders become adults or not, their childhoods are extraordinarily formative. As Emerson has said "the childhood shows the man, as morning shows the day." Often the determining factor is what the father failed to do. Columbus's father was a poor weaver. His son set out to be a nobleman. Jefferson's father—a farmer and Western land surveyor—did not live long enough to survey the full extent of America's western boundary. Jefferson finished the job for him—and then some! Theodore Roosevelt's father dodged the draft for the Civil War, so TR made up for him on San Juan Hill. Winston Churchill's father's brilliant career in politics was cut short by his untimely death. Winston took up the reins where his father left off and rose to the commanding heights of British politics.
- However defiant as youths, leaders acquire an education, at some stage, largely by independently reading widely. Columbus, without formal schooling, devoured geographic and navigational texts when in his mid-thirties in Lisbon. Theodore Roosevelt read (and wrote) more books than any other American president. Winston Churchill educated himself in the field in India, reading the classics while playing polo with the British cavalry. Dean Acheson finally got going as a student in law school and read widely (with a preference for biographies) thereafter. Deng Xiaoping was a precocious and omnivorous reader.
- The self-education of leaders is often accompanied by a photographic memory. Theodore Roosevelt could recite entire chapters of books he had read only once. Winston Churchill drew spontaneously upon his readings as grist for the mill of his renowned rhetoric. Deng Xiaoping was famous for quoting book passages from memory.

- While leaders are commonly great readers, they also are great speakers. Columbus has been described as being "indefatigably loquacious" in peddling to monarchs his plan to sail west to Cathay. Theodore Roosevelt—even with his high-pitched voice and chattering teeth—was an inspirational speaker. Winston Churchill mastered the art of speaking by practicing in front of a mirror. Deng Xiaoping has been immortalized for his phrase making.
- While leaders cultivate the arts of rhetoric, they also cultivate an aura—a distinctive presence that commands attention. Columbus often fitted himself out as a Franciscan monk to present himself as a servant of God. Theodore Roosevelt charged up San Juan Hill in a custom-made outfit from Abercrombie & Fitch designed to immortalize him as a Rough Rider. Churchill's dress was retro, evoking the images of Britain's halcyon imperial days. Dean Acheson carried himself, and self-consciously dressed, like an aristocratic statesman.
- Luck in generous measure also is required to survive long enough to become a leader recognized in the annals of history. Columbus, as young mariner, was rescued at sea off the coast of Portugal by floating debris. Jefferson, as Governor of Virginia, was lucky to escape from Richmond with his life when the British sacked and burned that bastion of rebellion. Theodore Roosevelt's Rough Riders were mowed down left and right in the charge up San Juan Hill. He miraculously survived. Winston Churchill was the quintessential cat of nine lives, from his escape as a captive during the Boer War in South Africa, to his recovery from being struck by a car in New York City. Deng Xiaoping lived through anarchy, revolution, a world war, a civil war and communist party infighting to emerge to lead China's "second revolution" in his mid-seventies.
- The list could go on, but it is fitting to end it with the absolute requirement of preparation. Columbus prepared himself to be a master mariner. Captain Cook prepared himself to be a master cartographer. Jefferson prepared himself to lead the western expansion of his country. Theodore Roosevelt prepared himself to represent—as a "steam engine in trousers"—America as it burst forth upon the world. Much of Churchill's life turned out to be in preparation for seizing the opportunity that presented itself when his country had its back against the wall. It has been said of Dean Acheson that he

did his homework better than those with whom he dealt. So the Boy Scouts, with their motto of "Be Prepared," seem to have gotten it right from the start.

Appendix A

GUNS, GERMS AND STEEL

The Fates of Human Societies

Jared Diamond

A central question raised by this book is why did the West prevail over the East in the period under study. No value judgment is inherent in the observation that the West did prevail. It is simply a historical fact. Nor is any value judgment inherent in the explanation why. It is quite possible that the explanation resides in environmental and geographical factors largely beyond human control. The predominance of the West may be owed to the advantages of its real estate rather than to the endowments of its residents.

This is the thesis powerfully presented by Jared Diamond in his best-selling, Pulitzer Prize winning book entitled: *Guns, Germs and Steel: The Fates of Human Societies*. Diamond is an interdisciplinary scholar par excellence. He possesses, in depth, knowledge of geography, paleontology, cultural anthropology, linguistics, inter-societal history, epidemiology, agriculture and biology. He has a marvelously equipped and finely tuned deductive mind. And he commands the King's English.

Diamond sets out to explain "history's broadest patterns." These patterns produce a picture of a world dominated by Eurasia, the world's largest contiguous landmass that happens to feature an east-west geographic axis or orientation. His core query involves the examination of why Eurasia came to dominate the world rather than Africa, Australia or the Americas (before the Americas were "discovered" by Eurasians from western Europe).

His answers—presented in a 400-page tome—are arresting. They consist of the following:

1. Eurasians were the first to develop food production extensively enough to afford a class of craftsmen and inventors.
2. They were able to do this because their indigenous supply of plants and domesticated animals were greater and more diverse than competing landmasses and because the east-west axis of the Eurasian landmass led to the easier spread of agricultural capability (inasmuch as crops and animals were migrating at roughly the same latitudes).
3. This agricultural productivity supported larger populations which, living in close proximity with themselves and their domesticated animals, developed and transferred germs which at first killed large numbers of them and then immunized them.
4. The close proximity of people not only transferred germs. They transferred inventions—such as writing. And they perforce developed forms of political organization to manage large-scale, essentially sedentary, agriculturally based (vice hunter–gatherer) societies.
5. When the inventions of agriculturally rich Eurasia—guns and steel, for example—were coupled with germs and with centralized systems of communication and political organization, they formed a formidable phalanx of weapons that overwhelmed the opposition of hunter–gatherers in their path.

This is not only how the whites from Western Europe took over the "New World." It is how the blacks took over Africa centuries before. The Bantu in Central Africa were more advanced agriculturally and technologically than their neighbors to the south and they basically overran and exterminated them.

For centuries—and until about five hundred years ago—the Chinese were the most advanced of the Eurasian peoples. They had the most advanced agriculture utilizing domesticated animals, superior technology featuring the water wheel, the compass, gunpowder, paper and printing, and advanced political organization, periodically led by an impressive Confucian meritocracy. Why then didn't China emerge from Eurasia, instead of Western Europe, to dominate the globe during the last half-millennium?

The answer offered by Diamond (and reinforced by another interdisciplinary macro-historian, David Landes in his book entitled *The Wealth and Poverty of Nations: Why Some Are So Rich and Others So Poor*), is to be found in the difference between enforced unity and conformity and operational diversity and dissent. In the 15th century, when the "age of discovery" was launched, China was unified and subject to centralized decision-making. Europe was fragmented and subject to the authority of autonomous, competing entities.

Geography helps explain the basis of the difference. China is a big chunk of real estate with an essentially even coastline. Western Europe is a patchwork of promontories, peninsulas and islands. Geographically it is easier to get a grip on China than it is to get a grip on Western Europe. Thus in the fifteenth century when all of embraceable China was controlled by the Soong Dynasty, hard to grip Western Europe was in the hands of contending kings and princes.

A single decision could determine the destiny of China. Not so, in Western Europe. And so it was that in the early 15th century, the Confucian dominated Soong Emperor decided that China should turn inward and that its impressive—even awesome—maritime capability (indeed superiority) should be mothballed, thereby freezing all of China in its tracks. Several decades later, ideas for maritime exploration were being shopped about in Western Europe; and, if they were rejected by one monarch they were simply taken to the next and eventually there was—as we know by studying Columbus—a sale (if you will excuse the pun). Diversity in Western Europe created opportunities that were closed by command to the Chinese.

The importance of diversity was later underlined in the subsequent competition among Western European powers for maritime supremacy. Portugal and Spain, which merged in 1580, led the way in the "age of discovery." But following the Spanish Inquisition, which was imposed the very year Columbus "discovered" the "new world," and the subsequent insistence of King Philip of Spain on doctrinal religious purity, the Iberian Peninsula was sapped of its diversity and of its openness to ideas beyond its borders. Nonconformists and so-called heretics, most notably the talented Jews, fled to more tolerant venues, which included quite prominently the United Provinces of the Netherlands. With the assistance of this infusion of mercantile and inventive talent, the Dutch rapidly and decisively overtook Iberian maritime superiority.

BIBLIOGRAPHY

Diamond, Jared. *Guns, Germs and Steel: The Fates of Human Societies*. New York: W. W. Norton & Co., 1999.

Appendix B

THE WEALTH AND POVERTY OF NATIONS

Why Some Are So Rich and Some So Poor

David S. Landes

This book offers an explanation of why the world's economic and cultural epicenter moved west over the last half millennium. Based on an economically oriented historical review of the great empires and cultures—Chinese, Indian, Arab, European—David Landes explains why the West came out on top—as it most surely did. He attributes the rise and success of the West to the following principal factors:

(1) The complacency—and in some cases—sense of superiority—of potential contenders for world power. The Chinese—the Celestial Kingdom—offers the lead case study in this department. But Indian and Arab cultures were also similarly afflicted. Europe had no reason to be complacent and no reason to feel superior. It entered the second half of the millennium as the world's laggard, commercially and culturally.

(2) A corresponding lack of curiosity about an external realm that was viewed as inferior. Europe, in contrast, located Eden in the East, and was eager to get there! Europe literally overflowed with curiosity about the world elsewhere. It also overflowed with greed and, periodically, with missionary zeal!

(3) Centralized tyranny's which demanded conformity, discouraged innovation and withheld incentives and rewards for initiative. Again China is a leading case study where the heavy hand of a pervasive Confucian bureaucracy stifled independence of thought and action. Europe, for its part, was disunited, fragmented and fundamentally freer on the ground.

(4) A religious orthodoxy or monopoly—or its functional equivalent—requiring conformity—Islam in the Arab world, Confucianism in the Chinese world. Theocracies and doctrinaire bureaucracies are congenitally inhospitable to scientific discovery and technological advance. In Europe, the Reformation ended a monopoly of Roman Catholicism and attendant conformity. Protestantism broke new ground for work, experimentation and reward. The split in the West between the secular and the religious—"the distinction between God and Caesar"—divided authority. And where authority is divided, dissent and inquiry flourish.

(5) Europe was first with key inventions, or the significantly improved application of old inventions. It was first with the mechanical clock that revolutionized the workplace, making it more efficient, more productive. It was first with eyeglasses, effectively doubling the life of the skilled craft workforce. It significantly improved upon gunpowder and cannon and upon the printing press, all first invented by the Chinese. Europe also made significant improvements in navigational techniques and ship and sail design. By the middle of the millennium, Europe had the best printing presses, the best ships and the best cannon in the world. The printing presses excited an interest in the external realm and the ships and cannon combined to provide Europe with the means to overpower that realm. Meanwhile, the printing presses, all by themselves, made it well nigh impossible to prevent new ideas from getting out of the box.

(6) European diseases assisted the ships and cannon. The diversity of European climate from the tundra of Scandinavia to the beaches of the Mediterranean—and the contact among peoples from these diverse regions over the centuries—bred a heartier stock. In consequence, and in the event, the native peoples whom the Europeans fought on their way to empire, were more susceptible to European diseases than the other way around. The correlation of pathogenic forces favored the West. In Mexico, for example, the "coming of the white man and his fellow-traveling pathogens (smallpox, influenza, etc.) brought death to nine tenths of a Mexican Indian population of perhaps 25 million."

(7) In general Europe, especially Western Europe, has a better climate than the East and South—more temperate, more rainfall, better agricultural land, fewer parasites. Its people were bigger, more vigorous, lived longer and "worked closer to their potential." The European horse also was bigger and stronger. "The European horse, carrying an armored war-

rior, amounted to a living tank, irresistible in charges, unbeatable in combat."

(8) Non-western societies tended to confine women to the home. In Europe they were also in the field and, when the manufacturing revolution kicked in, in the sweatshops. The West used its women more productively than the East.

(7) In the non-Western regions, regimes did not actively concert public and private capabilities and resources. The former normally got in the way of the latter. In the West, public and private instruments and means found a way to reinforce each other, becoming, in the process, more than the sum of their parts. At the core of this relationship were the concept of private property and the security thereof. The greatest progress was led in the West by "the mercantile community" that developed an independent capability to use the state when advantageous and to bypass it when it was not. Elsewhere a labyrinth of regulations and practices, including pervasive corruption or outright tyranny, prohibited, inhibited or sapped private enterprise.

(8) Northern Europe won out over southern Europe. Because the north developed via Protestantism a new "business breed"—rational, ordered, diligent, productive—emerged. Calvinism's secular code of behavior prevailed: "Hard work, honesty, seriousness, the thrifty use of money and time (both lent to us by God)." The Protestants stressed "instruction and literacy, for girls as well as boys" and "the importance of time." And the North, abjuring the "inquisition," was more open to ideas, knowledge, talent that drove a scientific and industrial revolution. Meanwhile, censure and censorship prevailed on the Iberian Peninsula. Protestant Europe led in "the growing autonomy of intellectual inquiry." "Around 1900, for example, when only 3% of the population of Great Britain was illiterate, the figure for Italy was 48%, for Spain 56%, for Portugal 78%. The religious persecutions of old—the massacres, expulsions, forced conversions and self-imposed intellectual closure—proved to be a kind of original sin."

BIBLIOGRAPHY

Landes, David S. *The Wealth and Poverty of Nations: Why Some Are So Rich and Some So Poor*. New York: W. W. Norton, 1998.

Appendix C

THE HUNGRY SPIRIT

How Fear and Yearning Drove World History

Ying Gao

Economic world history, it seems, is a chain reaction of the Hungry Spirit. This Spirit is a unique historical mixture of fear and yearning. My thesis is that fear triggers development, its direction set by people's shared yearning. When fear and yearning coincide in the way the Hungry Spirit does, we can expect nations to embark on a dynamism that maximizes speed, achievement and transformation.

The Spirit has four launchers: universal fear, geographical danger, a sense of single direction, and acceptance of technology. Also, over the timespan of unfolding development, the Spirit evolves. First, fear spreads among the population and is shared across all classes. Next, the source of fear approaches—often from the east—with a sense of only one way out and one means to achieve security. This vitalizes a nation much like when a person under pressure performs beyond their norm: the challenge is here, the requirement understood, and one only needs action to break through.

As economic development takes place, the population loses its initial fear and the sense of external danger begins to quiet down, leaving a general feeling of contentment and an altered collective identity through the experience. But the rapid development of one nation can be seen as a threat by its neighbor. This causes the Hungry Spirit to evolve rather than to dissipate. For six hundred years, the world has developed in a geographical chain reaction from region to region, from Ming China, advancing through the world of Islam, Western Europe, and North America and returning to present-day Asia. The Spirit has traveled westward.

The journey of development started from China in a somewhat gradual manner, because the perils—the Mongols, plague, territorial losses—though widespread, did not penetrate the kingdom's enormous population. Still, the Mongolian occupation had jolted the Han mindset even far from the frontiers, and once an emperor, who was orphaned in a plague outbreak, overthrew the conquerors, there was a moment of openness when people could accept new ideas. "Confucian influence fell to an all-time low" and trade—traditionally thought of as a lowly activity—looked like the way to reestablish a prosperous Middle Kingdom.[1] Besides, with the Mongolian blockade of trade routes in the north, where could China go but overseas? The succeeding Ming emperor therefore developed the largest naval fleet up until this time, dispatched eunuch emissaries far westward via the ocean, calling for tribute trade. As a result, "China's formidable presence would be felt in the coming years from Japan to the east coast of Africa."[2]

But this was a brief burst. Consider the traditional Chinese worldview against the global scene in history. During the rule of Mongols, who had expanded on the Sung dynasty's overseas trade, all seagoing became associated in the Han mindset with barbarians and their ways.[3] The international trading system actually flourished with the crucial link from Mongol-ruled Yuan China. A mismatch had occurred: China's economic importance had risen abroad while the cultural significance of the world outside fell in the Chinese establishment mind. People's sense of fear from outside was never acute to begin with; soon it would pass away, leaving the Hans no reason to expand outward, and free to focus instead on domestic affairs, which they believed was a wiser act anyway.

As the middle kingdom sunk into a deep and prolonged drowse, the Hungry Spirit sparked in another set of people: the Ottoman Turks. Pressed from the northeast by the earlier conquest of Mongolians, who were in turn retreating from China, the Islamic world experienced "more and more refugees."[4] Although wealth and knowledge poured in via sea routes, the land-based Mongolian threat compromised the geographical security of Turkic-speaking Central Asians. This "hunger" was particularly acute for the Ottomans, who were sandwiched between the incoming population and the Christian empire of Byzantium. The Ottoman Sultan Mehmet believed that to break the deadlock he had to strike the

Byzantine capital lying to his west, and his people, it seemed, agreed: "Pressure and faith alike urged them on to attack the Christians."[5] With a singularly focused objective and aided by the siege cannons and attack fleet expertly prepared, Mehmet captured the city once believed impregnable, thereby achieving security for his empire.

The Ottoman's victory was Europeans' calamity, however. Located at the western edge of the Eurasian continent, Europe had lost a large portion of its population to the Black Death and was now under siege by the seemingly reinvigorated infidels from the east. Here was a region in relative deprivation. It knew of the dazzling Oriental spices, silk, and porcelain, but could only access them at inflated prices through middlemen. Commoners and aristocrats alike were ravaged by the plague: after "the Black Death of 1348 and 1349, and the recurrent epidemics," Europe had experienced so many deaths that it "could have counted barely more than a third of the people it contained one hundred years before."[6] The richer the Ottoman Empire became, the hungrier Europe felt by comparison. The despair seems to have intensified the Hungry Spirit at this historical place and moment, producing more dramatic consequences.

Widespread fears like a plague can unite people—if not in highly articulated ideology or individual interests, then at least in vaguely millenarian sentiments. People can feel that they share the same destiny, even if it is an apparently doomed one. As the news that "the Christian Empire was ended" in the east shot through the continent, European fear and yearning gained a directionality: away from the infidels, and around, somehow, to the Orient![7] The keener the fear, the more radical a reaction it seems to trigger in economic history. After much improvement in maritime technology in a short period, when the Europeans finally outran their doom, they could hardly contain themselves. European colonists sought total monopoly of trade benefits, pouring capital, strategic attention, and power into the global game of colonial control. But the Spirit would pass westward to America,

The Puritans, fleeing from religious persecution, transported the Hungry Spirit from Europe to the New World. Here, ultimately, Americans invented a blended idealism in the Spirit, renaming it "Manifest Destiny." The Puritans' possessed clear attitudes about the world outside of their community: The natives should be feared, the land needed to be cultivated and made productive, and the progress forward must be away from Europe. Thus, the complex concoction of fear, geography and yearning for development was spelled out as a single, idealized, and collective destiny. With this Manifest thrust, the United States yearned at first for shelter. It populated North America while attempting to dissociate itself culturally from the Old World. Once its territory had reached the Pacific, the geographical peril diminished. The Manifest Destiny therefore was gradually redefined as yearning rather than fear.

All things being equal, the end of history was American democracy as enshrined in the trinity "free government, free commerce, and free men." Time was also accelerating and space diminishing, witness isolationist China, sunk in Oriental stagnation and corruption. It was essential, therefore, always to be on the move. Destiny required constant, purposeful intervention in time and space.[8]

People were no longer allergic to the Old World: security had been achieved. Not only could they counter Europe's influence now, they could correct its wrongs. Theodore Roosevelt was a leader who signaled this new ambition in history. Roosevelt built the Panama Canal exactly where the French had failed, built up the U.S. Navy to show off its reach, declaring with power politics that America was on its way to fulfill a divine promise. Sure enough, the United States accomplished hegemonic peace of sorts by rejecting the European system—colonialism and secret alliances—and boomed at the expense of two European World Wars. America today runs the world system. It is the center that holds it all together. To the west, Europe hovers in second place. And to the east, East Asia rises rapidly.

I argue that the Hungry Spirit vitalizes regions, but national dominance and relations of nations within a given region may vary. The Spirit, which is historical sentiment and opportunity shared by a geographic region, motivates nations to compete. In a race for one common direction, management of yearnings—strategy—will cause some nations to break through while others may relatively lag behind. Whoever best utilizes its changing situation and harnesses emergent technologies will likely dominate the scene. Nonetheless, the region with the Hungry Spirit is far more energetic as a whole because of the common drive and competition within.

Speaking of which, when did the East Asian "miracle" begin? The region has shown steady and resilient growth in recent decades. In fact the Hungry Spirit rests in East Asia today. It is there mainly because Japan had embraced it.

For the past 150 years, since it opened up to the United States, Japan seems to have embraced the Hungry Spirit. Indeed, the island nation has irreversibly changed East Asia with the heat of its vision, force and atrocity—a shock no other region had experienced. First, Japan's quick Meiji Restoration is striking. The Japanese conservatives may complain that this shows their nation's weakness to foreign pressures. Yet rather, it is a hypersensitivity. News and sentiments travel among people like a chemical reaction; and this occurred fast in Japanese society because its population shared one ethnicity, its land was compact and urbanized, and its transportation system well-developed. Theoretically, Japan was in no greater danger than its neighbors in the late colonial period.

Landes presents an impressive array of facts proving Japan's "pre-factory industry," "competitive economic world" with its samurai lords and a culture committed to "work rather than to wealth."[9] All these supported Japan's development after the Restoration. The spark, however, was the hypersensitivity. While Asia as a whole was baffled, quarreling domestically and lamenting foreign colonialism, the Japanese burst into action by the mere sight of steam ships. And act it did. Urged on by the Spirit and determined to catch up with the West, Japan pursued security through ambitious militarism, relentlessly thrusting its technology and colonial policy westward and southward. As a result, the region's ancient geopolitical map was destroyed. The Japanese aggression—so ruthless, so close at home—astonished East Asia. The Westerners had come from afar; they looked different; they were another people. The new Japan shook the traditional mindset in other nations. Once the smoke of World War II cleared, Korea no longer saw China as a source of order, China in turn understood its weakness, and all East Asians yearned for the power to be safe—they felt the Hungry Spirit. Meanwhile, in the bombarded open cities the Japanese too could not believe what had happened, but they knew where they were: zero. Their Spirit yearned for security more than ever. Mixing the American commercialism with artisans' culture—a happier marriage than between European colonialism and samurai militarism—and devoting themselves to companies that Landes calls "the mother firms," the Japanese again skyrocketed their economy, speeding up regional competition.[10]

To the west, struck in fear by Japanese atrocities, lay China. Development of this populous, continental-sized and multiethnic nation would require a different path than the one the Japanese chose. For one thing, the foreigners had, after all, "barely scratched the surface of the porcelain kingdom."[11] The shock from the Japanese and other colonial forces had mobilized inland peasants, after many decades, leading to the communist takeover. Yet the Hungry Spirit could not take hold. The population of "this paradoxical mass—at once obedient and independent, submissive and self-reliant" did not naturally adopt one collective aim.[12] Thus, under an authoritarian rule, the leadership's understanding of the Hungry Spirit sets contemporary China's direction.

Mao forced the nation into self-denials and counter self-denials in the name of a Cultural Revolution, launched "ever more fierce campaigns to save his people from themselves," and exhausted China and its people.[13] Political instabilities can undermine development by drawing national energy inward. Deng Xiaoping, on the other hand, looked outward and to doing things: "Not to engage in debates: this was an invention of mine," declared Mr. Deng, "in order to get more things done." One of Deng's biographers found irony in that "the morality he advocated should resemble the morality preached by the puritans of central and northern Europe associated by many Western historians with the rise of capitalism."[14] Landes would point out its resemblance to the Japanese respect for ceaseless quality work. Deng articulated the general yearning that Chinese people ought to hold in late 20th century. It was a simple policy managed carefully. He admitted what China lacked, affirmed its priority, and welcomed Western science.

Today, the Spirit still drives the world. We have seen its impact on economic development followed by changing national identities, and the trajectory around the globe in a chain reaction. The future seems uncertain. Shaken in 9/11, Americans are jolted by fear, craving for safety and power that is necessary for security; the administration chose the Middle East as the new energy's destination. Muslims worldwide then face more pressures, a new source of frustrations. East Asia, on the other end, continues largely undisturbed in increasing global influence. But its identity is in doubts. The Japanese sense of singular aim, which urged the country through its two bursts of economic development, has faded. In a world of internet and globalization, with news traveling instantly, neither Europe nor Japan will decline like Ming China. Still the Japanese search for a quieter, post-developmental identity.

The Chinese, on the other hand, must deal with the world's rising expectations: "There is no greater threat to the world than the emergence of a major power in possession of a victim mentality. Has China readily dispelled the 'humiliation' and 'victim mentality' it has harbored during the past 150 years since the Opium War and 15 years of Japanese aggression?"[15] Fully developed, China's self-vision would affect the world just as the American Manifest Destiny has done; yet victim mentality is familiar to all Chinese, keeping them from admitting their real weakness and strength.

So we see fear everywhere in today's world: there seem to be sources for anxiety. But where is the sense of direction, that steady yearning, the Spirit?

Last spring I was in Beijing, passing my days before the television set thanks to the SARS epidemic. China's newly founded 24-hour news channel was on. It showed the opening of Three Gorges Dam; city workers sending earnings back home—inland; and young graduates avoiding job scarcity in coastal cities and moving west. Here the Spirit was found—within China, seeking to send its urban prosperity westward, with resources on the move. It may be less visible from the rest of the world. It may take a long time to reach around the world. Nevertheless, like six centuries ago, the Hungry Spirit travels on westward.

NOTES

1. See Louise E. Levathes, *When China Ruled the Seas* (New York: Oxford University Press, 1996), 49.
2. Ibid., 106.
3. Janet L. Abu-Lughod, *Before European Hegemony: The World System A.D. 1250–1350* (New York: Oxford University Press, 1989), 341.
4. Steven Runciman, *The Fall of Constantinople 1453* (London: Cambridge University Press, 1965), 2.
5. Ibid., 28.
6. David Herlihy, *The Black Death and the Transformation of the West* (Cambridge: Harvard University Press, 1997), 17.
7. See Runciman, op. cit., 154.
8. Anders Stephanson, *Manifest Destiny* (Canada: HarperCollins, 1995), 97.
9. See David S. Landes, *The Wealth and Poverty of Nations: Why Some Are So Rich and Some So Poor* (New York: W. W. Norton & Company, 1998), 363–68.
10. Ibid., 486.

11. Ibid., 344.

12. See Henry A. Kissinger, "The Philosopher and the Pragmatist," *Newsweek,* March 3, 1997.

13. Ibid.

14. Richard Evans. *Deng Xiaoping and the Making of China* (New York: Penguin Books, 1997), 14.

15. Yoichi Funabashi. "China's long-term strategy: peaceful ascendancy," *Asahi Shimbun* December 2, 2003.

BIBLIOGRAPHY

Abu-Lughod, Janet L. *Before European Hegemony: The World System A.D. 1250–1350.* New York: Oxford University Press, 1989.

Evans, Richard. *Deng Xiaoping and the Making of China.* New York: Penguin Books: 1997.

Funabashi, Yoichi. "China's long-term strategy: peaceful ascendancy." *Asahi Shimbun,* December 2, 2003.

Herlihy, David. *The Black Death and the Transformation of the West.* Cambridge: Harvard University Press, 1997.

Kissinger, Henry A. "The Philosopher and the Pragmatist." *Newsweek,* March 3, 1997.

Landes, David S. *The Wealth and Poverty of Nations: Why Some Are So Rich and Some So Poor.* W. W. Norton & Company, 1998.

Levathes, Louise E. *When China Ruled the Seas.* New York: Oxford University Press, 1996.

Runciman, Steven. *The Fall of Constantinople 1453.* London: Cambridge University Press, 1965.

Stephanson, Anders. *Manifest Destiny* Canada: HarperCollins Ltd., 1995.

Appendix D

FURTHER READINGS

THE VIKINGS

Barrett, James H., ed. *Contact, Continuity and Collapse: The Norse Colonization of the North Atlantic.* Turnhout, Belgium: Brepols Publishers, 2003.
Craughwell, Thomas J. *How the Barbarian Invasions Shaped the Modern World.* New York: Crestline, 2018.
Dale, Roderick and Marjolein Stern. *The Viking Experience.* London: Carlton Books Ltd., 2014.
Lowery, Brian. *The Conquest of the Ocean.* London: DK, 2013.
Magnusson, Magnus. *Vikings.* New York: E. P. Dutton, 1980.
Paine, Lincoln. *The Sea and Civilization: A Maritime History of the World.* New York: Alfred A. Knopf, 2013.
Pendlesson, K. R. G. *The Vikings.* New York: Mayflower Books, 1980.
Rosedahl, Else. *The Vikings.* London: Penguin Books Ltd., 1992.
Sawyer, P. H. *Kings and Vikings.* London: Methuen & Co. Ltd., 1982.
Winroth, Anders. *The Age of the Vikings.* Princeton: Princeton University Press, 2014.

THE MONGOLS

Craughwell, Thomas J. *How the Barbarian Invasions Shaped the Modern World.* New York: Crestline, 2018.
De Hartog, Leo. *Genghis Khan: Conqueror of the World.* London: The Folio Society, 2005.
Gabriel, Richard A. *Subotai: Genghis Khan's Greatest General.* Connecticut: Praeger, 2004.
Lamb, Harold. *Genghis Khan: The Emperor of All Men.* Philadelphia: The Balkiston Company, 1940.
Lister, R. P. *Genghis Khan.* New York: Dorset Press, 1969.
McLynn, Frank. *Genghis Khan: His Conquests, His Empire, His Legacy.* Boston: Da Capo Press, 2015.
Morgan, David. *The Mongols.* Oxford: Basil Blackwell, 1986.
Ratchnevsky, Paul. *Genghis Khan: His Life and Legacy.* Oxford: Blackwell, 1993.
Rossabi, Morris. *Kubilai Khan: His Life and Times.* London: The Folio Society, 2005.
Weatherford, Jack. *Genghis Khan and the Quest for God: How the World's Greatest Warrior Gave Us Religious Freedom.* New York: Viking, 2016.

BEFORE EUROPEAN HEGEMONY

Braudel, Fernand. *A History of Civilizations,* New York: Penguin Group, 1995.
Crosby, Alfred W. *Ecological Imperialism.* Cambridge: Cambridge University Press, 1986.
Diffie, Bailey W. *Prelude to Empire: Portugal Overseas Before Henry the Navigator.* Nebraska: University of Nebraska Press, 1960.
Kennedy, Paul. *The Rise and Fall of the Great Powers.* London: Fontana Press, 1989.

THE OTTOMANS AND MEHMET THE CONQUEROR

Atil, Erin. *Suleynanname: The Illustrated History of Suleyman the Magnificent.* New York: Harry N. Abrams, Inc., 1986.
Babinger, Franz. *Mehmed the Conqueror and His Time.* Princeton: Princeton University Press, 1978.
Barker, Noel. *The Lords of the Golden Horn.* London: Macmillan, 1973.
Beck, Brandon H. *From the Rising of the Sun: English Images of the Ottoman Empire to 1715.* New York: Peter Long Publishing, 1987.
Beg, Turson. *The History of Mehmed the Conqueror* (edited and translated by Halik Inalcik and Rhoads Murphy). Minneapolis: Biblioteca Islamica, 1978.
Betts, R. R. et al. *The Fall of Constantinople (A Symposium).* London: School of Oriental and African Studies, University of London, 1955.
Kristoboulos of Imbros. *History of Mehmed the Conqueror.* Princeton: Princeton University Press, 1994.
McCarthy, Justin: *The Ottomans: An Introductory History to 1923.* Essex: Addison Wesley Longman Ltd., 1997.
Wheatcroft, Andrew: *The Ottomans.* New York: Viking, 1993.

THE PORTUGUESE

Bell, Christopher. *Portugal and the Quest for the Indies.* New York: Barnes and Noble, 1974.
Boxer, Charles Ralph. *The Portuguese Seaborne Empire, 1415–1825.* New York: A. A. Knopf, 1969.
———. *Four Centuries of Portuguese Expansion, 1415–1825: A Succinct Survey.* Berkeley: University of California Press, 1969.
Cuyvers, Luc. *Into the Rising Sun: Vasco da Gama and the Search for the Sea Route to the East.* Collingdale, Pennsylvania: Diane Publishing Company, 2001.
Diffie, Bailey W. *Prelude to Empire: Portugal Overseas Before Henry the Navigator.* Nebraska: Nebraska University Press, 1960.
Hamilton, Genesta Mary. *In the Wake of da Gama: The Story of Portuguese Pioneers in East Africa: 1497–1729.* London: Skeffington Press, 1951.
Jayne, Kingsley. *Vasco da Gama and His Successors: 1460–1580.* New York: Barnes and Noble Publishing Company, 1970.
Ravenstein, Ernest George. *A Journal of the First Voyage of Vasco da Gama.* London: Hakluyt Society, 1898.
Russell, Sir Peter. *Prince Henry the Navigator: A Life.* New Haven: Yale University Press, 2000.
Sanceau, Elaine. *Good Hope: The Voyage of Vasco da Gama.* Lisbon: International Academy of Portuguese Culture, 1967.
Sanderlin, George William. *Eastward to India.* New York: Harper and Row, 1965.

THE WORLD AND VOYAGES OF CHRISTOPHER COLUMBUS

Bergreen, Laurence. *Columbus: The Four Voyages*. New York: Penguin Group, 2011.

Dugard, Martin. *The Last Voyage of Christopher Columbus*. New York: Little Brown and Company, 2005.

Fernández-Armesto, Felipe. *Before Columbus: Exploration and Colonization from the Mediterranean to the Atlantic, 1229–1492*. Philadelphia: University of Pennsylvania Press. 1987.

The Journal of Christopher Columbus (translated by Cecil Jane). New York: Charles N. Potter Inc., 1960.

Landstrom, Bjorn. *Columbus*. New York: The Macmillan Company, 1966.

The Log of Christopher Columbus (translated by Robert H. Fuson). Camden, Maine: International Marine Publishing Company, 1987.

Nebenzahl, Kenneth. *Atlas of Columbus and the Great Discoveries*. New York: Rand McNally and Company, 1990.

Symcox, Geoffrey and Sullivan, Blair. *Christopher Columbus and the Enterprise of the Indies: A Brief History with Documents*. New York: Palgrave Macmillan, 2005.

Thomas, Hugh. *Rivers of Gold: The Rise of the Spanish Empire from Columbus to Magellan*. New York: Random House, 2003.

FERDINAND MAGELLAN

Butterworth, Hezekiah. *The Story of Magellan and the Discovery of the Philippines*. Sydney: Wentworth Press, 2019.

Fleming, Fergus. *Off the Map: Tales of Endurance and Exploration*. New York: Atlantic Monthly Press, 2004.

Guillemard, Francis Henry Hill. *The Life of Ferdinand Magellan and the First Circumnavigation of the Globe*. Franklin Classics Trade Press, 2018.

Pigafetta et al. *The First Voyage Round the World* (translated by Lord Stanley of Alderly). London: The Hakluyt Society, 1874.

Thomas, Hugh. *Rivers of Gold: The Rise of the Spanish Empire from Columbus to Magellan*. New York: Random House, 2003.

Waldman, Stuart. *Magellan's World*. New York: Mikaya Press, 2017.

Zweig, Stefan. *Magellan*. London: Pushkin Press, 2013.

SIR FRANCIS DRAKE

Bradford, Ernle. *Drake: England's Greatest Seafarer*. New York: Open Road Integrated Media, Inc., 2014.

Brydges, Egerton and Charles Fitz-Jeffrey. *The Life and Death of Sir Francis Drake*. Palala Press, 2015.

Dudley, Wade G. *Drake: For God, Queen and Plunder*. Dulles, Virginia: Brasseys, 2003.

Thomson, George Malcolm. *Sir Francis Drake*. London: Secker and Warburg, 1972.

Vaux, William Sandys Wright. *The World Encompassed by Sir Francis Drake*. New York: Rutledge, 2016.

Williams, Glyndwr. *The Great South Sea: English Voyages and Encounters: 1570–1750*. New Haven: Yale University Press, 1997.

CAPTAIN JAMES COOK

Beaglehole, J. C. *The Life of Captain James Cook.* Stanford: Stanford University Press, 1974.
Cook, James. *The Journals.* London: Penguin Books Ltd., 2003.
Dugard, Martin. *Farther Than Any Man: The Rise and Fall of Captain James Cook.* New York: Washington Square Press, 2002.
Fisher, Robin and Hugh Johnston. *Captain James Cook and His Times.* Seattle: University of Washington Press, 1979.
Hough, Richard. *Captain James Cook.* New York: W. W. Norton and Company Inc., 1997.
———. *The Last Voyage of Captain James Cook.* New York: Morrow, 1979.
Skelton, R. A. *Captain James Cook After Two Hundred Years.* London: Trustees of the British Museum, 1969.
Williamson, J. A. *Cook and the Opening of the Pacific.* New York: The MacMillan Company, 1948.

THOMAS JEFFERSON AND THE LOUISIANA PURCHASE

Adams, Henry. *History of the United States During the Presidency of Thomas Jefferson.* New York: Library of America, 1986.
Ambrose, Stephen. *Undaunted Courage: Meriwether Lewis, Thomas Jefferson and the Opening of the West.* New York: Simon and Schuster, 1996.
Cogliano, Francis D. *Emperor of Liberty: Thomas Jefferson's Foreign Policy.* New Haven: Yale University Press, 2014.
Dumas, Malone. *Jefferson the Virginian.* Boston: Little Brown, 1948.
———. *Jefferson the President, First Term 1801–1805.* Boston: Little Brown, and Company, 1970.
Ellis, Joseph J. *American Sphinx.* New York: Vintage Books, 1996.
Merk, Frederick, *History of the Westward Movement.* New York: Alfred A. Knopf, 1978.
Onuf, Peter, ed. *Jeffersonian Legacies.* Charlottesville, Virginia: University of Virginia Press, 1993.
Stephanson, Anders. *Manifest Destiny: American Expansion and the Empire of Right.* New York: Hill and Wang, 1999.

THEODORE ROOSEVELT AND THE PANAMA CANAL

Auchincloss, Louis. *Theodore Roosevelt.* New York: Henry Holt, Tomes Books, 1997.
Donald, Aida D. *Lion in the White House: A Life of Theodore Roosevelt.* New York: Basic Books, 2007.
Grondahl, Paul. *I Rose Like a Rocket: The Political Education of Theodore Roosevelt.* New York: Free Press, 2004.
McCullough, David. *Mornings on Horseback.* New York: Simon and Schuster, 1977.
Morris, Edmund. *Theodore Rex.* New York: Random House, 2001.
Zimmerman, Warren. *First Great Triumph: How Five Americans Made Their Country a World Power.* New York: Farrar, Strauss and Giroux, 2002.

WINSTON CHURCHILL

Best, Geoffrey. *Churchill: A Study in Greatness.* Oxford: Oxford University Press, 2003.

Charmley, John. *Churchill's Grand Alliance: The Anglo American Special Relationship 1940–57.* New York: Harcourt Brace and Company, 1995.

Hastings, Max. *Winston's War: Churchill 1940–1945.* New York: Alfred A. Knopf, 2010.

Holmes, Richard. *In the Footsteps of Churchill: A Study in Character.* Cambridge: Basic Books, 2005.

Jenkins, Roy. *Churchill: A Biography.* New York: Farrar, Straus and Giroux, 2001.

Lord Moran. *Churchill: The Struggle for Survival: 1940–1965.* London: Heron Books, 1966.

Lukacs, John. *Five Days in May.* New Haven: Yale University Press, 1999.

Strawson, John. *Churchill and Hitler in Victory and Defeat.* New York: Fromm International, 1998.

DEAN ACHESON

Acheson, Dean. *Power and Diplomacy.* Cambridge: Harvard University Press, 1958.

Beisner, Robert L. *Dean Acheson: A Life in the Cold War.* Oxford: Oxford University Press, 2006.

Brinkley, Douglas. *Dean Acheson: The Cold War Years: 1953–71.* New Haven: Yale University Press, 1992.

Ferrell, Robert H. ed. *The American Secretaries of State and Their Diplomacy: Dean Acheson.* New York: Simon and Schuster, 1998.

Hopkins, Michael F. *Dean Acheson and the Obligations of Power.* Lanham Maryland: Rowman and Littlefield, 2017.

McLellan, David S. *Dean Acheson: The State Department Years.* New York: Dodd, Mead and Company, 1976.

McMahon, Robert J. *Dean Acheson and the Creation of an American World Order.* Washington, D.C.: Potomac Books, Inc., 2009.

Smith, Gaddis. *Dean Acheson.* Lanham, Maryland: Crown Square Publishers, 1972.

DENG XIAOPING

Baum, Richard. *Burying Mao.* Princeton: Princeton University Press, 1994.

Kristof, Nicholas D. and Sheryl WuDunn. *China Wakes: The Struggle for the Soul of a Rising Power.* New York: Random House, 1994.

Pantov, Alexander V. *Deng Xiaoping: A Revolutionary Life.* New York: Oxford University Press, 2015.

Salisbury, Harrison. *The New Emperors.* New York: Avon Books, 1992.

Vogel, Ezra F. *Deng Xiaoping and the Transformation of China.* Cambridge: Harvard University Press, 2011.

PERMISSIONS

CHAPTER 1

Hugh Kennedy/Mongols, Huns and Vikings/Introduction p. 19/excerpt of 22 words. Text copyright Hugh Kennedy 2002 for Mongols, Huns and Vikings. Design and Layout copyright Cassell & Co. 2002. With permission of The Orion Publishing Group, London

G.V. Scammell/The World Encompassed: The first European maritime empires c. 800–1650/p. 10/excerpt of 22 words. Copyright 1981 G.V. Scammell for The World Encompassed: The first European maritime empires c. 800–1650 published by University of California Press.

Felipe Fernández-Armesto/Pathfinders: A Global History of Exploration/ p. 42/ excerpt of 24 words. Copyright 2006 by Felipe Fernández-Armesto for *Pathfinders: A Global History of Exploration* published by W.W. Norton & Company, Inc.

CHAPTER 2

Jack Weatherford/Genghis Khan and the Making of the Modern World/p. xxviii/excerpt of 34 words. Penguin Random House grants one-time, non-exclusive permission to use the material/Contract ID: 31725 [CREDIT LINE: Excerpt(s)from *GENGHIS KHAN AND THE MAKING OF THE MODERN WORLD* by Jack Weatherford, copyright 2004 by Jack Weatherford. Used by permission of Crown Books, an imprint of Random House, a division of Penguin Random House LLC. All rights reserved.]

William H. McNeill/The Rise of the West/p. 530–531/excerpt of 50 words. University of Chicago Press: We consider 50 words from pages 530–531 in "The Rise of the West" by William H. McNeill fair use, provided Peter Krogh gives proper credit and citation in his forthcoming book. [CREDIT: William H. McNeill for *The Rise of the West* copyright 1963, 1991 with permission of the University of Chicago Press]

CHAPTER 3

Janet L. Abu-Lughod/Before European Hegemony: The World System A.D. 1250–1350/p. 361/excerpt of 32 words. The following notices and acknowledgements must be reproduced prominently alongside each reproduction and must include title and author of Licensed Material, the copyright notice must be included in the Licensed Material and the statement: [Janet Abu-Lughod for *Before European Hegemony* Copyright 1989 by Oxford University Press, Inc. Reproduced with permission of the Licensor through PLSclear.]

John M. Hobson/The Eastern Origins of Western Civilisation/p. xii/excerpt of 9 words. The following notices and acknowledgements must be reproduced prominently alongside each reproduction and must include title and author of Licensed Material, the copyright notice must be included in the Licensed Material and the statement: [Copyright John M. Hobson 2004 for *The Eastern Origins of Western Civilisation* with written permission of Cambridge University Press, reproduced with permission of the Licensor through PLSclear.]

Feliipe Fernández-Armesto/Pathfinders: A Global History of Exploration/p. 120/ excerpt of 13 words. Copyright 2006 by Felipe Fernández-Armesto for Pathfinders: A Global History of Exploration published by W. W. Norton & Company, Inc.

William H. McNeill/The Rise of the West/p. xxviii/excerpt of 24 words. University of Chicago Press: We consider 24 words from page xxvii in "The Rise of the West" by William H. McNeill fair use, provided Peter Krogh gives proper credit and citation in his forthcoming book. [CRED-

IT: William H. McNeill for The Rise of the West copyright 1963, 1991 with permission of the University of Chicago Press]

CHAPTER 4

William H. McNeill/Plagues and People/p. 179/excerpt of 24 words. Penguin Random House grants one-time, non-exclusive permission to use the material/Contract ID: 31725 CREDIT LINE: Excerpt(s)from PLAGUES AND PEOPLES by William H. McNeill, copyright 1976 by William H. McNeill. Used by permission of Doubleday, an imprint of Knoph Doubleday Publishing Group, a division of Penguin Random House LLC. All rights reserved.

Jared Diamond/Guns, Germs and Stee: The Fates of Human Societies/p. 197/excerpt of 17 words. W.W. Norton grants nonexclusive license to use the following material (17 words as submitted) in paperback and ebook in the US. CREDIT LINE: From GUNS, GERMS AND STEEL: THE FATES OF HUMAN SOCIETIES by Jared Diamond. Used by permission of W.W. Norton & Company, Inc.

Feliipe Fernandez-Armesto/Millennium: A History of the Last Thousand Years/p. 123/excerpt of 23 words. Copyright 1995 by Felipe Fernández-Armesto for *Millennium: A History of the Last Thousand Years* published by Charles Scribner's Sons a trademark of Simon & Schuster, Inc.

CHAPTER 5

Jason Goodwin/ Lords of the Horizon: A History of the Ottoman Empire/ p. 91/excerpt of 14 words. Copyright 1998 by Jason Goodwin for *Lords of the Horizon: A History of the Ottoman Empire.* Henry Holt and Company, LLC A John Macrae/Owl Book

Lord Kinross/The Ottoman Centuries: The Rise and Fall of the Turkish Empire/p.613/excerpt of 42 words. CREDIT LINE: [. . . from the Ottoman Centuries by Lord Kinross. Copyright 1977 by Lord Kinross. Used by permission of HarperCollins Publishers]

Philip Mansel/Constantinople: City of the World's Desire 1453–1924/p. 31/excerpt of 12 words. Copyright 1995 by Philip Mansel for *Constantinople: City of the World's Desire 1453–1924*. Published by St. Martin's Griffin Press.

Stanford J. Shaw/History of the Ottoman Empire and Modern Turkey/p. 57/ excerpt of 18 words. Copyright Cambridge University Press 1976 for Stanford J. Shaw and the *History of the Ottoman Empire and Modern Turkey*. Reproduced with permission of the Licensor through PLSclear.

John M. Hobson/The Eastern Origins of Western Civilisation/p. 135/excerpt of 22 words. Copyright John M. Hobson 2004 by Cambridge University Press/ John M. Hobson for *The Eastern Origins of Western Civilisation*. Reproduced with permission of the Licensor through PLSclear.

CHAPTER 6

Bailey W. Diffie and George D. Winius/Foudations of the Portuguese Empire: 1415–1550/p. xiii/13 words. Copyright 1977 by the University of Minnesota Reference# 19090601 for Bailey W. Diffie and George D. Winius, *Foundations of the Portuguese Emire: 1415–1550.*

George D. Winius (ed.)/Portugal, The Pathfinder/p. 19/14 words . Copyright 1995 by The Hispanic Seminary of Medieval Studies, Ltd. at the University of Wisconsin-Madison for Portugal, *The Pathfinder* Edited by George D. Winius. Email contact is John O'Neill at hsmsbooks@gmail.com.

Eric Axelson (ed.)/Dias and his Successors . *Dias and his Successors* Edited by Eric Axelson Published by Saayman & Weber Ltd. P.O. Box 673 Cape Town South Africa.

CHAPTER 7

Felipe Fernández-Armesto/Columbus/p. 15/ excerpt of 15 words. Credit Felipe Fernández-Armesto 1991 for *Columbus*, published by Oxford University Press.

G.V. Scammell/The World Encompassed: The first European maritime empires c. 800–1650/p. 155/excerpt of 7 words. Credit G.V. Scammell for *The World Encompassed: The first European maritime empires c. 800–1650.*

William D. Phillips, Jr. and Carla Rahn Philllips/The Worlds of Christopher Columbus/p. 3/excerpt of 27 words. Copyright Cambridge University Press 1992. William D. Phillips, Jr. and Carla Rahn Phillips for *The Worlds of Christopher Columbus.* Reproduced with permission of the Licensor through PLSclear.

Felipe Fernández-Armesto/Columbus/p. 15/ excerpt of 15 words. Credit Felipe Fernández-Armesto 1991 for *Columbus*, published by Oxford University Press.

CHAPTER 8

Samuel Eliot Morison/The European Discovery of America: The Southern Voyages A.D. 1492–1616/p. 320/excerpt of 11 words. Copyright 1974 by Samuel Eliot Morison T*he European Discovery of America Volume 2: The Southern Voyages A.D. 1492–1616.* Oxford University Press, Inc. Reproduced with permission of the Licensor through PLSclear.

Daniel J. Boorstein/The Discoverers. p. 261/excerpt of 17 words. Excerpt(s) from THE DISCOVERERS by Daniel J. Boorstin, copyright 1983 by Daniel J. Boorstin. Used by permission of Random House, an imprint and division of Penguin Random House LLC. All rights reserved.

Felipe Fernández-Armesto/Millennium: A History of the Last Thousand Years/p. 74/excerpt of 24 words. Copyright 1995 by Felipe Fernández-Armesto for *Millennium: A History of the Last Thousand Years* published by Charles Scribner's Sons, a trademark of Simon & Schuster, Inc.

CHAPTER 9

Samuel Eliot Morison/The European Discovery of America: The Southern Vouages A.D. 1492–1616/p. vii/excerpt of 11 words. Copyright 1974 by Samuel Eliot Morison *The European Discovery of America Volume 2:*

The Southern Voyages A.D. 1492-1616. Oxford University Press, Inc. Reproduced with permission of the Licensor through PLSclear.

G.V. Scammell/The World Encompassed: The first European maritime empires c. 800–1650/p. 466/excerpt of 19 words. Copyright 1981 G.V. Scammell for *The World Encompassed: The first European maritime empires c. 800–1650* published by University of California Press.

Admiral Sir Robert Mansell/Francis Drake: The Lives of a Hero/p. 305/ excerpt of 12 words. Copyright 1995, 1997 by John Cummins, St. Martin's Press.

CHAPTER 10

Lynne Withey/Voyages of Discovery/p. 10/excerpt of 11 words. Copyright 1987 by Lynne Withey for *Voyages of Discovery* First paperback ptrinting 1989 University of California Press

Daniel Conner and Lorraine Miller/Master Mariner: Captain James Cook and the Peoples of the Pacific/p. xi/excerpt of 25 words. Daniel C. Conner ad Lorraine Mller for *Master Mariner: Captain James Cook and the Peoples of the Pacific*. 1978 Unversity of Washington Press. Permission granted by author.

CHAPTER 11

Robert Tucker and David Hendrickson/Empire of Liberty/p. 109/excerpt of 26 words. Robert Tuker and David Hendrickson for Empire of Liberty 1990 Oxford Publishing Limited. Reproduced with permission of the Licensor through PLSclear.

Patrick C.T. White (ed.)/Conducting the Diplomacy of the New Nation, 1793–1815. Copyright 1971 by Jerome S. Ozer, Publisher, Inc. for Patrick C.T. White (ed.) *Thomas Jefferson and the Louisiana Purchase.*

CHAPTER 12

Edmund Morris/The Rise of Theodore Roosevelt/p. 717/11 words. Copyright 1979 by Edmund Morris 2001 Modern Library Paperback Edition] Permission for excerpt sought 11/12. Quotation may be in the public domain.

David McCullough/The Path Between the Seas: The Creation of the Panama Canal 1870–1914/p. 12/excerpt of 16 words. Copyright 1977 by David McCullough for *The Path Between the Seas: The Creation of the Panama Canal 1870-1914*. A Touchstone Book published by Simon & Schuster. All rights reserved.

David McCullough/The Path Between the Seas: The Creation of the Panama Canal 1870–1914/p. 383/excerpt of 15 words of Theodore Roosevelt as quoted by David McCullough. Copyright 1977 by David McCullough for The Path Between the Seas: The Creation of the Panama Canal 1870–1914. A Touchstone Book published by Simon & Schuster. All rights reserved.

CHAPTER 13

John Charmley/Churchill: The End of Glory/p. 10/excerpt of 25 words. Copyright 1994 by John Charmley *Churchill: The End of Glory* published by Harcourt Brace & Company.

Sir Winston Churchill Direct Quotation as recorded by the BBC November 30, 1954/excerpt of 29 words. Public Domain Quotation available via https://news.bbc.co.uk/onthisdy/hu/dates/stories/november/30/news.

CHAPTER 14

James Chace/Acheson: The Secretary of State Who Created the American World/p. 12/excerpt of 34 words. Copyright 1998 by James Chace. *Acheson: The Secretary of State Who Created the American World* published by Simon & Schuster.

Felipe Fernández-Armesto/Columbus/p. 184–185/ excerpt of 32 words. Credit Felipe Fernández-Armesto 1991 for *Columbus*, published by Oxford University Press.

CHAPTER 15

The Economist February 22, 1997/excerpt of 40 words. *The Economist*. February 22, 1997.

Michael Dillon/Deng Xiaoping: The Man who Made Modern China/p. xv/excerpt of 7 words. Copyright 2015 by Michael Dillon for *Deng Xiaoping: The Man who Made Modern China* I.B. Tauris, an imprint of Bloomsbury Publishing Plc.

Feliipe Fernández-Armesto/Pathfinders: A Global History of Exploration/p. 115/ excerpt of 16 words. Copyright 2006 by Felipe Fernández-Armesto for *Pathfinders: A Global History of Exploration*. W.W. Norton & Company, Inc.